Precis

Manchester University Press

Precision

A history of American warfare

James Patton Rogers

Manchester University Press

Published by Manchester University Press
Oxford Road, Manchester M13 9PL

www.manchesteruniversitypress.co.uk

British Library Cataloguing-in-Publication Data
A catalogue record for this book is available from the British Library

ISBN 978 1 5261 2588 0 paperback

First published 2023

The publisher has no responsibility for the persistence or accuracy of URLs for any external or third-party internet websites referred to in this book, and does not guarantee that any content on such websites is, or will remain, accurate or appropriate.

Typeset
by Cheshire Typesetting Ltd, Cuddington, Cheshire
Printed in Great Britain
by TJ Books Ltd, Padstow, Cornwall

To Brittany and Caroline, without whom this book would have remained unfinished

Table of contents

Prologue: The pursuit of precision

[T]he U.S. public standard for military action now seems to resemble the ethic that prevailed on old TV Westerns: The good guy – the one in the white hat – never killed the bad guy. He shot the gun out of his hand and arrested him. Modern air power may not solve every military problem, but thanks to the innovations of the last decade, it is the weapon in the U.S. arsenal that comes closest to fulfilling that goal.

Phillip S. Meilinger, A Matter of Precision (2009)[1]

It's quite the ambition. To kill precisely, yet without ever needing to inflict unnecessary suffering on innocent civilians. To take out the bad guy, while saving the good. A beguiling prospect. Such ambitions have a tendency to feel incredibly familiar and definitively modern, yet they are far from new. The term 'precision strike' may evoke the image of a drone pilot lining up crosshairs on a computer screen before launching a lethal strike, but precision has a much longer history involving much more than strike accuracy or advanced weapons systems. Instead, precision is best described as an ethos, one which enshrines the long-held ambition in American strategic thought to mitigate the cost to life in conflict, while still achieving a rapid American victory. Although often illusory, it has been vehemently pursued (sometimes to a fault) for over one hundred years.

Those who seek to achieve such an ambition, which is by no means all those in the US military, speak about it in moral, ethical, and strategic terms. They argue that 'precision' epitomises the push to be *better* than other nations, to hold oneself to a higher moral standard in times of both peace and war. In terms of a definition, the 'precision ethos' can be defined by the ambition to be proportionate and discriminate in the targeting of the enemy from the air, to rapidly end conflict, and to reduce the cost to civilian and American military life as much as possible. This does not mean that such aims are always achieved in

1

war. In fact, as this book will show, precision can sometimes be a strategically counter-productive ambition. Despite this, the American pursuit of precision is as fascinating as it is troubling. It is a phenomenon – an obsession – which when analysed as a century-spanning pursuit, reveals rare insights into the intellectual history, evolution, and character of American warfare.[2]

As American air power historian Tami Biddle explained to me early on in this project, 'the American desire for precision in war is part of the narrative of 'American exceptionalism'. It is the want to hold oneself to a higher standard than others do, to be better than others are. Such ambitions have driven the American people, in one way or another, since they first arrived on Plymouth Rock'.[3] Thus, the drive for precision in American strategic thought is a product of the society from which it emerged. It is, in essence, a social construction – a very American idea and ideal, one which has most often manifested as an agonising struggle.

So, what does it mean to be *better* at bombing? Well, as explained in the following chapters, the ambition to achieve increased levels of precision was born to early American airpower thinkers during the First World War as a reaction to the horror of that conflict and the emergence of European 'area bombing' strategies. It was then chased across the twentieth century and pursued well into the twenty-first. Yet, it is within this space – between the original pursuit of precision bombardment in the early twentieth century and the so-called 'perfection' of precision missiles and drones in the twenty-first – that this book finds its place and purpose. The origins of precision have been well documented. Chapter 1 and Chapter 2 build upon studies by Tami Biddle, Conrad Crane, Paula G. Thornhill, Mark Clodfelter, Paul Gillespie, Michael Sherry, Stephen MacFarland, Stephen Bourque, Raymond O'Mara, Phil Haun, and Malcolm Gladwell.[4] In these texts, each author explains in their own way how early American air power thinkers operationalised their pursuit of precision bombing after the First World War and through the Second World War. Yet it is here that the wealth of studies into precision, along with the pursuit of precision bombing itself, appear to pause.

This is until the 1990s. During this period, at the other end of the history on American precision warfare, a considerable number of books began to emerge. Each author presented technical and policy insights into how and why US policymakers, pioneers of industry, and military thinkers were able to build upon the Revolution in Military Affairs (RMA) and achieve never-before-seen levels of precision bombardment during the Gulf War (1991), Kosovo Campaign (1999), and well into the War on Terror (2001). In this first wave of renewed precision scholarship, Richard P. Hallion, Stephen D. Wrage, and Benjamin Lambeth (among others) captured the moment where the United States harnessed a new precision air power capacity to devastating effect. As Hallion argued in 1995, '[b]ecause of precision, decision-makers have a freedom to use military force closer to non-combatant-inhabited areas in an enemy homeland (or in enemy-occupied territory) than at any previous time in military history'.[5] Although not wrong in terms of the technical precision achieved during this period, critics of American precision air power condemned the suggestion that war could ever be waged in such close proximity to civilians without innocent people getting caught in the crossfire. It was in reaction to such suggestions that a critical wave of scholarship arose. Spearheaded by experts like Michael Ignatieff and James Der Derian, these authors derided the US for its 'precision' and high-tech computerised ambitions, accusing the US military (and select allies) of seeing war as a sanitised practice. As Ignatieff wrote in 2001, '[w]e see war as a surgical scalpel and not a bloodstained sword. In so doing we mis-describe ourselves as we mis-describe the instruments of death.'[6] Despite these protestations, however, the quest to achieve ever greater levels of precision air power continued along with numerous publications on the topic.

In the post-9/11 world, and as the Obama administration deployed drones across the globe in the hunt for suspected terrorists, studies on the use of drones and their precision strike capabilities ballooned into their hundreds, if not thousands. Just a few of the notable works published during this period include those by Sarah Kreps, Medea Benjamin, Michael Boyle, Gregoire Chamayou, Thomas, G. Mahnken, Chris Fuller, J. Wesley Hutto, Kelly A. Grieco, Caroline Kennedy-Pipe, Talat Farouk, Tom Waldman, Chris Wood, Kathrine Chandler, Daniel Brunstetter, Megan Braun, Hugh Gusterson, Jacqueline L. Hazelton, Michael J. Williams, Stephanie Carvin, Michael P. Kreuzer, and Azmat Khan.[7]

Much like in my own work during the 2010s, many of these authors focused on modern drone technologies and their strategies of deployment. Of particular interest were the claims of infallible precision and guaranteed accuracy in warfare – a puzzling assertion given the rising number of documented civilian casualties and the 'collateral' aspects of war, which ran contrary to official claims.

In May 2013, for instance, President Barack Obama announced to the National Defense University in Washington, DC that, 'conventional air power or missiles are far less precise than drones and are likely to cause more civilian casualties and more local outrage'.[8] In that same speech, President Obama doubled down on his claims, arguing that drones were part of a 'just war – a war waged proportionally, in last resort, and in self-defense'.[9] In fact, Obama administration officials had a particular passion for precision when it came to solving the dilemmas of the War on Terror. As John Brennan, Obama's Homeland Security Advisor (and future head of the CIA) stated in 2012, it was the 'surgical precision' of the drone that was a vital ability with its 'laser-like focus to eliminate the cancerous tumour called an al-Qaida terrorist, while limiting damage to the tissue around it'.[10] With a surprising lack of irony, Brennan was fulfilling the prophetic warning laid out by Ignatieff over a decade before. War, it appeared, had become surgical, sterile, and too easy to wage.

Dissenting voices continued to criticise these sanitised takes on dealing death from above. This included some of those who had worked in the Obama administration. As Obama's former Secretary of Defense, Robert Gates, stated in 2015, once he had left office, '[f]or too many people, including defence "experts", members of Congress, executive branch officials and ordinary citizens, war has become a kind of video game or action movie: bloodless, painless and odorless'.[11] In hindsight he was correct. Civilian casualties from Obama-era drone strikes are now documented into the thousands. Precision often meant guaranteed death, destruction, and immeasurable suffering for the communities under persistent overwatch by drones, not just the suspected terrorists and insurgents. A precision strike, it turned out, was only as precise as the intelligence at hand.[12]

Precision was not always imprecise. There can be little doubt that Obama's drone wars were partly responsible for supressing al-Qaeda by taking out high-value terrorist targets. Osama bin Laden, for instance, detested drones. These seemingly omnipotent, ubiquitous systems forced him and his followers to hide or die, 'devastating al-Qaeda'.[13] Obama's drones also provided a valuable Intelligence, Surveillance, Target Acquisition, and Reconnaissance (ISTAR) capacity and close air support to allies and US troops on the ground. In addition, they helped mitigate the need for increased numbers of troops in contested regions of the world, reducing the risk to American lives.[14] As such, conflict became less about en masse ground deployments and more about waging war by remote control, at a distance, where precision missiles could be released against enemies, from thousands of miles away, with minimal risk to US military personnel.

In fact, it was due to these perceived successes, and despite the broader concerns of civilian harm, that from 2017 the Trump administration kept drones as the spearhead of force deployment around the world. To silence critics, Trump officials simply removed the requirement to report on civilian casualties, while keeping drone strikes at a similar level to the Obama presidency.[15] President Biden continued along a similar path, decreasing drone deployment in some regions (such as Afghanistan), while still maintaining the drone programme and expanding the supply of drones to key allies around the world. Indeed, there can be little doubt that it was the perceived successes of the US drone programme under Obama, Trump, and Biden that acted as a catalyst for a growing global demand and proliferation of drones in the late 2010s and early 2020s.[16]

As new 'drone powers' emerged around the world, drawn in by the allure of the drone's precision strike capabilities, my work evolved to focus on this new drone era. Inspired by scholars, such as Agnes Callamard, Paul Lushenko, Ulrike Franke, Dan Gettinger, Sam Bendett, Delina Goxho, Zachary Kallenborn, Emil Archambault, Yannick Veilleux-Lepage, Lauren Kahn, Ash Rossiter, Brandon J. Cannon, Anna Jackman, Michael Horowitz, Dominika Kunertova, Joshua A Schwartz, Ingvild Bode, Matthew Fuhrmann, Arthur Holland Michel, Kerry Chavez, and Ori Swed (among others),[17] I focused on how drones and precision missiles were being used and misused in both internal and international conflicts. These included Russia's offensive war against Ukraine – where drones, precision missiles, and a clambering for deep precision strike capabilities defined the early conflict – but also the Second Libyan Civil War, the Nagorno-Karabakh conflict, the Ethiopian Tigray War, and the terrorist use of drones and precision strikes across the Middle East.[18]

Today, over 113 nation states have a military drone programme and at least 65 violent non-state actors have access to weaponised drones.[19] According the Center for the Study of the Drone, only 60 nation states possessed drones in 2010, meaning there has been an 88.2 per cent increase in drone-owning states in just over a decade.[20] As a result, academic research into drone warfare has become a global endeavour. From what started as analysis of US precision technologies, my own attempt to keep track of the escalating and uncontrolled proliferation of military drones has taken me from the Middle East to the Arctic, the Sahel to the Baltic. As part of this research journey I have been able to inspect captured terrorist drones and learn how precision weapons,[21] such as 'kamikaze drones', are spreading into the hands of proxy actors who do the bidding of hostile nations.[22] Not only this, but as climate change warms regions of the Arctic four times faster than the global average – opening up new economic opportunities to rival nations – drones allow governments and their militaries to project sovereign power across hard-to-reach places and cast a watchful eye over unwanted guests.[23]

Precision

In February 2022, Russia's invasion of Ukraine sparked a new rush across Europe to acquire military drones from any available source. While the Kremlin chose to target Ukraine's major cities with Iranian-manufactured weapons, China supplied armed military drones to Serbia and the US sent high-tech loitering munitions to support Ukraine and provide persistent overwatch of Russia's borders. In addition, Turkey provided its Bayraktar TB2 drones to Latvia, Ukraine, Lithuania, Poland, and any European nation that wished to possess a loitering and lethal precision strike capacity.[24] All this activity has pointed to the rapid spread of precision drone systems across Europe, one which shows no signs of abating.

It is for this reason that when I was afforded the opportunity to address the UN Security Council in New York, I chose to focus on how weaponised drones now pose a major threat to international security. Attacks, I argued, now take place over thousands of kilometres against state military assets, diplomatic sites, chokepoints of international trade (at sea and on land), and the civilian centres of nation states.[25] This is the current state of the world, one of global drone diffusion.

Why is this important? How is it relevant or indeed useful to include in a book on the history of precision and American warfare? Termed 'The Second Drone Age', this new security environment has played host to the uncontrolled proliferation of precision strike technologies that now allow a range of hostile actors to deploy drones and missiles with pinpoint precision from the safety of their own territorial domains. In an ironic, yet predictable, twist of fate, it is the very precision technologies, pioneered by the US, that now threaten deadly precision attacks back onto the nation that first developed them.[26] The threat, therefore, has travelled full circle, and to understand the character of contemporary warfare we must turn to history.

Where did the search for precision begin? How did it evolve over time? And how have we ended up where we are today?' The book's purpose is to fill a gap in the established body of literature that presents a less than clear answer to the questions posed. Although there are many excellent studies that explore parallel stories of weapons development and strategic evolution during this nuclear period – not least those by Fred Kaplan, Scott Sagan, and David A. Rosenberg (to whom I own a special debt for their eye-opening analysis) but also Donald McKenzie, Peter W. Singer, Stephen Budainsky, Sterling M. Pavelec, Maja Zehfuss, Brent Ziarnick, David Axe, Robert Pape, John Andreas Olsen, Matthew Evangelista, and Henry Shue – there are still gaps in the literature.[27] As such, I went in search of answers:

Prologue

- What happened between 1945 and the high-tech advancements of the 1990s which kicked off the new 'drone world' we live in today?
- Who continued to push for this seemingly impossible and illusory prospect of 'precision' in American warfare after 1945 and the shortfalls of the Second World War?
- What factors – moral or strategic – drove such ambitions? Who challenged them?
- Finally, what can we learn from their experiences – and from the history of precision – to help us understand modern precision warfare and the uncontrolled proliferation of precision strike technologies around the world today?

It is these questions that I hope to provide answers to in *Precision: A History of American Warfare*.

1
Genesis (1917–41)

What victory can cheer a mother's heart,
When she looks at her blighted home?
What victory can bring her back
All she cared to call her own.
Let each mother answer
In the years to be,
Remember that my boy belongs to me!
'I Didn't Raise My Boy to Be a Soldier', Alfred Bryan (1915)[1]

It was the unique social, political and strategic reaction to the horror of the First World War that gave birth to the genesis of precision as an ambition in the minds of early American air power thinkers.[2] During the initial post-war period, unlike the British and German militaries who had developed a penchant for area bombing, for the Americans it was the nature of the target that was most important.[3] An area bombing strategy was believed to be 'unbridled savagery'[4] by the people of the United States who saw it as both morally corrupt and strategically flawed.[5] To be proportionate and discriminate in the targeting of the enemy became the mantra of the American public, many of whom had watched aghast as the 'Old World' of Britain and Germany had drawn out a disproportionate and indiscriminate war of attrition.[6] This war had not only cost the death and injury of over 300,000 Americans,[7] but had seen mass killing,[8] and the terror bombing of civilians.[9] As Dominick Pisano, curator at the Smithsonian National Air and Space Museum, stated, 'one factor that affected the evolution of [American] bombardment thought was the general public opposition to mass civilian bombing'.[10] In essence, the American people blamed the brutal character of the First World War for 'the death of a lost generation' and for the unnecessary death of civilians throughout Europe.[11] It was the damnation of the indiscriminately brutal and disproportionately horrific suffering of the First World War which dominated the American societal perception of war as the conflict drew to an end. In fact, so widespread, dominant, and forceful was this sentiment that it had a great influence on the way in which those at a strategic level in the United States began to perceive the very nature and characteristics of American warfare, and the form it would take in the future. Specifically, it led American strategic thinkers, backed by public sentiment, 'motivated by the horrors of trench warfare ... repulsed by the thought of targeting civilian population centres through Area Bombing' and sceptical as to its strategic utility, to develop a new air power strategy – a very American strategy.[12]

Colonel Edgar S. Gorrell

the carnage and waste ... sparked the beginning of a progressive effort that was unique – an attempt to reform *war*

Mark Clodfelter (2010)[13]

One strategic thinker directly influenced by the horror of the First World War and palpable public sentiment was Colonel Edgar S. Gorrell.[14] Gorrell was an early American air power strategist whose role during the First World War was as Chief of the Technical Section in the air service of the American Expeditionary Force (AEF) in Europe. As the Great War drew to a close, Gorrell was uniquely aware of the growing public perception of war and receptive to the demands to mitigate its 'cost'.[15] Based on what he had witnessed in relation to the use of the aeroplane in the Great War, Gorrell believed that investment in air power, and new military strategies to accompany its deployment, could provide a possible means by which to fulfil growing American societal demands, while strengthening American military power. To highlight the potential of his proposal, as the war came to a close Gorrell began to construct an early American air power strategy. Unlike the British and German strategies, Gorrell's strategy would seek to avoid indiscriminate and disproportionate bombing of the enemy. Instead, he would put at its very core the motivation to reduce the cost to both civilians and to American military life, while still securing victory. It was here that the desire for precision began to emerge.

As stated in his war and post-war writings, Gorrell's idea was simple. Instead of area bombing the enemy, the aim was to precision bomb the specific warmaking industry within the enemy's 'commercial centres'.[16] In Gorrell's mind such a plan had two virtues. The first was the avoidance of bombing the 'populace and its livelihood', thereby reducing civilian casualties.[17] The second was the rendering of 'the enemy forces impotent' by cutting off supplies, making victory easier.[18] Thus, put quite simply, through the destruction of specific strategically important targets, a reduced cost to American military and civilian life would occur and victory would be assured. Unsurprisingly, such notions proved popular. As Gorrell made clear, 'the American public ... and financial purse-strings lend themselves to this idea'.[19] As such, Gorrell set about developing his 'precision bombing' strategy further.[20]

Using his experiences from the First World War to support his argument, Gorrell pointed to the precision targeting of 'German manufacturing centres and means of transportation' from the air as a specific way to end the war rapidly and mitigate the cost to life.[21] As he stated, 'for practically three years the artillery has constantly shelled German positions and the infantry has sacrificed an enormous number of human lives, only to gain an insignificant number of miles along the front'.[22] Such loss of life without strategic gain was absurd to Gorrell who believed that 'with a similar expenditure in aerial bomb-dropping ... the transportation in the rear of the German lines and the supplies of all sorts of material to the German troops could long ago have been cut off'.[23] For Gorrell, precision through air power, for reasons of strategic utility and to reduce the cost to life, was most important.

There were those who agreed with this line of thought. Building on an earlier US Navy project, in 1918 the US Army tested the first pilotless air-to-ground attack weapon – the Kettering Bug. Developed by the engineer and inventor Charles F. Kettering, with the help of some of the greatest inventors, military leaders, and industrialists of his generation (such as Orville Wright, Elmer Sperry, Henry Ford, and Henry 'Hap' Arnold) the weapon aimed to mitigate the need to put America's young soldiers at risk on the battlefield.

Often called an early drone or cruise missile, Kettering himself referred to it as an 'aerial torpedo'. It was an unmanned device, set on rails, and would speed up along a ramp to take off. It's level would be maintained by an early Sperry gyroscope. When its engine had gone through a preset number of revolutions, the wings would detach and the Bug would plunge to earth 'like a bird of prey' (or so its advocates hoped). In reality, the short range and unreliability of this futuristic machine made it of little strategic use, but it marked the start of a search for high-tech solutions to the risks and dilemmas of ground warfare.

As the initial post-war years progressed, perhaps in recognition of his unique insight and perception of the conflict, Gorrell was appointed Chief Historian

Figure 1.1 Kettering 'Bug' Aerial Torpedo

for the Air Service of the AEF. He was charged with preparing a 'final report on U.S. air activities in Europe during the war'.[24] In his report, Gorrell again detailed his own strategic recommendations, while also analysing what lessons could be taken from the AEF's experiences during the wartime period. This document, influenced by the costs of the previous war, builds on his original strategic thoughts.

Specifically, in his 1919 documentation of the AEF's history, Gorrell's thoughts continued to build on the idea that it was beneficial to target enemy 'commercial centres and the lines of communications in such quantities as will wreck the points aimed at and cut off the necessary supplies'.[25] He believed that the specific and discriminate targeting of military-industrial sites, such as chemical plants and aircraft engine plants 'without which the armies in the field cannot exist', should be the primary focus of any future American air power strategy.[26] Gorrell expanded upon his idea of a direct link between the specific targeting of the industrial sites and the reduction in the enemy's military power. As Mark Clodfelter stated, 'Gorrell aimed to render the enemy forces impotent.'[27] This, Gorrell believed, would give all sections of the American military the advantage on the ground, rapidly ending the conflict and reducing the cost to American military and civilian lives, all, to the pleasure of the American people, without the abhorrent targeting of civilians. Such an ambition would become ingrained in the history of the AEF due to Gorrell's report, and it continued to influence American strategic thought as the years progressed. In fact, its most high-profile advocacy came from none other than Brigadier-General William 'Billy' Mitchell.[28]

Brigadier-General William 'Billy' Mitchell

Writing from an American perspective ... he [Mitchell] thought, air warfare did not necessarily have to be particularly cruel. Indeed, he nurtured the hope that civilian casualties could be kept relatively limited ... The targeting he advocated also aimed less at the populations than at production centres.

Beatrice Heuser (2014)[29]

Whereas the Italian air power strategist, Giulio Douhet, believed in indiscriminate area bombing to ensure 'no distinction between soldier and civilians' when bombing the enemy, Mitchell was driven by the mission to achieve precision, although in a slightly different way to Gorrell.[30] Like Gorrell, Mitchell believed that the precision targeting of vital enemy infrastructure, such as fuel depots, was far more strategically and morally beneficial than striking civilians directly.[31] Yet whereas the military-industrial sites were the main focus for Gorrell to weaken the teeth of the enemy, for Mitchell there was also an added bonus in terms of pressuring the enemy populous. With fuel being vital for light, heat, transportation, and food preparation, Mitchell's view was that by destroying these targets, the enemy's standard of living and morale would drop. As he stated, 'targeting the means of communication, the food products, even the farms, the fuel and oil ... [n]ot only must these things be rendered incapable of supplying armed forces, but the peoples' desire to renew the combat at a later date must be discouraged'.[32] Mitchell believed bombing with precision would achieve the same effect as Douhet's area bombing and bring a rapid end to conflict, but without the cost to civilian life. Mitchell also wanted to mitigate the cost to American military lives through this strategic concept. He believed the deployment of precision would weaken the strength of the enemy military, as without items such as fuel, the enemy would be unable to cook, see at night, keep warm, or power its vehicles. As Mitchell stated, 'aircraft operating in the heart of an enemy's country will accomplish this objective in an incredibly short space of time ... and the months and even years of contest of ground armies with a loss of millions of lives will be eliminated in the future'.[33] In essence, Mitchell believed that proportionate and discriminate precision through air power had tremendous strategic utility and was 'a distinct move for the betterment of civilisation' and 'really much more humane' than an area bombing strategy.[34]

Of course, it is odd to think that starvation and general human suffering were acceptable consequences of precision bombardment. Yet this did not prove of major concern to Mitchell. These factors would (in theory) pressure 'the people' into forcing their politicians to end war before suffering became unbearable. Consequently, precision strike, in this context, covered a multitude of sins in Mitchell's mind. It was a moral and strategic notion, below the threshold of direct civilian bombardment, and it would in time become a driving factor in Mitchell's strategic thought during the inter-war period.[35] A persistent challenge for Mitchell throughout this period, however, was the fact that the American military did not have a separate air force, making it impossible for American air power strategists to autonomously shape their own military strategies and invest in armaments.

Despite early limited autonomy and success as the AEF in Europe, once the Great War had ended in 1918 American military air power was placed as a subordinate military arm resulting in a dramatic decrease in funding.[36] It was at this time that the US Army Air Service was formed as a combat arm of the US Army, with the US Navy having their own Division of Naval Aeronautics.[37] For both the US Army and US Navy, this was the perfect arrangement as they perceived air power to be an auxiliary arm for their own strategic need – namely reconnaissance or air-to-air combat.[38] Consequently, the military and political leadership within these departments either perceived air power to be of little strategic use on its own, or damaging and a threat to their own resources and funding which had been dramatically cut due to the peacetime context of the period. As Franklin D. Roosevelt, the then Assistant-Secretary of the Navy, stated, Mitchell's notions were 'pernicious' and thus damaging to the American military.[39] Yet this did not stop Mitchell, now Army Air Service Chief of Training and Group Operations, and his advocacy of precision through air power.

In fact, such negative rhetoric by the US Army and US Navy infuriated Mitchell, who believed that he was 'righter than hell'.[40] He felt that 'Army bureaucracy' mixed with the 'stupid or immoral' and those that 'feared innovation' were holding back American air power and potentially risking American national security.[41] He believed that air power, and its ability to achieve precision, were not only vital for the future offensive capability of the American military, but also for its future defensive capability and for American national security as a whole. When talking about potential threats to the United States,

Mitchell expressly stated that precision through air power would put any attacking 'Navy under the water ... [and could] ... have a great effect on land operations'.[42] Consequently, for Mitchell, air power was neither a high-tech novelty nor an auxiliary sideshow (as many in the US Navy and US Army believed). Instead, it was the future of American warfare and vital for the security and military effectiveness of the United States. As such, to ensure his vision would come to fruition, it was Mitchell's view that the American military should have 'a separate air force', like the flourishing independent British Royal Air Force (RAF).[43] He believed that if 'allowed to expand' autonomously, American air power and the vital notion of precision could progress unimpeded.[44] Consequently, during the 1920s, Mitchell set about the fight for air power independence, a fight which would firmly cement his place as the 'pioneer and prophet of air power' and embed precision into the strategic thought of the United States.[45]

To win this political battle, it was Mitchell's plan to showcase air power's most dominant, useful, and publicly popular trait: precision. The ambition to wage warfare through precision was already popular with the American public (and thus increasingly so with politicians). Therefore, Mitchell aimed to bypass the internal politics of the military and utilise precision's popular support to coerce Congress and the White House into supporting the idea of an independent air force.[46] As the military historian Stephen Bourque stated, 'precision was a code word for "we don't need the Army, make us an independent air force"'.[47] To succeed, however, Mitchell needed to generate as much support for precision as possible. Thus, he embarked on a Congressional lobbying, public lecturing, and newspaper article campaign in an attempt to embed precision's strategic and moral characteristics into the mind of American military and political elites and highlight the strategic utility of air power. As the historian Robert Futrell stated, 'Mitchell hoped that he could modify the military policy of the United States by laying "aeronautical facts" before Congress and the people.'[48] Subsequently, in 1921 Mitchell released his seminal text, *Our Air Force*, which comprised much of the material for his campaign.

In this text, Mitchell focused specifically on air power's ability to discriminately strike 'objects on the ground or on the water ... with great accuracy'.[49] Moreover, he chose to cherry pick American experiences from the First World War to complement his arguments regarding air power and its proportionate and discriminate targeting. For instance, when recalling one bombardment mission during the First World War Mitchell stated that in a 'Day Bombardment attack *which missed the town*, [the bomb] hit among the troops of a division which was drilling at a short distance from the city, killed over 200 men, and wounded a corresponding number [emphasis added]'.[50] Here, as shown by his reference to missing the town, Mitchell highlighted that, for both moral and strategic reasons, precision through air power can strike military targets without civilians paying the ultimate cost. Furthermore, Mitchell also highlighted how air power can precisely deploy attacks 'against ground troops and against navies' to end conflict rapidly.[51] In fact, Mitchell even explained how air power can improve the precision of the US Army and US Navy, as 'no artillery can fire accurately now any distance without having observation from the air, and the observers are taught to gauge the fall of the projectiles from the artillery with a percentage of accuracy which amounts to a very few yards' error in each shot'.[52] Consequently, throughout this public campaign Mitchell proclaimed to the people and politicians of the United States that air power and its ability to achieve precision was a strategically and morally superior strategy.

As 1921 progressed, such arguments became increasingly compelling and Mitchell's notions of air power and precision were increasingly supported by the American press and public. As the air power historian Walter Boyne stated, 'the term "Mitchellism" was coined by the press to symbolise the concept that air power was now the dominant military factor and that sea and land forces were becoming subordinate'.[53] Progress had been made. Now demand grew to see this fabled precision in action. As such, the next step was to move from espousing precision's utility, to showing how it would work in practice. This was something Mitchell himself had been campaigning for and he was happy to oblige, although the US Navy was not. After playing 'to the press and to Congress', however, the pressure caused by Mitchell's campaign 'went all the way to the top'.[54] As a result, a test of the strategic worth of air power's precision was eventually approved, forced upon the US Navy.[55] This test was a high-profile spectacle with fifty members of the press, eighteen members of Congress, and military representatives from around the world attending.[56] Yet more importantly for Mitchell's political fight for autonomy, the Secretary of War, Secretary of the Navy, General of the Army, and even President Warren G. Harding were in attendance to see American air power and its lauded precision in action.[57] If Mitchell could prove that air power really did possess the virtue of precision, his mission, he hoped, would be accomplished and air power, along with precision, would be cemented into the very foundations of American strategic thought.

This he achieved on 20 July 1921, during the second day of tests at Langley Field in Virginia.[58] Here Mitchell ordered 'eight Martins and three Handley Page' bomber aircraft to be loaded with 2,000-pound bombs which he 'had personally monitored' being developed.[59] Their target was the USS (formerly SMS) *Ostfriesland*, a First World War German vessel chosen and recommissioned by the US Navy to make it difficult for Mitchell, as this vessel was 'considered by some to be unsinkable'.[60] This Mitchell knew, so to ensure maximum damage he ordered his pilots to 'try for a near miss'[61] as this tactic would create 'water hammer shockwaves'[62] against the ship's hull and cause considerable damage.

Happy with his tactics, Mitchell took to the sky in his own plane named the *Osprey* to have a bird's-eye view of the action. What he witnessed not only pleased him, but most importantly impressed the great, the good, and the powerful who were watching. Dropped with precision at 12:18 p.m., the first bomb made a perfect 'near miss', as Mitchell had ordered, and the five bombs that followed were equally as impressive.[63] As Mitchell stated, 'we could see her [the *Ostfriesland*] rise eight or ten feet between the terrific blows'.[64] Consequently, by 12:40 p.m. the once great German naval vessel had sunk. Furthermore, to highlight the utility of precision one more time, the seventh of Mitchell's bombers dropped a bomb precisely at the point where the ship had gone down. As the historians Stephen Budiansky, Arthur Wagner, and Leon Braxton have stated, it was 'gone in twenty-two minutes'[65] and 'the sinking of the Ostfriesland was well on its way to becoming a legend.'[66]

In the days following, both press and politicians relished the success of precision through air power. As the *New York Times* stated, 'Brigadier General William Mitchell's dictum ... no longer seems fanciful'.[67] Adding political support, Senator William Borah, a leading figure in military debates, declared, 'the battleship is practically obsolete'.[68] He went on to state that 'with sufficient airplane and submarine protection this country was perfectly safe from attack'.[69] In time, even the Joint Army and Navy Board, which analysed the tests, stated air power and its deployment of precision could be 'the decisive factor' in future American conflicts.[70] Mitchell had not only embedded the utility of precision into the foundations of American strategic thought, but had secured the future of American air power.

Over the inter-war years, a steady evolution of the American military structure and strategy occurred, with a greater focus on precision by all arms of the American military.[71] As Richard P. Hallion, the former Air Force Historian stated, measures were being brought into place which would see that 'in 1926 the Army Air Corps was established, and in 1934 the Baker Board directed the formation of the General Headquarters Air Force, giving the Army air arm a measure of autonomy'.[72] As such, progress was being made and both precision and air power were becoming firmly integrated into American warfare. For Mitchell, however, the corresponding years were not so positive.

Instead, by 1925 it seemed to Mitchell that very little had happened to progress his cause, despite his ardent campaigning.[73] Conversely, due to the media circus he had generated around the need for air power precision, Mitchell found himself ostracised by the Army, Navy and political elites. By 1925 he had effectively been demoted and 'assigned to be Air Officer, Eighth Corps Area, in San Antonio, a dead end job' with little power, influence, or prospects.[74] Mitchell became 'increasingly impatient' and frustrated by his treatment and the lack of progress being made.[75]

As a result, Mitchell attempted to do all he could to get himself and his air power crusade back into the American limelight. Specifically, when the suspected loss of an American patrol plane occurred and the 'very real crash of the airship Shenandoah' came to light, Mitchell took the opportunity to try one more time to fast-track the changes he proposed in the military and get his career back on track.[76] In an attempt to generate media attention he proclaimed that the losses were 'the direct result of the incompetence, criminal negligence and almost treasonable administration of our national defence by the Navy and War Departments'.[77] This was 'a splashy public confrontation with the highest authorities' and, unfortunately for Mitchell, such slanderous remarks were merely the opportunity his enemies had been waiting for to remove him from the service.[78]

He was court-martialled for his actions on charges under the 96th Article of War, such that his statement was 'insubordinate ... to the prejudice of good order and military discipline' and was 'highly contemptuous and disrespectful'.[79] Despite Mitchell's closest allies (such as Henry 'Hap' Arnold) speaking in his defence, Mitchell was found guilty and 'sentenced to be suspended from rank, command, and duty with forfeiture of all pay and allowance for five years', later amended to half pay.[80] For Mitchell, this was the final straw and he resigned, a move supported by those in the air service who believed he was unjustly treated.[81] From this point onwards, however, Mitchell's direct influence in strategy and policymaking continued to decrease until his death in 1936. Yet, although his direct influence had dropped, by resigning in such a public fashion and due to the perceived unjust nature of his court-martial and harsh punishment, Mitchell became a martyr in the name of air power. Seen as a 'missionary and a visionary', Mitchell's message of precision air power became immortalised in the strategic thought of the next generation of American air power strategists who were inspired by his 'noble cause'.[82] This new generation of thinkers would pave the way for the development of an official precision-based strategy to be integrated within American warfare prior to the start of the Second World War. As Boyne stated, 'he [Mitchell] inspired devotion in the airmen who would follow in his footsteps and ... would be vital in winning World War II'.[83]

Air Corps Tactical School

From 1931, it was at the Air Corps Tactical School (ACTS), located in Maxwell Field, Alabama, that this new generation of Mitchell-inspired American strategists would devise an official precision-influenced air power doctrine.[84] It was here that Air Corps instructors, such as Major General Donald Wilson and Lieutenant Colonel Harold L. George,[85] would carry on the baton from Mitchell by establishing new doctrine and influencing future high-ranking American officers like Carl A. Spaatz, Haywood S. Hansell, Ira C. Eaker, and, most prominently, the future General of the Army (and the first head of an independent US Air Force) Henry 'Hap' Arnold: the most loyal devotee of Mitchell's doctrine and an ardent pursuer of precision.[86]

Officially named Industrial Web Theory, the doctrine these men devised was more commonly referred to as 'precision bombing' due to its precision attributes in the targeting of the enemy.[87] This evolution in strategic thought encompassed the essence of Mitchell's desire for precision, which they sought to engrain into official doctrine. Precision bombing hoped to achieve the proportionate and discriminate deployment of force to ensure maximum damage to targets deemed pivotal to the enemy war effort. Therefore, in the same vein as Mitchell and Gorrell, and in line with American public demands, the direct targeting of civilian centres was intended to be avoided. Instead, often in daylight conditions, with high visibility to ensure precision, the aim was to 'attack the enemy population indirectly, by disrupting' as opposed to 'blasting and burning' the civilian centres.[88] As historian Conrad Crane stated, 'precision bombing doctrine, attacking factories instead of women and children, offered a way for the Air Corps to be decisive in war without appearing immoral'.[89] Examples of indirect targets included the basic foundations of enemy industry, such as 'raw material, plant machinery [and] power supplies'.[90] By discriminately targeting these sections of infrastructure the aim was to cause 'the breakdown of the industrial and economic structure'.[91] This intended not only to weaken the military might and war-making capacity of the enemy, but also to break the morale of the population and force the enemy leadership to halt hostilities rapidly. If such an outcome could be achieved, it was hoped that it would ultimately reduce the cost to American military and enemy civilian lives. With the details of precision bombing comprehensively theorised at ACTS during the inter-war period, by 1941 it had been ingrained into official American documents on air power doctrine such as Air War Planning Documents AWPD-1, AWPD-4, and AWPD-42. Known as the ACTs doctrine, for all intents and purposes, these were the first official American attempts at a strategic air power doctrine influenced by the attributes of precision.[92] As direct quotations from these documents highlighted, it was now the textbook strategic practice of American bombing raids to ensure the precise targeting of 'objectives vital to the [enemy] war effort' as a means to guarantee 'the breakdown of the industrial and economic structure' of the enemy.[93] Thus, by the time the inter-war period came to an end and America joined the Second World War in 1941, a doctrine based on precision had been cemented within the core of a new American air power strategy. The next step was to prove the doctrine worked in battle.

The overreliance on technology

Pre-war tests, such as the sinking of the 'unsinkable' USS (SMS) *Ostfriesland* with precision targeting during test conditions, had settled many concerns about the achievability of precision.[94] In fact, such weight was placed on the achievement of precision through air power that a seemingly endless stream of funding and support was thrown at the development of technology to ensure its operational success. Quite simply, 'to obtain the utmost accuracy in bomb drops' by investing vast sums of money into the research and development of precision technologies became the philosophy of American political and strategic thinkers.[95]

At the princely sum of $1.5 billion, the most prominent of these investments was the Norden bombsight.[96] From as early as 1920, an evolution of technologically improved versions of this bombsight were created at exceptional cost to keep up with the American demand for greater precision, with the C-1 and M-9 partially automated onboard computers being seen as the peak of precision. When the declassified Air Force Systems Command papers on American bombing systems are studied, it can be seen that the aim of the Norden bombsight was to allow the bombardier perfect accuracy by simply adjusting 'the sight for bomb ballistic data obtained from bombing tables, which allowed for true airspeed, altitude, and the type of bomb to be dropped'.[97] Once these variables had been taken into account, it was deemed that if the bombardier 'synchronized his crosshairs from 25,000 feet altitude so that they remained absolutely centred on the target for the last portion of the bomb run' then the bomb would hit the target precisely.[98] Thus, if successful, the precision bombing doctrine would be achieved.

This was an assumption which was proven time and time again in peacetime testing of the equipment, but never under wartime pressures. As the official Air Force Historical Division records stated, 'practice bomb drops under ideal weather conditions by trained and highly skilled crews gave fantastically good results'.[99] Such faith was put into the bombsight that it was widely promoted that it could achieve sufficient precision to 'put a bomb in a pickle barrel from twenty thousand feet',[100] or hit an apple barrel, or 'the mailbox on the corner'.[101] As a result, by the time the Second World War began, the US had the utmost confidence in its precision bombing doctrine and the new technology designed to help implement it in practice.[102] This was despite the fact it had never been deployed under wartime realities.[103] As historian Tami Biddle stated, 'technology [in a self-proclaimed 'high-tech' nation] seemed to make all things possible and, equally, seemed to solve all potential problems'.[104] In reality, this was just not the case.[105]

2

Evolution (1941–45)

The ruthless bombing from the air of civilians in unfortified centres of population ... has sickened the hearts of every civilized man and woman, and has profoundly shocked the conscience of humanity.

President Franklin D. Roosevelt (1939)[1]

President Roosevelt's comments were declared at the dawn of the Second World War as an appeal for European nations to discontinue the area bombing of civilians. This strategy, he argued, was uncivilised and shocking to the conscience of humanity.[2] The United States, if required, would not deploy force in such a manner. Instead, over the inter-war period American strategic thinkers had, they believed, developed the perfect mix of force deployment, targeting criteria, and precision technologies as a means to avoid such brutality. Thus, when the United States joined the war in 1941 they continued to advocate this 'American way' of bombing.

Precision bombing played a pivotal role in American military strategy. Its success was not only important to those who had pioneered its moral and strategic aims, but also played a vital role in bolstering the reputation of the United States Army Air Forces (USAAF). The first attempt to implement this bombardment strategy in wartime conditions had, however, fallen 'far short of expectations', with only minimal precision achieved and insufficient damage caused (Ploesti, 1942).[3] This early attempt had, due to its failures, not been made public, and plans were put in place to ensure that such failure would not be repeated for the following mission.

Between 1942–43 pressure had already begun to mount on the USAAF leadership from the British who believed such ideas were strategically flawed and less productive when compared to area bombing. Yet, for the USAAF leadership it was imperative – almost personal – to ensure precision's success. Henry 'Hap' Arnold, now Chief of the Army Air Forces, was perhaps the most important proponent of precision. Arnold, it is important to remember, had been taught to fly by the Wright Brothers, had worked on the Kettering Bug, and had even risked his career to defend Billy Mitchell during his court martial in 1925. He was a devoted champion of American precision bombing, and was determined to make it a success. As Arnold stated to his fellow ACTS graduates, precision advocates, and USAAF leaders, General Spaatz and General Eaker:

> [w]e know that the primary function of bombardment is to destroy vital enemy facilities, factories, etc., which are making it possible for him to continue to fight against us. We know that the selection of the most vital targets must come as a result of thorough analysis. We know that the strength of our striking force will always be relatively limited. We must, therefore, apply it to those specially selected targets which will give the greatest return. We cannot afford to apply it where, or in such manner that, the return is not eminently worth the cost. We know that there is room for doubt as to whether friend or enemy is worn down faster by bombing unless it is applied with precision against vital objectives.[4]

Therefore, the outcome of the next mission was of vital importance to reaffirm positive perceptions of the American air war and maintain a precision bombing doctrine. It was for this reason that the results of the next mission were not left to chance.

When the first publicly promoted and reported deployment of precision bombing by the USAAF took place on 17 August 1942, it was what can only be described as a 'PR stunt' – a simulated and exaggerated achievement of the American drive for precision. It was designed for the press, politicians, and public. It was also carried out in conditions which facilitated the mitigation of risks from fighter planes and ground flak. The military and press records from 1942 provide insight into these events. For instance, the records show that the target the USAAF leadership selected for bombardment was chosen specifically for its considerable size, a surprising choice for the inaugural test of precision. These were the locomotive marshalling yards at Sotteville-lès-Rouen, 'one of the largest and most active in northern France'.[5] The choice of this target was important. With such a large target to hit, even if precision bombing failed to hit the primary target it could still be claimed to be proportionate, discriminate, and precise by striking secondary targets in the yard.[6] Furthermore, Sotteville-lès-Rouen was chosen because of its geographic location, which protected the USAAF B-17 Flying Fortress bombers from the risks of war. This was due to the target being sufficiently distant from heavily defended population centres. As such, the USAAF bombers could avoid anti-aircraft fire from dense ground-based flak weapons systems,[7] reducing the risk to life and increasing the chance of a low-cost, high-success first mission. It must also be mentioned that the proposed target was within the British Royal Air Force (RAF) heavy fighter support limit. An unprecedented nine RAF squadrons of Spitfire IX and V fighters were sent alongside a small, and thus easier to defend, group of eighteen USAAF B-17 bombers.[8] This would ensure that no enemy planes would be able to interfere with the USAAF bombardiers and their ability to achieve precision.[9] As such, bearing these factors in mind, historian Stephen Bourque stated, 'if there was a PR stunt, it was Rouen. Military historians sometimes underestimate the power of the home front in sustaining the war. The "Rouen show" was part of entertaining Congress and the American people' with the perceived ability to achieve precision.[10] In fact, the USAAF leadership were so confident of their success and the little risk they faced, that Spaatz was happy to allow fellow proponent and pioneer of precision, Brigadier-General Eaker, to command the mission himself in-flight. This was a highly irregular move which, in regular wartime conditions, would have been highly dangerous and not the place for a high-ranking officer who could have been captured or killed in a high-profile manner. The USAAF leadership, however, knew every measure had been taken to mitigate the risks of war and ensure precision bombing's success. Thus, by sending Eaker along, when he returned, Spaatz could reward his bravery with the distinguished Silver Star – a story which was popular, widely promoted by the press, and helped further justify air power, promote precision bombing, and highlight the achievement of the desired precision back in the United States.[11]

Thus, on reading the American press reports after the 'first' wartime deployment of a precision bombing doctrine (and the precision technologies created to support it), you would be forgiven for thinking that the US Army Air Forces alone were well on their way to winning the war in Europe. The *New York Times* wrote of the precision bombing raid and stated that 'American air power in Britain [was] growing daily in a manner capable of causing the deepest concern in the Reich.'[12] Such assertions were backed by some of the highest-ranking USAAF officers. Spaatz stated that 'this is the real start of our bombing effort and we are going to keep it up',[13] while General Arnold declared that 'the attack on Rouen again verifies the soundness of our policy of the precision bombing of strategic objectives rather than the mass bombing of large, city size areas'.[14] One American pilot quoted in the press even hailed precision as being so successful that 'to see all the bombs making dead hits was like all the Fourths of July I have ever known'.[15] Thus, publicly, precision bombing and its ability to achieve the long-held moral, ethical, and strategic ambitions had not only passed its first wartime test, but to those looking in, it had passed with flying colours.[16] There are some, such as historian Richard P. Hallion, who disagreed with this appraisal.

As Hallion stated, 'this [Rouen] is a baby step ... the force was having to learn how to operate as a team, something you only do gradually'.[17] Furthermore, he asked 'what would have been better? Taking an inexperienced force straight into the Ruhr or to Schweinfurt? That would have simply thrown ill-trained and ill-experienced airmen away.'[18] Hallion is of course correct. This study does not wish to suggest that the USAAF leadership would have been better to go for a direct hit on the Führerbunker on their first run. In an attempt to identify, adapt, and learn from the mission. However, it is suggested that a more realistic initial test of daylight precision bombing should have been undertaken, one which allowed the pilots and strategists to experience and learn from the realities of the dense German anti-aircraft defences and the enemy fighter planes which would come to hamper later USAAF efforts to achieve precision as the war progressed. If carried out in this manner, the inaugural mission would have highlighted some of the flaws and failures of precision bombing, many of which would become all too clear over the corresponding months. It was due to this fabrication of wartime realities that an overreliance and faith in precision bombing ensued from the 'Rouen Show'. As historian Paul Fussell argued, due to the seeming success of precision bombing 'only a cynic or sadist could have predicted in 1942 that before the war ended the burnt and twisted bits of almost 22,000 of these Allied bombers would strew the fields of Europe and Asia'.[19]

Strategic reality

They were dropping them all over the fucking landscape. Maybe it was true that they could hit a pickle barrel with that Norden bombsight, but there were no pickle barrels in the Liri Valley that day.
Observer of US precision bombing, Liri Valley/Monte Cassino (1944)[20]

The American manipulation of wartime conditions to ensure the success of precision bombing contributed to an overdependence on the doctrine. As such, when precision bombing went from theory into practice without any substantial tests of its utility in wartime realities, the United States exposed itself to a litany of technological and strategic failures. This led directly to an unnecessary loss of life and an eventual deviation from precision, towards area bombing. Indeed, if the real results of the Sotteville-lès-Rouen raid had been made public, it might have become clear that precision bombing, although viable in theory, was not capable of fulfilling the demands required in war.

Press reports depicted the Sotteville-lès-Rouen raids as a success, and thus the raids have often been synonymous in American military history with success and 'exceptional accuracy'.[21] When the French reports are studied, however, it is clear that precision bombing, despite the measures taken to ensure its success, was far less precise than publicised. Records show that out of a total '36,900 pounds of general-purpose bombs dropped on the marshalling yards' only around half fell in the area of their proposed target.[22] Although proclaimed as precise by the USAAF leadership, the French historians Edward Florentine and Claude Archambault took a different perspective and stated that the attack 'killed 52 civilians and injured another 120'.[23] This claim is further supported by Stephen Bourque, who added that 'bombs tumble everywhere, but only about five actually hit the rail line'.[24] As such, despite all the hype, press fanfare, technological investment, and operating in daylight to ensure precision through the best possible visibility, precision bombing was unable to drop the vast majority of its ordnance on one of the largest marshalling yards in Europe, let alone a mailbox or pickle barrel. The unreliability of the vastly expensive Norden bombsight in combat conditions may go some way to explaining why precision bombing was unable to successfully fulfil the levels of precision required of it

The author of *Wired for War*, Peter. W. Singer, stated that precision bombing was 'typically hitting targets within 100 to 1000 feet'.[25] As such, despite being able to achieve 'pinpoint' precision on the majority of occasions in tests, the accuracy in combat situations was far from guaranteed. The declassified US Air Force review of Second World War bombing systems offered a number of reasons why this precision technology underperformed. For instance, it argued that when exposed to combat situations many shortcomings were spotted in the Norden bombsight, not least of which was its 'inability to bomb except under conditions of good visibility'.[26] In detail, the report stated that 'cloud cover, haze, fog, smoke from fires and explosions in the target area: any of these made the optical bombsight worse than useless'.[27]

As such, it can be seen how, in times of war, a precision bombsight which is inoperable in cloud or in smoke from fire and explosions, can render useless a precision bombing doctrine and its aim to be proportionate and discriminate in its targeting of the enemy. The technological failure of precision equipment led to the strategic failure of precision bombing. The USAAF leadership were, however, not ready to give up on its central notion. Thus, as the war progressed, and even more damning examples of precision's technological ineffectiveness

Figure 2.1 Original Norden bombsight used on Enola Gay for the atom bomb drop on Hiroshima

emerged, USAAF strategists attempted to modify their bombing doctrine to ensure increased levels of precision.

This was the case in regard to the targeting of the strategically vital German occupied Ploesti oil fields in Romania, which took place on 1 August 1943.[28] Two years prior to this attack, on 14 July 1941, Soviet air forces had conducted an air raid against the Unirea Orion refinery in the Ploesti region. By flying in at an altitude of between 2,000 and 3,000 feet, the Soviet air forces had not only been able to achieve the element of surprise and encounter little resistance from ground-based flak crews, but were also able to identify and strike their targets without the need for high-tech precision equipment.[29] These aircraft were able to drop their bomb loads with accuracy and destroy their targets rapidly without the need for subsequent sorties. In total, the forces caused damage 'amounting to more than a million dollars' (1940s prices, equivalent to roughly $20 million today) and put the refinery out of action for a total of four months.[30] For the USAAF in 1943, with high-altitude precision bombing not achieving the successes they had hoped, such successes were compelling. One US report stated, 'much more effective was the [Soviet air forces] raid of 14 July, a surprise attack …'.[31] Furthermore, the USAAF had previously attempted to strike the Ploesti oil fields with high-altitude precision bombing a year after the Soviet air forces low-level attack, but with little success.

In this instance, the American attempt at precision bombing was limited by poor weather which was 'broken overcast at 10,000 to 12,000 feet which practically obscured the targets'.[32] As a result, the bombs dropped by the Middle East-based Halverson Detachment of 13 American B-24 bombers caused minimal damage. As the Assistant Chief of Air Staff's report stated in 1944, 'at any rate, the damage inflicted fell far short of expectations'.[33] As for the rest of the bombs, they were scattered over the city of Constanta, with some hitting 'unidentified targets' and others falling 'in the woods' or hitting 'a railway station'.[34] Thus, when the USAAF wanted another attempt at these vital oil supplies, seen as a 'panacea target'[35] which could act 'as a means to strike hard at the Germans',[36] they chose to take heed of their previous mistakes and adopt Soviet air force tactics.[37]

Specifically, due to the litany of technological flaws seen in high-altitude precision bombing and the importance of the target, General Jacob E. Smart helped to create the tactic 'of having planes fly exceedingly low' to bomb with increased levels of precision, but without the need for unreliable technology.[38] Known as 'zero altitude' or 'minimum altitude' bombing, the aim of the tactic was to achieve strategic aims while maintaining the proportionate and discriminate characteristics of precision.[39] It would achieve this through low-level flying, allowing little opportunity for error and the unintentional targeting of civilians in the nearby cities of Constanta. It would be comparatively low-cost to American life through the element of surprise achieved by flying under German radar.[40] It would also be rapid in its achievement of aims by hitting all targets with precision in one mission, eliminating the need for subsequent costly sorties. In theory, it was to be the pinnacle of proportionate, discriminate, rapid, and low-cost precision.[41] In practice, however, this was not the case.

Even before the mission began, plans started to unravel. Unbeknown to the USAAF, during the planning stages Ploesti had become one of the most heavily defended sites in Europe. As Robert Modrovsky stated, in the time since the previous American high-altitude precision bombing mission, 'Luftwaffe Colonel Gerstenberg had done his work well making the city – Festung Ploesti – an unconquerable fortress … [with] … 237 antiaircraft guns … barrage balloons, light-flak towers, and hundreds of machine guns.'[42] On top of this the Germans had an 'efficient radar detection net … coupled with a Signal Interception Unit near Athens which was decoding' the American transmissions.[43] Thus, on the day of the mission, as historian Leon Wolff reported in a somewhat understated manner, 'it began badly'.[44]

Not only did some aircraft fail to take off, with one crashing on the runway,[45] but due to the German interceptions of American transmissions, the USAAF bombers were being tracked as soon as they were in the air.[46] With the American pilots flying low and 'well within anti-aircraft range'[47] into a region teeming with poised defences, it is unsurprising that this day came to be known as 'Black Sunday'.[48] Specifically, on the raids of 1 August, 180[49] USAAF B-24 Liberator bombers were sent to carry out their attacks at a 'tree top level'.[50] As one pilot stated, 'we came in right on the deck – 20 feet or less'.[51] The raid, without the element of surprise, resulted in 310 airmen being killed,[52] 108 captured,[53] and only 88 (48.8 per cent) of the total bombers, 'most badly damaged',[54] managing to return to base.[55] Furthermore, when the declassified US Enemy Oil Committee reports of the attack from 1943 are analysed, it can be seen that, despite the low-level bombing contributing to some increase in accuracy and temporary damage to the refineries,[56] attempts to achieve the precision aims of the bombardment were unsuccessful, with heavy cost to life and 'no curtailment of overall product output'.[57] As such, despite tactical and technical adjustment, American attempts had fallen wide of the mark once again. Such shortfalls, however, did little to change the American reliance and dependence on precision.

Motivated by a long-held dedication to precision, and the vast investment that had already been put into achieving it, the USAAF leadership refused to deviate from their primary ambition and move to a strategy unconstrained by such moral, ethical, and strategic limitations.[58] Instead, the USAAF leadership did as they had done before and portrayed the Romanian raids as a victory.

This, the leadership hoped, would not only give them time to try to devise a successful precision-based bombing strategy, but would also allow them to keep the pivotal notion of precision as the core of their development plans. As such, referred to as Operation Tidalwave, these attacks were spun in the official press releases and in the international press as being a 'success' which 'cut off Hitler's oil tap at the mains' and made 'the enemy rock back on his heels'.[59] The official reports labelled it 'an epic of American valor' and a 'masterpiece of detailed and careful planning'.[60] While promoting precision, Spaatz even stated that his plan could 'reduce to the point of surrender any first-class nation now in existence, within six months'.[61] Thus, the USAAF mantra was that precision, through either high or low altitude bombing, was fulfilling the American ambitions for precision. Such stories had of course been embellished, but they were important for the USAAF to maintain.

These reports of success allowed the US Army Air Forces leadership to continue to posture in the face of significant pressure by the British Air Ministry to adopt area bombing.[62] This was an option which had always been available to the USAAF as part of its official military doctrine. Nevertheless, due to such an option being perceived as largely disproportionate and indiscriminate by the USAAF leadership, it was only 'to be undertaken solely as a last resort, and only if precision bombing proved unfeasible or failed to do the job'.[63] For the USAAF leadership this was not yet the case. In Henry 'Hap' Arnold's memoirs he recalled a meeting with Prime Minister Winston Churchill about the matter. As Arnold stated:

> [O]n January 19th, I had lunch with the Prime Minister … The Prime Minister seemed willing to let the matter drop. It was quite evident to me he had been harassed by some of his own people about our daylight bombing program and had to put up a fight on the subject … [however,] the Prime Minister told me he was willing for us to give it a trial … That was a great relief to me and to my command. We had won a major victory, for we would bomb in accordance with American principles, using the methods for which our planes were designed'.[64]

Indeed, ACTS alumni, such as Ira Eaker, believed he and his fellow precision advocates had 'built up slowly and painfully and learned [their] job'.[65] In a position paper (1943), Eaker even went on to ask for the British to be patient with precision bombing, and stated, 'give us our chance, and your reward will be ample'.[66] Thus, it is clear that within the USAAF it was believed that precision bombing, if given time, could still learn from its mistakes and achieve its aims. As such, the USAAF leadership was refusing to abandon its highly inconsistent, yet core, principle of precision.

While pushing for victory in the Pacific theatre, the USAAF attempted to prove precision bombing's utility one final time by showing it could target the strategically vital Japanese aircraft manufacturing works.[67] Many of these missions were carried out by the American XXI Bomber Command, under the control of Major-General Haywood S. Hansell Jr., another former ACTS man who had originally helped draw up the ACTS Doctrine.[68] As such, if anyone could make precision bombing work, it was him. Yet despite precision bombing's continued use throughout 1944 and into 1945, vast improvements did not occur. Hansell was encouraged to use incendiary bombs in his precision bombing of the Japanese aircraft works. The intent was to maximise the damage of the bombs which were successful in striking the military-industrial target. Although an increased level of fire damage occurred, increased precision did not. For instance, on 27 December 1944 Hansell ordered the targeting of the *Nakajima* Aircraft Engine Plant in *Musashino* (a city in the Tokyo area) with incendiary bombs. Seventy-two USAAF B-29 bombers were sent out to conduct daylight precision bombing raids. During these attacks, however, only thirty-nine of the bombers managed to gain sufficient visibility to release their bombs. Yet what is perhaps most astonishing is that out of the bombs these aircraft dropped, a mere twenty-six landed in the general area of the target.[69] As such, only minimal success was achieved, and only minor damage caused (other than setting a hospital alight).[70] As the historians Wesley Craven and James Cate stated, 'by any reasonable standards the attack was a failure'.[71]

Precision bombing attacks continued throughout the opening months of 1945 with the majority producing similar levels of failure. As a result, it was during this period that even Hansell conceded, 'it was apparent our preferred strategy (destruction of selected targets through precision optical bombing) could not be sustained'.[72] Therefore, targeting improvements had to be made and technological advancements found, or the attempt to achieve precision bombing had to be abandoned. In a final attempt to improve precision bombing, Hansell was replaced by General Curtis LeMay (a decision taken by Arnold and Eaker).[73] LeMay continued where his predecessor had left off, and, in a final attempt, tried to achieve the American strategic aims with precision bombing. Yet, LeMay was, like those before him, unsuccessful. As Hansell stated in his memoirs, 'for about six weeks, General LeMay carried forward the operations I had started – with almost identical result[s] [precision bombing] ... could not be sustained'.[74] Thus, with no technological advancement currently available to allow for improvements in precision bombing, the only option was for it to be replaced after almost three decades as the primary American air power strategy.[75] Subsequently, it was relegated to a secondary strategic aim. In its place the 'last resort' of area bombing was reluctantly brought into action in Japan.

American area bombing: precision distorted

USAAF devoted the bulk of its effort to 'area raids' that used incendiary bombs to burn down Japanese cities and to kill hundreds of thousands of Japanese civilians.
Thomas R. Searle (2002)[76]

To describe the USAAF adoption of area bombing as a last resort is no understatement. Nor is it an attempt to try to justify the use of a bombing strategy that President Roosevelt himself had described as 'ruthless bombing from the air'.[77] As highlighted in examples above, it was clear that every attempt had been made to try to ensure precision bombing remained the core component of American air power doctrine, even at a substantial cost to American military and enemy civilian lives. As previously stated, however, area bombing had always been an option of last resort within American military strategy if precision bombing failed, and it was now the common consensus that precision bombing was no longer fit for purpose. As such, Arnold, now General of the Army, reluctantly side-lined precision bombing and took the task in hand to mitigate the ever-growing death toll to enemy civilians and the American military by ending the war as quickly as possible and through any means available.

Consequently, with no alternative precision-based strategy deemed adequate or available, the British mantra that 'in order to destroy anything, it is necessary to bomb everything' was adopted as part of an American area bombing strategy.[78] As the military historian Thomas Searle stated, the 'USAAF devoted the bulk of its effort to "area raids" that used incendiary bombs to burn down Japanese cities and to kill hundreds of thousands of Japanese civilians'.[79] This potent deployment of incendiary weapons on Japanese cities was approved by General Arnold and given the highest priority by the Committee of Operations Analysts.[80] As Arnold stated in his writings to Spaatz, 'of particular interest to me would be some idea as to the most effective mixture of high explosives and incendiaries against heavily built-up areas'.[81] As such, the strategic intent of such attacks was clear. It was perceived by the US that in Japan 'much of the manufacturing process was carried out in homes and small "shadow" factories' which were often close to the larger central factory.[82] Thus, for the USAAF leadership, such a strategy was justified by stating it was a strategic necessity to target the home factories of the skilled Japanese workforce to diminish the war-making capacity of Japan. Furthermore, it was argued that this level of barbarity was necessary to end the war against an enemy which, as the Allied 'Magic' radio interceptions had indicated, was prepared to 'fight to the bitter end'.[83] A study of selected sections of the 1946 United States Strategic Bombing Survey (USSBS) 'Summary Report Pacific War' highlights the destructive nature of this strategy of last resort.[84]

Starting on 9 March 1945, during the first ten days of area bombing the USAAF conducted a total of 1,595 sorties on the great cities of Japan.[85] During these sorties, a total of 9,373 tons of predominantly incendiary bombs were deployed upon the urban areas of Kobe, Nagoya, Osake, and Tokyo.[86] As the USSBS stated, these raids destroyed '31 square miles of those cities'.[87] In Tokyo on 9 and 10 March 1945, the infamous 'firestorm' or 'firebombing' of the city occurred. This 'boiled water in Tokyo's rivers and canals' and even melted glass windows.[88] In fact, the city was burnt to such an extent that after the raid one eyewitness stated, 'I thought I saw some black work gloves. When I took a closer look, they were hands that had been torn off' by the fire storm and intense heat.[89] Due to the inferno caused by the USAAF area bombing, this raid alone was responsible for between 130,000 and 185,000 fatalities.[90] Yet, despite the horror, terror, and death caused by this new strategy, an unconditional surrender from the Japanese still needed to be achieved. As such, the USAAF invested further in its use of area bombing to 'terrorise the rest of Japan' into unconditional surrender.[91]

Over the next four months an intense effort was made by Arnold to increase the 'burning of Japanese cities'.[92] The monthly tonnage of ordnance deployed increased from 13,800 tons in March 1945 to 42,700 tons in July 1945.[93] Along with this, the rules of engagement were amended. No longer were just the great cites of Japan open for attack; instead, smaller secondary cities were made legitimate targets to apply further pressure on the Japanese to surrender.[94] Unsurprisingly, during this period the number of Japanese fatalities saw a significant increase. If we remove the lower 9–10 March Tokyo area bombing estimates of 130,000 from the total number killed from the USAAF area bombing of Japan, Sherry stated, 'one arrives at a death toll of 550,000' from the remaining American area bombing raids.[95] Such civilian fatality figures are hard to comprehend. Yet after the failure of USAAF precision bombing, these tactics, condemned by history as indiscriminate and disproportionate, were seen as a justified strategy of last resort to end the war rapidly and save lives in the long term.[96] Nonetheless, unfortunately for the USAAF leadership, after these raids an unconditional surrender and rapid end to the conflict had still not emerged. Consequently, it seemed that the strategy of last resort was failing to achieve its ultimate objective and, as such, General Arnold began to talk of drastically increasing the area bombing and the burning of Japanese cities.

During this desperate period, General Arnold is quoted as wanting to 'continue firebombing'.[97] When the projected increase in bomb tonnage is studied for the period going into August 1945, this notion rings true. As the USSBS stated, the US area bombing 'would have continued to increase thereafter to a planned figure of 115,000 tons per month'.[98] Although exact figures cannot be ascertained, it can be stated with a degree of certainty that such an increase – from 13,800 tons in March to 42,700 tons in July and 115,000 tons in August – would have seen a drastic increase in Japanese fatalities as a result of American desperation. Yet this was but one escalatory measure being prepared to put pressure on the Japanese. Alongside this proposed increase in the heavily destructive area bombing, it should be recognised that, within all departments of the American military, plans were being laid for a cost-heavy and prolonged ground invasion of the Japanese homeland.[99]

As Secretary of War Stimson stated, American strategists predicted that if such a textbook case of total war was to come to fruition, it would have seen the Allied forces take on the Japanese who 'commanded forces of somewhat over 5 million' troops and 5,000 Japanese aircraft which were predicted to be utilised for kamikaze purposes.[100] Yet despite the size of the enemy, plans continued to be developed for the 'final offensive'. Named Operation Downfall, the assault would see a combined ground, air, and sea attack staged upon Japan as early as November 1945, with victory not coming 'until the latter part of 1946 at the earliest'.[101] Fatalities among the Allied forces alone were estimated at one million, with at least equal that for the Japanese.[102] Such a line of strategic thought is undoubtedly a cost-heavy strategy of last-resort during a period of desperation. It was not, however, the only alternative proposed.

Alongside this, another cost-heavy strategy (for the Japanese at least) was being devised. This was to starve Japan into submission through the increased targeting of its transport system.[103] Richard B. Frank, author of *Downfall* (2001), stated that such a strategy would have 'had the most effect'.[104] As he explained, '[a]t first glance, the new directive, which substituted selective attacks on transportation targets for the area-incendiary campaign, appears far more humane'.[105] In the long term, however, Frank estimated that 'the new directive would have caused far more loss of life by starvation'.[106] Quite simply, as he concluded, the implementation of this strategy would have caused the transportation of already limited food supplies to cease and thus would have unleashed 'mass starvation' which, by the highest estimates, would have resulted in the death of up to '10 million Japanese' in an attempt to force the nation's leadership to end the war.[107] Such a line of strategic thought epitomised the desperate mindset of the period. In fact, when all proposed strategies are considered individually (or combined), it is clear to see that to bring the Second World War to a victorious conclusion, the United States and its allies would stop at nothing. Whether it was the potential starvation of millions, the sacrifice of a generation in a sustained invasion, or the expansion of a prolonged, indiscriminate, and cost-heavy air power strategy, American strategic thinkers were willing to consider all lines of strategic thought to end the war – no matter the cost. This was epitomised by the destructive means ultimately chosen by the Truman administration to end the war in the Pacific. Successfully tested in the deserts of New Mexico, a new weapon offered the potential for a rapid victory. Its singular destructive capacity, however, would be like that never seen before.

Why the atomic bomb?

the project might even mean the doom of civilization or it might mean the perfection of civilization; that it might be a Frankenstein which would eat us up or it might be a project by which the peace of the world would be helped in becoming secure.

Secretary of War Henry L. Stimson (1945)[108]

The ultimate decision was taken on 2 August 1945 aboard the USS *Augusta*.[109] It was here that, after weeks of discussion with military, political, and scientific elites, President Truman came to issue the order for the deployment of atomic bombs on Japan.[110] By 9 August, after said bombs had been dropped on the cities of Hiroshima and Nagasaki, 200,000 Japanese had been killed and scores of additional casualties had been exposed to life-altering burns and the life-shortening effects of radiation poisoning.[111] As Hiroshima survivor Keiko Ogura explained to me during my research, 'everywhere fire started ... people in the centre of the city caught fire'.[112] By 15 August the war was over.[113]

Often defined by their 'traditional' or 'revisionist' approaches, scholars have made it their life's work to analyse and identify the motivation behind the deployment of these enormously destructive weapons.[114] Although in-depth study of each argument is beyond the scope of a project concerned with the evolution of precision, the most prominent explanations from these two schools of thought are analysed here. When these differing schools are analysed they highlight the multitude of complex factors which contributed towards the deployment of the atomic bomb. They also highlight the strategic complexity of the period and help us to understand that there was no one dominant line of strategic thought, nor strategic motivation behind the deployment of the atomic bomb: a multitude of reasons lay behind the use of such a weapon. Precision is analysed within this complex context and it is argued that a distorted understanding of precision bombing strategy was but one of these motivations. The study starts by outlining the traditional interpretations offered by both Truman and Stimson.

When selected segments from Truman's diary and correspondence (both of which are steeped in contestation over their accuracy and legitimacy) are studied, it would seem that moral and ethical motivations lay behind the deployment of the atomic bomb. From the moment news of its successful testing broke, the notion of deploying the bomb to save lives was at the forefront of the narrative (or perhaps rhetoric) espoused by Truman. As he entered in his diary on 25 July 1945, 'he [Stimson] and I are in accord. The target will be a purely military one.'[115] This suggests a mutual feeling of abhorrence at the thought of targeting civilians. His later statements support such a line of thought. As selected Truman papers highlight, it was the nature of the target and its pinpoint destruction which were seemingly at the centre of atomic preparations. As he again stated in his diary on 25 July 1945:

> the weapon is to be used against Japan between now and August 10th. I have told the Sec. of War, Mr. Stimson, to use it so that military objectives and soldiers and sailors are the target and not women and children. Even if the Japs are savage, ruthless, merciless and fanatic, we as the leader of the world for the common welfare cannot drop this terrible bomb on the old capital or the new [Kyoto or Tokyo].[116]

Consequently, as history tells us, instead of causing maximum destruction by striking Kyoto or Tokyo, it was Hiroshima and Nagasaki that were struck with this new weapon. Specifically, it was the Headquarters of the Second Army (Hiroshima) and the Mitsubishi Steel and Arms Works (Nagasaki) that were targeted through the crosshairs of the latest M-9 Norden bombsight. This was allegedly due to their smaller overall population numbers and the high profile of these military targets.[117]

As for Stimson, his thoughts on conventional strategic bombardment had long been focused on precision. As his diary entry concerning a conversation with Truman on 6 June 1945 stated:

I told him that I was busy considering our conduct of the war against Japan and I told him how I was trying to hold the Air Force down to precision bombing but that with the Japanese method of scattering its manufacture it was rather difficult to prevent area bombing. I told him I was anxious about this feature of the war ... because I did not want to have the United States get the reputation of outdoing Hitler in atrocities[118]

Such a narrative, especially incorporating a wish to not outdo Hitler, demonstrated an ambition to ensure strategic bombardment was carried out in line with the original ethos of precision bombing. More importantly, it highlighted such an ambition was, it seems, apparent at the highest levels of American political thought just two months before the atomic bomb was deployed in 1945. When certain select post-war statements are studied it appears that these same goals drove Stimson's (and Truman's) personal motivations behind the deployment of the atomic bomb in late 1945.

Recalling his motivations behind the deployment, Stimson stated that he believed the atomic bomb to be 'a great new instrument for shortening the war and minimizing destruction'.[119] In addition to this, Stimson stated that he thought 'such an effective shock would save many times the number of lives, both American and Japanese, than it would cost'.[120] Truman espoused similar statements in the initial post-war days. Directly after the bombs were successfully deployed, Truman declared to the American people via radio:

[t]he world will note that the first atomic bomb was dropped on Hiroshima, a military base. That was because we wished in this first attack to avoid, insofar as possible, the killing of civilians ... We have used it in order to shorten the agony of war, in order to save the lives of thousands and thousands of young Americans[121].

Again, such a statement from the President highlights the supposed discriminate nature of the target and the President's drive to mitigate the cost to civilians. As such, it would appear to add credence to the notion that ambitions akin to precision, no matter how misplaced and illusory, may have in part contributed towards the deployment. Of course, this could also simply be populist rhetoric put forward by a president to a population concerned with discriminate precision. On further analysis, however, it would seem that similar ambitions fuelled the motivations (and the practicalities of the atomic bomb deployment) at the military level of strategic thought.

The USAAF pursuit of precision is well documented. When select details from the day of the deployment are studied, it is likely that, although having to deviate from the doctrine in early 1945, precision bombing doctrine played a role in the strategy behind the deployment of the atomic bomb in August of the same year. Colonel Paul W. Tibbets Jr. was the man chosen to command, pilot, and train the crew of the B-29 Superfortress which would ultimately strike the first of these targets.[122] It would seem that this fact in itself is not particularly noteworthy. What is often overlooked, however, is that Tibbets was recognised as 'a superb pilot', regarded as the most accomplished operator of the latest precision bombsights, and had led the first ever precision bombing raid on Sotteville-lès-Rouen back in 1942.[123] He was, in essence, 'the best of the best' when it came to precision. By choosing such an experienced precision pilot, it could be proposed that it was the accurate striking of the desired military targets which was key to the bomb's deployment. Additionally, it is interesting to note that, in training for these attacks, Tibbets was ordered to carry out a number of test runs for the use of the bomb which Cate and Craven have expressly stated were centred on perfecting 'a precision attack against pinpoint targets'.[124] Although it is by no means uncommon to carry out practice runs before a bombardment, it is evident that elements of precision were included when planning for the attack. This is not the only factor worthy of mention when discussing precision.

When the USAAF deployed the atomic bombs, it would appear that it was out of intention not coincidence that precision was given a level of priority. For instance, if the weather had not allowed for visual precision deployment (a more precise means of targeting than the rudimental radar available) of the atomic bombs on 6 and 9 August 1945, then the release of the bombs would not have been allowed. As Acting Chief of Staff General Handy stated in a letter to General Spaatz, '20th Air Force will deliver its first special bomb as soon as weather will permit visual bombing'.[125] Furthermore, on the day of the first raid, in a preflight briefing, Tibbets was ordered to 'bring the bomb back if all three cities were hidden by cloud'.[126] Such an order adds credence to the notion that merely to deploy the bomb and cause indiscriminate destruction was not good enough. Instead, it was the precision striking of a military target which was one aspect of the strategy and strategic thought at play. Extra support for this notion is provided by the reports of the bombs' precision strike 'success' on the day of the attacks.

As stated, clear weather for visual precision deployment had been outlined as a prerequisite for the use of the atomic bomb on the two Japanese cities. During the attacks, visibility over Hiroshima was rated 2/10[127] and thus extremely clear, while the pilot over Nagasaki 'found a hole in the cloud'[128] to deploy his bomb visually with his bombsight. As such, a surprisingly high level of precision was achieved in both attacks. In Nagasaki the bomb landed precisely within the radius of the Mitsubishi Arms Plant (500 yards north of the plant),[129] while in Hiroshima, ground zero was 'near a bridge at the end of the island and quite close to the aiming point'.[130] The aiming point was designated as slightly south of the Second Army base (as mentioned by Truman).[131] This was struck with relative precision at the Aioi-bashi bridge, 800 feet from the designated target, obliterating the military headquarters based at Hiroshima Castle.[132] Thus, analysis of all the above aspects would suggest that a drive for precision at a political, military, and technical level influenced the way the US Air Force deployed atomic bombs on Japan in August 1945.

Of course, there are alternative understandings of this period. For instance, although from the study of one set of documents it may seem that planners did seek the achievement of a long-held precision bombardment strategy, the predeployment damage estimates put forward in differing planning documents paint a contrasting picture. As stated in Cate and Craven, military planners calculated for a '7,500-ft radius of destruction' (1.4 miles).[133] They believed that 'a bomb exploding … would wreck all important parts of the city except the dock areas'.[134] Areas directly targeted within their destructive radius were densely built-up sections of Hiroshima consisting of 'a mixture of residential, commercial, military and small industrial buildings'.[135] Thus, it would appear discriminate targeting was far from a military goal.

An explanation for such targeting, however, may come from General Arnold's statement to Stimson earlier in 1945 when justifying why precision bombing was increasingly being extended to civilian areas. In conversation with Stimson (who, as aforementioned, was concerned about reports of a mounting Japanese death toll from American bombing), it is documented that Arnold argued:

> the Air Force was up against the difficult situation arising out of the fact that Japan, unlike Germany, had not concentrated her industries and that on the contrary they were scattered out and were small and closely connected in site with the houses of their employees; that thus it was practically impossible to destroy the war output of Japan without doing more damage to civilians connected with the output than in Europe.[136]

When Stimson raised his concerns further about said destruction – directing that he had been informed 'there would be only precision bombing in Japan' – Arnold clearly replied that he and the USAAF leadership were 'trying to keep it [the destruction of civilian centres] down as far as possible'.[137] Thus, it was argued by Arnold that, in Japan, it was simply not possible to achieve previous levels of precision against targets of a differing nature to those in Europe. Quite simply, practical targeting issues meant that the scope of the precision remit had to broaden. Of course, given the complexity of this subject matter, many revisionist scholars would argue such a point of view naive.

In *American Arsenal* (2014), Patrick Coffey argued a more prosaic point. He made it clear that precision bombing had reached merely rhetoric status by late 1945, and argued that 'the atomic bomb is, of course, the perfect weapon for area bombing, but the AAF still *pretended* that it practiced precision bombing [emphasis added]'.[138] As the controversial use of the word 'pretended' suggests, Coffey argued that the USAAF had long abandoned precision bombing and had now branded all forms of bombing 'precision' to keep in line with public and political demands. As he stated, even incendiary raids were now presented as 'pinpoint incendiary bombing' to the American public.[139] Such an argument is compelling. In addition to this, when the destruction wrought is outlined, it is clear why any consideration of precision as a motivation would be dismissed. With 4.7 square miles (24,816 ft) of Hiroshima destroyed, the destruction was vast, unforgiving, and far from any justifiable incarnation of precision bombing.[140] Thus, it is clear to see why the idea of 'precision' as a military motivation behind the deployment of the bomb is a contested issue. A similar state of affairs is apparent at a political level. Further reasoning for the rejection of any precision intent comes from the study of additional motivations espoused at a political level within a differing set of Truman and Stimson papers and the work of scholars who have interpreted them.

After studying additional Truman and Stimson papers, scholars have hypothesised a plethora of explanations as to why the atomic bombs were deployed in August 1945. Sherry, author of *The Rise of American Air Power* (1987), argued the more obvious motivations to 'hasten victory over Japan', 'to placate a war-weary and grumbling public', and to 'close off any need for a land invasion' form part of this narrative.[141] None of these motivations counter the idea that precision may have also been part of the discussion and decision-making process. Indeed, the ambition to reduce American casualties and to rapidly end the war could be considered a core part of the said process. Nevertheless, when additional motivations are put forward (identified by scholars such as Alperovitz, Coffey, Freedman, and Fussell), it is clear to see that a complex narrative around the deployment of the atomic bomb persists.

Gar Alperovitz, a revisionist historian, put forward the most prominent of these narratives. In *Atomic Diplomacy* (1965) and *The Decision to Deploy the Atomic Bomb* (1995) he argued that, at a political level, decision-makers understood that the deployment of the bomb was unnecessary to win the war. Instead, Alperovitz proposed that the decision was primarily motivated by Great Power politics. Utilising his study of alternative sections of the Stimson Papers, he stated that long 'before the atomic bomb had been tested, American leaders had begun to calculate that the new force might greatly strengthen their hand against their wartime ally, the Soviet Union'.[142] Citing Stimson's remarks from May 1945 that 'it may be necessary to have it out with Russia' and that 'S-1 [i.e., the atomic bomb] secret would be dominant' as support for his argument, Alperovitz proceeded to build a compelling case.[143] He moved to consolidate his argument through the study of remarks made by key figures at a military level. Alperovitz posited that the Truman administration rejected the advice (both ethical and strategic) of senior military officials and proceeded with the deployment of the bomb as a means to send a powerful message to the Kremlin. Two of his foundational supporting statements originated from Admiral Leahy and General Eisenhower. Although neither are directly part of the USAAF leadership charged with deploying the bomb, their post-war statements on the bombs' deployment give us pause for thought. Admiral Leahy made his views abundantly clear within his memoirs:

> [i]t is my opinion that the use of this barbarous weapon at Hiroshima and Nagasaki was of no material assistance in our war against Japan. The Japanese were already defeated and ready to surrender ... My own feeling was that in being the first to use it, we had adopted an ethical standard common to the barbarians of the Dark Ages. I was not taught to make war in that fashion, and wars cannot be won by destroying women and children.[144]

Leahy was not alone in this line of thought. General Eisenhower made a similar and equally emotive declaration. In reaction to 'factual' remarks made by Stimson during the initial post-war period, Eisenhower chose to make his own opinions and discussions with Stimson public. As he stated:

> [d]uring his recitation of the relevant facts, I had been conscious of a feeling of depression and so I voiced to him my grave misgivings, first on the basis of my belief that Japan was already defeated and that dropping the bomb was completely unnecessary, and secondly because I thought that our country should avoid shocking world opinion by the use of a weapon whose employment was, I thought, no longer mandatory as a measure to save American lives. It was my belief that Japan was, at that very moment, seeking some way to surrender with a minimum loss of 'face'.[145]

Although such thoughts are espoused in a post-war context and are thus a retrospective take on the events and motivations, such statements lend support to

Alperovitz's line of argument. As he declared, '[s]omething clearly had caused Leahy and Eisenhower to break the unwritten rule that required high officials to maintain a discreet silence'.[146] In Alperovitz's eyes, this 'something' was the falsity and myth being put forward by Truman and Stimson. Thus for Alperovitz, supported through substantial study, it was 'diplomatic considerations related to the Soviet Union [which] played a significant part in the Hiroshima decision'.[147] This is an argument that, since the publication of Alperovitz's thesis, has become a common point of view within the literature. Yet this is but one explanation for why the bomb was deployed.

Alternative studies found differing motivations. For instance, in *American Arsenal*, Coffey proposed that the Truman administration sought revenge against Japan for 'waging war in an inhumane fashion'.[148] Referring to the argument that Truman detested the Japanese for their treatment of American prisoners of war, Coffey argued that, at a political level, it was regarded that '[b]urning their [Japanese] cities was simply what they deserved'.[149] Lawrence Freedman listed other motivations in his 2003 edition of *The Evolution of Nuclear Strategy*. He argued that the deployment of the new 'experimental' bomb was part of a strategy of 'maximum shock'.[150] Freedman explained how, at a military and political level, it was believed only a 'sudden shock' would have forced the entrenched and 'culturally honour-bound' Japanese elites to finally capitulate.[151] To support his argument, Freedman quoted Stimson's 1947 remarks that 'to extract a genuine surrender from the Emperor and his military advisers they must be administered a tremendous shock which would carry convincing proof of our power to destroy the Empire'.[152] In addition to this, Freedman quoted General Marshall who, like Stimson, is said to have believed in the shock value of the bomb. As Marshall remarked, '[i]t's not good warning them. If you warn them there's no surprise. And the only way to produce shock is surprise.'[153] Thus, for Freedman, a motivating factor was the administering of a 'shock' through the atomic bombs' deployment to force the entrenched and honour-bound Japanese political elites to end the war.

A final explanation as to why the bomb was deployed is seen in the work of Paul Fussell, who brought a controversial and highly contested point to the fore.[154] In *Thank God for the Atom Bomb* (1981), Fussell tentatively put forward the unsettling idea that not only was the atomic bombing of Japan intended to cause maximum destruction, but that such destruction was partly motivated by racist hatred of the Japanese people. To support his argument Fussell vividly depicted the American military's perception of the Japanese prior to the bombs' deployment. Describing the routine decapitation and dismembering of captured Japanese prisoners, Fussell argued, '[a]mong Americans it was widely held that the Japanese were really subhuman, little yellow beasts, and popular imagery depicted them as lice, rats, bats, vipers, dogs, and monkeys'.[155] Quoting the Marine Corp journal *Leatherneck* from May 1945, Fussell suggested that it was not uncommon to hear talk of 'a gigantic task of extermination' and 'annihilation' of the Japanese people. Thus, he concluded:

> Hiroshima seems to follow in natural sequence ... Since the Jap vermin resist so madly and have killed so many of us, let's pour gasoline into their bunkers and light it and then shoot those afire who try to get out. Why not? Why not blow them all up, with satchel charges or with something stronger? Why not, indeed, drop a new kind of bomb on them, and on the un-uniformed ones too.[156]

Overall, it is clear to see that a complex set of conflicting motivations complicates the narrative and, in turn, our understanding of the motives behind the atomic bombs' deployment. These range from the idea that it was a racist attack against the Japanese people, that it was an experiment and aimed to deter the rapid advance of Russian forces, that it was a 'sudden shock' intended to force the Japanese to surrender, or that it was a misguided continuation of the long-held precision bombing strategy designed to end the war and save American and Japanese lives.[157]

Although we may never know the main reason why this action was taken, the 'truth' is most probably that each of these factors, and many more yet understudied contributing elements, were a core part of the personal motivations of those who were involved in the deployment of the atomic bomb. What can be agreed on, however, is that the indiscriminate and destructive impact of these weapons on Japan was unparalleled by any singular weapon seen before in history. To say that such an atomic bombardment marked the ultimate deviation from a once ingrained precision doctrine may be an understatement. The first of these weapons destroyed 'close to 100 percent'[158] of Hiroshima and indiscriminately ended the lives of 130,000 people.[159] In the second use of the atomic bomb, on the city of Nagasaki, 70,000 people perished.[160] Recalling the horror of the latter attack, the mayor of the region stated:

> Nagasaki became a city of death where not even the sound of insects could be heard. After a while, countless men, women and children began to gather for a drink of water at the banks of nearby Urakami River, their hair and clothing scorched and their burnt skin hanging off in sheets like rags. Begging for help they died one after another in the water or in heaps on the banks ... Four months after the atomic bombing, 74,000 people were dead, and 75,000 had suffered injuries,

that is, two-thirds of the city population had fallen victim to this calamity that came upon Nagasaki like a preview of the Apocalypse.[161]

Such a statement evokes vivid imagery. The impact of the bomb was, of course, more destructive in Hiroshima. As a Japanese schoolchild, Sakamoto Hatsumi, succinctly surmised in a poem written in 1952:

[w]hen the atomic bomb drops
day turns into night
people turn into ghosts[162]

Ghosts – mere shadows left on cold dark stone – are truly what people became. Those 'lucky' enough not be boiled alive, or enveloped by the ensuing blast of heat and all-consuming fire, were killed instantly. Their bodies – blood, bone and flesh – were turned to dust in an instant.[163] As Frank described in *Downfall*:

an American officer later found the etched shadow of a man with one foot in the air pulling a laden two-wheeled cart. The man's shadow had shielded the blacktop from the heat, but elsewhere the surface melted to tar and absorbed dust. The only vestige of another man idling at a bank building was his shadow on the granite. Both had been vaporized at or near the speed of light.[164]

Such remarks evoke unimaginable and horrific imagery. They highlight the real-life impact of Truman's decision and the immense power of the atomic bomb.

Chapter 3 outlines how the indiscriminate horror of the atomic bomb went on to have far-reaching political and military implications post-war. Specifically, it is argued how, within the military, disciples of Mitchell (such as Arnold) attempted to avoid the reoccurrence of such indiscriminate and disproportionate levels of atomic destruction in future wars by readopting a precision ethos. In addition, I explain how the Truman administration reacted in stark contrast to this by moving away from a reliance on military means to achieve policy. Instead, a move towards international control and political containment took place at a political level. In essence, political thought and military thought pertaining to the atomic bomb diverged during the initial post-war period.

3

Continuation (1945–49)

> The greatest need facing the world today is for international control of the human forces that make for war. Pending the establishment of such controls, the mission of the Air Forces is the protection of the United States by the employment of airpower.
>
> H.H. Arnold, General of the Army (1946)[1]

Moral turmoil, strategic confusion, and a demand for the international control of atomic weaponry collectively dominated American political, social, and strategic thought post-Hiroshima and Nagasaki.[2] Such a unique atomic context created a time when the outlaw of war was seriously considered and all thought regarding the future recourse to atomic force was side-lined and even ceased at a political level.[3] When we consider the horror, death, and destruction resulting from a prolonged period of total war, it appears to be common sense that such peaceable notions would have prevailed. Yet, as the opening quotation's reference to future airpower suggests, the reality was far more complex.

At a political level there was a short-lived movement, led by President Truman and supported by political leaders, atomic scientists, and people of conscience that sought to establish the international control of atomic capabilities. In policy planning circles, academic discussion, and wider public debate there was a certain amount of uncertainty, division, and even confusion about how best to proceed in the atomic age.[4] Some, such as George F. Kennan (Director of Policy Planning and future US Ambassador to the Soviet Union), highlighted the preference for the political containment of the USSR, not a military containment based on atomic weapons.[5] Such a policy would become the spearhead of Truman's attempts, alongside international control, to avoid future war and a reliance on military means.[6] At the level of military strategic thought, however, the experience was somewhat different.

44

There was neither a cessation, nor a side-lining, of American strategic thought pertaining to the future deployment of the atomic bomb.[7] Nor was there any strategic confusion regarding the way in which atomic weapons would be deployed in future warfare.[8] In fact, the moral and strategic ambition that drove the evolution of American nuclear strategy after the horror of Second World War was a continuation of that sought in reaction to the brutality of the First World War. This was the ambition for precision manifested through the precision strategic bombardment of specific military and industrial targets, not civilians.

Specifically, it was through General Arnold's pugnacious drive for precision in lieu of international control, and due to the overall reappraisal of precision bombing as a successful Second World War doctrine, that precision was able to continue as a core ambition after 1945. Furthermore, it was this reappraisal of precision which led the Joint Chiefs of Staff (JCS) and their planning staff to adopt it quickly as a morally justifiable and strategically sound line of strategic thought – one which could be relied on to guide American nuclear strategy through the greater uncertainty of the period. Consequently, at a military strategy level it was precision which was perceived as the panacea to the strategic complexities and moral uncertainties that arose in the atomic age, not notions of international control and political containment that had dominated the policy direction of the Truman administration.[9] Starting with Arnold's own drive for precision in this post-war context, each of these contributing factors is analysed in turn as a means of providing the reader with a cogent study in support of the core argument that the ambition for precision continued into the post-war period.

Precision in the context of international control

> I am not at all pessimistic on the final outcome. We shall have a permanent peace in the world.
>
> President Truman (1945)[10]

As details of the bomb's devastating power emerged in late 1945, the rhetoric of public intellectuals, people of conscience, and political elites in America became dominated by notions of atomic regulation through international control.[11] Nobel Prize winner Albert Einstein stated that only through a 'supranational organization … can we have some assurances that we shall not vanish into the atmosphere, dissolved into atoms'.[12] Phillip Morrison, a fellow of the atomic project at Los Alamos and (sent at the request of the War Department) a recent

45

returnee from the devastation of Hiroshima, stated in 1946, '[i]f the bomb gets out of hand, if we do not learn to live together so that science will be our help and not our hurt, there is only one sure future. The cities of men on earth will perish.'[13] The President himself pioneered such a quest. Through a United Nations-led commission, he hoped to 'achieve an enduring peace [and] ... deal adequately with the atomic bomb'.[14] As he concluded in a letter to Clark Eichelberger (Director of the American Association for the United Nations) in 1945, '[w]e are, I believe, on the threshold of the greatest age in the history of mankind'.[15] Such expectation was dominant. This makes Arnold's overt argument for the future employment of atomic weapons through air power (in the chapter's opening quotation) seem out of place. In fact, his comments are so differing to the peaceable context of the period that they are somewhat novel, worthy of analysis, and in need of justification.[16]

Arnold's statement on future atomic warfare appeared, perhaps surprisingly, alongside those averse to the future deployment of atomic weapons in the popularised book *One World Or None* (1946),[17] a publication which quite literally advocated the notion of there being one united world, or none at all. Edited by Dexter Masters and Kathrine Way, the volume's contributors included Nobel Prize winner Hans Bethe, the pre-eminent chemist and physicist Irving Langmuir, and the 'pulse of public opinion' Walter Lippmann,[18] not to mention atomic scientists like Leó Szilárd, who had lobbied President Truman prior to the bomb's deployment in an attempt to warn of an 'era of devastation on an unimaginable scale'.[19] Yet, although at first it may seem as if these peaceable contributors had conflicting ambitions to Arnold's, on further study what soon becomes clear is that each person had three things in common. Each contributor's view of the world had been influenced by the horror of the atomic bomb, each had the desire to try and mitigate future destruction abroad and at home, and each was trying to ensure the future security of the United States. These were virtuous aims for which Arnold was praised, alongside his fellow contributors, in the American press.[20] As the *New York Times* declared, '[f]ifteen of the world's most distinguished scientists, a solider, and a political commentator have combined to produce an important, authoritative, and ominously challenging book ... No book of our time treats a more important subject.'[21] Yet, as may be clear, although Arnold shared similar ends to his fellow contributors, his means of achieving them were not directly in line with the majority. Instead, for Arnold there was one clear way to secure the United States and mitigate future destruction. This was through the ability to deploy atomic bombs with precision, not international control. It was this desire which would, in Arnold's eyes, drive the strategic thought of 'tomorrow'.[22]

Continuation (1945–49)

The reappraisal of precision

We must think in terms of tomorrow.
H.H. Arnold (1951)[23]

Arnold saw a moral and strategic utility in atomic weapons and thus he saw a place for them in American strategic thought. This was especially the case when the weapons were combined with his long-held ambition for precision.[24] Specifically, for Arnold it was the achievement of precision strategic bombardment through air power and missile development which was pivotal to future American nuclear strategy and security.[25] Therefore, soon after the Second World War, Arnold began highlighting the reasons why precision should once again be adopted as the core driving factor at the heart of American military strategy in the atomic age.

One might think that this would be an uphill battle, especially because of the perceived underachievement of precision bombing in the previous war. Arnold's efforts, however, were helped considerably by an unlikely advocate of precision. This was Herman Göring, the (now incarcerated and soon to be sentenced) successor to Hitler and the Commander-in-Chief of the Luftwaffe. As a result of his vast experience of allied bombardment, Göring had insight into the successes and failures of the Allied bombing campaign against Germany.[26] Therefore, when General Spaatz was offered an opportunity to interview him about the impact of American bombing, he accepted. In an interview at the headquarters of the US Seventh Army (housed in the Ritter School in Augsburg, Germany) just three days after the official German surrender (10 May 1945), Spaatz questioned Göring for two hours about American precision bombing and British area bombing.[27] Specifically, he asked Göring, '[w]hich had the most effect on the defeat of Germany: area bombing or precision bombing'.[28] Much to the delight of Spaatz, Göring's reply was clear and absolute.[29] He unequivocally stated that it was '[t]he precision bombing, because it was decisive. Destroyed cities could be evacuated, but destroyed industries were difficult to replace.'[30] These remarks were significant. Although historians may question the intent behind Göring's conclusions, there can be little doubt that they went on to have a lasting impact.[31] It also helped that they were later somewhat supported by the US Strategic Bombing Survey's final report on Allied bombing in Europe. The report, although its findings have been challenged in recent years, supported Göring's claims regarding the success of American precision bombing compared to British area bombing.[32]

Figure 3.1 General Henry 'Hap' Arnold

Unsurprisingly, it was not long before Spaatz sent a letter directly to Arnold informing him of the good news.[33] Although expressing regret at not being able to question Göring himself, the revelations delighted Arnold.[34] As he recalled in his memoir, '[i]t was a remarkable interview'.[35] Quite simply, the interview had brought vindication for Arnold and had seemingly justified the price paid (in men, money, and reputation) in the previous war when the achievement of precision was attempted. Yet, perhaps more importantly for the future of precision, such a reappraisal would be useful for any future American adoption of precision within nuclear strategy.

In fact, this is exactly how it was used. Although Göring's testimony pleased Arnold, it was not he who needed convincing as to the utility of precision. Nor was it the American public, the majority of whom saw atomic weapons as virtuous and pivotal to the facilitation of peace.[36] Instead, it was the politicians, those in competing branches of the American military, and even some American air power thinkers who needed persuading that precision was the way forward, or even necessary, in such peaceable times. Thus, as a means to convince the sceptical that it was precision and not solely international control which should be sought after, the 'resounding success' of American precision bombing became the narrative of how the Second World War was won. As Arnold stated (with a certain amount of euphoric recall) in 1946, '[in] Germany the decisive air blows were aimed at oil and transportation; and although the total value of the destruction in dollars might not have been so large as for cities, the effect was to paralyze the whole German war machine and make land conquest practical'.[37] Thus, Arnold adopted Göring's revelations. It was now the proportionate and discriminate striking of enemy military and industrial targets which had ended the Second World War rapidly and at a reduced cost to both civilian life and American soldiers on the ground. This was how the war in Germany was won and, for Arnold, it was how the wars of the future could and should be fought.

Thus, Arnold went on to describe the ambition for precision bombardment with atomic weapons as akin to the ambition for precision which had emerged after the First World War.[38] As such, like Gorrell and Mitchell, who had promoted precision as a means to mitigate trench warfare and civilian causalities, Arnold went on to promote atomic precision as a means to mitigate any future indiscriminate atomic horror and ensure a moral and strategic American victory in any future war. This was what he believed and sought to achieve. Thus, from 1945 until his death in 1950, Arnold made it his mission to reappraise precision and persuade the political and military elites to incorporate it into the heart of American nuclear strategy, a strategy which he believed should be prioritised over international control. In particular, Arnold's 1946 contribution to *One World or None* entitled 'Air Force in the Atomic Age' (an article which was his 'last official public statement as head of the Air Forces'[39]) provided a detailed insight into this reappraisal and continued to push for precision in an atomic context.

Why precision with atomic bombs?

[N]ot only must we prepare to fight an atomic war, but – strange though it may seem at first – we must also prepare to fight a war in which no city may feel the blast of an atomic bomb.

H.H. Arnold, General of the Army (1946)[40]

Arnold began his contributing article by outlining an apocalyptic vision of the future. He declared that the 'cheapness of destruction … has been multiplied manifold by the sudden, extensive, pulverizing force of the atomic bomb'.[41] He went on to envision 'how terrible ... [future] war would be', and stated that such horror 'is indicated by the factual appraisal of what atomic explosives mean in comparison with the most deadly materials men have devised before them'.[42] As he declared, 'even before the creation of the atomic bomb ... mass air raids were obliterating the great centres of mankind'.[43] Arnold then proceeded to give British and Japanese cities as key examples of such past horror,[44] allowing readers to imagine for themselves what an indiscriminate attack with atomic weapons 'six times more economical than conventional bombing' may 'achieve' in the future.[45] It was not, however, all doom and gloom for Arnold. For him the means to avoid this apocalyptic scenario were clear and he wanted others to see the light.

Branding the famous joint statement by President Truman and Prime Ministers Clement Attlee (UK) and Mackenzie King (Canada) that 'the only complete protection for the civilized world from the destructive use of scientific knowledge lies in the prevention of war'[46] as a 'blunt assertion',[47] Arnold quickly moved to outline his reality and his alternative. As he pointed out, '[i]n the past no effective weapon of war has remained long unused'.[48] The alternative option for Arnold was simple, 'the Air Forces must maintain a program of preparedness giving the best possible protection'.[49] As such, preparation for war (not the prevention of war) lay as the key to a future free from an atomic apocalypse. Yet how would such preparations for future war manifest themselves? And who would devise them? For Arnold the fate of civilisation was 'subject to the goodwill and the good sense of the men who control the employment of air power' (of which he was one).[50] How must these good men act? Arnold made this clear as well.

Unsurprisingly, in the event of atomic warfare Arnold outlined that the targeting of the enemy should be both proportionate and discriminate through precision. With passion and clarity he stated, 'not only must we fight an atomic war, but – strange though it may seem at first – we must also prepare to fight a war in which no city may feel the blast of an atomic bomb'.[51] Combining notions from Göring's beguiling comments with his own experiences during the Second World War, Arnold went on to explain his reasoning behind such notions of city avoidance.[52]

For Arnold, if atomic weapons were to be used by the American military, it was the enemy's strategic military and industrial targets which must be the primary focus of any atomic strategy, not cities and civilians. As he stated, '[t]he destruction of cities is not the aim of a strategic air force. The aim is to weaken the enemy's military strength.'[53] Arnold especially thought this was case, as he believed in the future such vital military and industrial targets would be dispersed, heavily fortified, or even underground.[54] As Arnold wanted the political and military establishment to realise, in this evolved strategic context, the drive for precision took on a role of increased importance.

In detail, and contrary to the peaceable political will of the period, Arnold dictated that at the current time 'with relatively unimportant exceptions all of the centres of civilization in the northern hemisphere are within reach of destruction at the hands of any major nation in that hemisphere'.[55] This made the total destruction of civilian centres a zero-sum game and thus morally and strategically null and void. In Arnold's opinion this created a unique strategic situation for America in which isolation and mere fortification would not provide salvation. Instead, in a world where both America and its enemies could equally strike one another, it was the dispersal of targets desired by one's enemy which was key.

Specifically, Arnold recommended to his military colleagues and political leaders that American industry should either be placed underground or widely dispersed across the nation. As he stated, '[o]ur passive defence of great importance consists of dispersing or burying below ground essential war industry'.[56] This is something Arnold recognised other potential aggressors (such as the Soviet Union) had already worked towards during the previous war and were continuing to incorporate when 'rebuilding destroyed industry'.[57] So, for Arnold, the future was thus. In a situation where the total destruction of cities would be avoided due to mutual capabilities of atomic destruction, the most important defence was dispersal, and the key to offence was the ability to strike individual enemy military/industrial sites with precision from great distance.

As Arnold declared, 'the achievement of range alone is of little strategic value unless it leads to effective and economical destruction of specific targets'.[58] He then went on to explain that '[o]btaining satisfactory accuracy' and 'achieving these or greater accuracies at much larger ranges' should become a core strategic goal and ultimately a reality.[59] By achieving such precision with atomic capabilities, 'the effort required to knock out completely all phases of an enemy's war industry is within practical reach'.[60] Thus, for Arnold, his argument for precision was clear. Much like the ethos of precision bombing in the previous war, he believed that in the atomic age, if the precise striking and destruction of the enemy's industry through air power was achieved, a rapid victory and reduction to the cost to life would follow. This is how he believed the atomic wars of the future would be won (and lost).

Arnold retired in 1946, and although he continued to be a passionate (and active) advocate of precision, official war planning was no longer his responsibility.[61] Instead, his arguments were clear and it was now up to those who remained on the JCS and in the Truman administration to decide if they agreed.

The age of uncertainty

> In a war with the USSR is our purpose to destroy the Russian people, industry, the Communist party, the Communist hierarchy, or a combination of these? … Will there be a requirement to occupy, possibly reconstruct, Russia after victory, or can we seal off the country, letting it work out its own salvation?
>
> General Hoyt Vandenberg (1947)[62]

Fortunately for Arnold, his reappraisal of precision as a recipe for strategic success was deemed compelling. As the (flippant) comments above suggested, strategic certainties were in short supply during the initial post-war period.

Of course, such uncertainty is a common context in which generals must plan for and conduct warfare. As Carl von Clausewitz stated, '[w]ar is the realm of uncertainty; three quarters of the factors on which action in war is based are wrapped in a fog of greater or lesser uncertainty'.[63] For American military thinkers and planners within the JCS, such comments would have resonated with their own experiences during the initial post-war years. For them, however, it was not the traditional Clausewitzian 'fog of war' during conflict which hindered them; instead, it was a fog inflicted by the American political elites which hampered their planning. In particular, it was extreme secrecy regarding the American atomic capacity and a lack of high-level policy guidance which led to such uncertainty during this period.[64] The reasons behind such secrecy and lack of guidance are now outlined. Furthermore, the impact this uncertainty had on the adoption of Arnold's continued ambition for precision by the JCS, and its subsequent inclusion within the JCS war plans, are explained.

In regard to the atmosphere of extreme secrecy, the historian David Alan Rosenberg stated that the 'obsessive secrecy surrounding all atomic information during this period meant that even the highest policymakers did not have ready access to information about American nuclear capability'.[65] As he declared in his seminal 1983 article, *The Origins of Overkill*, even 'President Truman remained very much isolated from the entire issue of nuclear strategy'.[66] In fact, it is surprising to realise that Truman was 'not officially advised on the size of the American nuclear stockpile' until mid-1947.[67] Such secrecy is telling.

It is particularly indicative of the ill-informed environment in which JCS strategic thought was devised during this period. At the secondary level of strategy development – behind the President and his National Security Council (NSC) – the JCS was left to devise their war plans without knowing many of the realities in regard to American atomic capacity.[68] As the historian Steven Ross stated, the JCS 'did not in fact know how many atomic bombs the United States possessed. [They] presumed that there were twenty to thirty A-bombs available. The actual figure was much smaller.'[69] Such secrecy was undoubtedly a contributing factor to the uncertainty of the period. A second (and equally influential) feature was the lack of high-level nuclear policy guidance and guidelines provided to the JCS.

Such an insufficient level of guidance occurred as a result of President Truman's reluctance to consider the possibility that his efforts for international control would not come to fruition and his reliance on political and diplomatic containment would not be sufficient. His inflexibility manifested itself in a lack of guidance in regard to militaristic notions of nuclear strategy. As Rosenberg highlighted, Truman had an 'unwillingness, or inability, to conceive of the atomic bomb as anything other than an apocalyptic terror weapon, a weapon of last resort'.[70] Such a mindset influenced the move for international control and political containment which became the focus of Truman's diplomatic efforts during this period.[71] As Rosenberg went on to explain, Truman's 'official policy initiatives through 1948 focused exclusively on the goals of establishing civilian control over American nuclear resources, including production facilities and the weapons stockpile, and seeking international control of atomic energy in the United Nations'.[72] Such a reticent approach from the President undoubtedly contributed to a lack of high-level policy guidance in regard to the direction of American nuclear strategy. As Director of the Office of Far Eastern Affairs W.W. Butterworth recommended in 1948, 'I wonder if it would not be helpful to our National Military Establishment if … thought were more fully developed and guide lines – if any are possible – laid out for aid in strategic planning.'[73] Thus, as Butterworth suggested, the JCS and its staff were limited and in need of more information in regard to what could (and should) be achieved with atomic weapons. Consequently, this lack of presidential and NSC guidance, mixed with extreme secrecy during this pivotal period of Cold War American history, combined to create a difficult environment for the JCS war planners – one in which little knowledge of American atomic capacity and advances in atomic technology was imparted, and little guidance as to the direction in which such strategic thought should move, was disclosed.

Such concerns were shared by Vice Chief of Staff of the Air Force, General Vandenberg (a former ACTS man in the 1930s and a future Chief of Staff of the Air Force).[74] As the opening quotation of this section highlighted, Vandenberg raised a number of concerns regarding this issue in his 'Memorandum to the Secretary of the Air Force' in 1947.[75] Specifically, he called for the highest levels of government to provide guidance on objectives desired in the event of future American atomic conflict. He also called for guidance on how such a war would be fought, taking time to mention the need for direction on what should be targeted (and why) if such a war were to take place.[76] In response to this, the NSC released NSC-30 which was approved by the President in September 1948.[77]

This document was intended to dictate the official stance regarding 'United States Policy on Atomic Warfare'.[78] It merely, however, outlined two broad guidelines in regard to American nuclear strategy. The first was that the military 'must be ready to utilize promptly and effectively all appropriate means available, including atomic weapons' if war was to arise.[79] This assisted the military planners within the JCS as it gave them the green light to plan for future atomic war (something which had already started, but had only been implicitly granted). What NSC-30 did not do, however, was go into detail about how 'the bomb' should be deployed in the event of war, thus leaving an array of pivotal questions regarding targeting open for interpretation. The second piece of guidance within NSC-30 clarified that, although the military must be ready, it was 'the Chief Executive' who would make the final 'decision as to the employment of atomic weapons in the event of war'.[80] Again, this guidance assisted all military and policy planners as it outlined the hierarchical framework through which an atomic war would be declared. Yet it did not clarify what conditions might determine or trigger a decision. As may be clear, although these broad directives provided some clarity, they did not come close to answering more specific concerns, especially the strategic and tactical concerns raised by Vandenberg.[81] As such, NSC-30 was soon followed by NSC-20/4 in November 1948 as a means to provide increased clarity.

Yet this additional document only provided marginal clarity, while leaving a further litany of unanswered questions. Specifically, NSC-20/4, again approved by the President, broadly outlined to the military planners three more aspects in regard to American nuclear policy and the 'broad U.S. objectives vis-à-vis the Soviet Union'.[82] First, it stated that in the event of war there would be no 'predetermined requirement for unconditional surrender',[83] yet it did not explicitly clarify what would be sought in place of unconditional surrender. Secondly, it broadly concluded that no situation was foreseen where the US would 'need to occupy the Soviet Union'.[84] It did not, however, outline what level of force and enforcement would be needed. Finally, it suggested that the aim of such a war would be to eliminate 'Bolshevik' control of the Soviet Union. Yet it did not define what measures should be taken to 'eliminate', nor did it define what elimination would look like. As such, NSC-20/4 failed to comprehensively answer the questions raised by Vandenberg. Yet, together with NSC-30, this would be all the guidance the JCS and its military planners would receive during this period. As Rosenberg concluded, 'NSC-30 and NSC-20/4 embody the ambiguous if not schizophrenic character of Truman's strategic policy.'[85] Thus, it was uncertainty and ambiguity which defined the broader context of this period.

In fact, when taken as a whole, such an environment could understandably be seen as one which would trickle down and generate confusion for American strategic thinkers and complicate the construction of war plans. It would seem common sense that when faced with little information, vague guidance, and no clear perception of American atomic capacity, clarity regarding the course of strategic thought would be hard to come by. What may seem surprising, however, is that such uncertainty did not translate in this manner. Instead, when the strategic thought of the JCS and the wider community of strategic thinkers is studied between 1945 and 1950, it is not confusion which is apparent. In contrast, the uncertainty of the period only goes on to galvanise a desire for the perceived certainties of a long-held precision bombing strategy and an increased reliance on the atomic bomb.

Precision through the fog

Here is the panacea which enables us to be the greatest military power on earth without investing time, energy, sweat, blood and tears.

Walter Lippmann (1946)[86]

Quite simply, it was the tried and tested methods of the previous war which were sought to provide strategic certainties. As has been highlighted in the study of Arnold (and largely as a result of Arnold's efforts), it was specifically the notion of precision which was being reappraised as a shining example of success.[87] Therefore, it was deemed only natural that such a notion should become the pivot around which an atomic strategy should be developed for the next war. In fact, it was the historian Fred Kaplan who most suitably summed up the strategic and moral ambition for precision in American strategic planning between 1945 and 1950. As he stated, the aim was to 'devise a targeting plan that would aim at destroying particular types of industries, the specific sectors of the Soviet economy on which the war machine uniquely and critically depended'.[88] As such, there was a general 'lack of enthusiasm for city bombing'.[89] It was considered a strategic failure of the previous war (area bombing) that could, and should, not be repeated. As Kaplan sharply concluded, 'the most ineffective elements of bombing in World War II should not dominate the strategic bombing of World War III'.[90] Consequently, the JCS war plans of the period relied on, and sought, precision as a means to guarantee victory in line with American values.[91] Arnold had prevailed, and the longstanding ambition for precision continued.

PINCHER (1946)

Released on 2 March 1946, the PINCHER plans were an initial attempt by the JCS's Joint War Plans Committee (JWPC), in consultation with the intelligence and logistics committees,[92] to outline the 'foundation for detailed war planning' in regard to future atomic war.[93] As the introduction to PINCHER outlined, the purpose of these initial plans was to:

> determine a concept of operations upon which to base a joint outline war plan, providing for action to be initiated during the next three years by the United States, in conjunction with her allies, to defeat the U.S.S.R. or, as a minimum, to impose upon the U.S.S.R. surrender terms acceptable to the United States.[94]

With its broad objective outlined, the document quickly moved to detail the core assumptions about future atomic war on which the document had been based.

The first assumption was that for 'planning purposes, M-day is assumed to be 1 July 1947, and the date of US entry [into the war], 1 January 1948'.[95] Secondly, the context behind the US entry into war was assumed to be that the Soviet Union had committed 'an act or series of aggressions vitally affecting the security of the British Empire, of the United States or both'.[96] As a result, and 'through miscalculation by the Soviets of the risks involved', such an act of aggression had led to war 'between the U.S.S.R. on the one side; and the United States and the British Empire on the other'.[97] Thus, PINCHER was in essence an initial planning document to outline the best way to approach the Soviet Union in the event of future warfare.

Early in the document, notions of a ground offensive by a combined British, French, and American force were dismissed. As the document outlined, at the outbreak of hostilities on 1 July 1947, the predicted strength of the Soviet

Union would consist of 3,311,000 personnel,[98] within '113 divisions backed by eighty-four satellite units'.[99] As such, it was predicted that the 'initial Soviet advance to the west could be made with a force approximately three times the strength of the combined British, French and United States occupation forces'.[100] Due to such superiority in numbers, and against what was commonly held to be an accomplished fighting force, it was concluded that the British, French, and American forces 'would be forced to fight Soviet ground forces under conditions which would favour the U.S.S.R. since it would permit her to bring her preponderance of ground forces to bear'.[101] Thus, with these conclusions in mind, it was decided that the 'direct application of our ground armies would be prohibitive'.[102] In other words, it would result in a cost-heavy loss of American and allied military personnel. As a result, the JWPC set about devising plans which played to the American military strengths and strategic ambitions.

With a ground offensive off the cards the JWPC planners stated that it was 'necessary to select operations which are more in consonance with our military capabilities and in which we can exploit our superiority in modern *scientific warfare* methods [emphasis added]'.[103] Although subsidiary plans were made to utilise the superior American and British naval capacity to blockade Russia and sabotage its merchant and military fleets, the centrepiece of the plan relied on a strategic air offensive that included the use of atomic weapons.[104] As a continuation of aims intrinsic to American precision strategic bombing, the planners believed that in any future atomic bombardment it was the industrial war-making capacity which should be the primary target. Reminiscent of the strategic ambitions proposed in the 1920s, the JWPC proposed initiating 'an air offensive against important strategic targets within the U.S.S.R.' from 1 January 1948 (the day the planners proposed America joined the war).[105] At the heart of these plans was the aim of ensuring the 'destruction of the war making capacity of the U.S.S.R.'.[106] As the planners went on to state, the precision striking of these targets was vital to victory as the 'Soviet armed forces, like any armed forces, are directly dependent upon these war industries'.[107] Such plans could have been uttered by Gorrell or Mitchell themselves.

In fact, one cannot ignore the relationship between the early ambitions of Gorrell and Mitchell and the strategic ambitions in 1946. For instance, Mitchell explicitly stated that American air power should target the 'means of communication, the food products, even the farms, the fuel and oil … [to render them] … incapable of supplying armed forces',[108] while Gorrell pointed to the precision targeting of 'German manufacturing centres and means of transportation'.[109] The aims intrinsic to this early drive for precision, which progressed through the Second World War, can be seen mirrored in this later development of atomic war plans. Thus, as a continuation of this early ambition, the PINCHER paper moved to highlight the importance of discriminately hitting specific industrial targets and sectors of the Soviet economy, not whole cities. Furthermore, the demand for precision was such that the planners even proceeded to outline the shortcomings that must be overcome if this ambition was to become a reality in the near future.

With the 'apparent early objective of allied military effort' set as 'the destruction of the war making capacity of the U.S.S.R', the JWPC moved to highlight the lack of accurate targeting data available to them.[110] As they stated, '[d]etailed target system analysis is not attempted in this study'.[111] Not to be deterred from precision, however, they indicated that it should and 'will be included in the eventual War Plan as it is evolved'.[112] As such, they proceeded to outline general regions in which the USSR's industry was believed to be located. As stated:

> [d]espite the dispersal of Soviet resources and industries and the paucity of information concerning the development of new industry, it is possible to delineate definite areas which contain a substantial proportion of vital resources, without which the Soviet war effort would be seriously curtailed (if not prevented).[113]

Specifically, they listed eight general regions for bombardment. These vital areas, listed in an estimated order of their importance, were as follows:

1 Moscow area
2 Caucasus area
3 Ploesti area
4 Ural area
5 Stalingrad area
6 Kharkov area
7 Lake Baikal area
8 Leningrad area.[114]

What is most interesting about this list is not the areas themselves, but the several 'apologies' made for the broad regions which were put forward and the insistence that in future war they must (and will) be narrowed in line with American moral, ethical, and strategic ambitions. As they stated:

> [a]n examination of these areas, together with a consideration of Russia's vast area, immediately indicates the *necessity for narrowing down our objective areas to the smallest possible field* ... neutralization of these areas would create conditions leading

to the defeat of the U.S.S.R. It would denude the field armies of the vital support necessary for them to continue effective organized resistance [emphasis added].[115]

By highlighting the 'necessity' to narrow the targeting areas of atomic bombing to the 'smallest possible field', these initial plans outlined the ambitions for precision in early American atomic war plans against the USSR and the advances that needed to be made to ensure these demands could become a reality.

Thus, it can be argued that the initial plans for atomic warfare, outlined by the JWPC in 1946, were not confused and did not lack clarity of purpose. Instead, as a continuation of the strategic ambitions which had driven American air power during the inter-war period and into the Second World War, it was the proportionate and discriminate targeting of enemy industrial sites, not civilians, which was seen as the key to ensuring a rapid end to war, without having to endure a cost-heavy ground offensive. Precision was seen as the core factor to guide the American military to victory through a period of such uncertainty. As the JWPC plans conclude, the PINCHER plans were a 'rapid and effective series of initial operations exploiting special weapons ... to bombard and to initiate the destruction of his war making capacity'.[116] Although not officially approved by the JCS due to the Truman administration's limitations on official war planning, it was the PINCHER plans, with the ambition for precision at their core, which provided the foundations for future war plans.[117] This continuation is clear to see within Joint Emergency War Plan BROILER (1948).

BROILER (1948)

Submitted by the Joint Strategic Plans Committee (JSPC) in March 1948, BROILER became the 'first operationally oriented atomic target list'.[118] Approved by the JCS for planning purposes, it built upon and expanded the PINCHER plans in two ways. First, BROILER set out a contingency strategy in the event that the core precision-based strategy was to fall short of its aims. Heeding lessons from the shortfalls of precision bombing during the previous war, the BROILER planners proposed that if precision atomic bombardment was to fail in its task of bringing the Soviet Union to its knees, 'it may become advisable to abandon the concept of destruction of the enemy's physical means to wage war in favour of a concept involving destruction of his will through selective attack with biological and chemical agents'.[119] As a continuation of this line of thought, the JSPC stated that it seemed logical 'to anticipate that the psychological effect, properly exploited, could become an important factor in the timing of and the effort necessary to cause the cessation of hostilities'.[120] Therefore, much like in the Second World War, a more indiscriminate strategy became the contingency. Yet despite such pragmatic planning, as within PINCHER, precision remained a core strategic goal within BROILER.

Specifically, the JSPC's second improvement on PINCHER was their attempt to narrow down the list of atomic targets from vague regions to a more discriminate target list. This new list stated the precise targets that should be struck to ensure a rapid end to war at a reduced cost to civilian and American military lives. Thus, with these ambitions in mind, the planners started BROILER by stating that for 'humanitarian reasons it is probable that initially atomic bomb attacks will be made only against targets within the U.S.S.R. proper'.[121] Expanding on this notion, the BROILER planners outlined those specific targets within the 'U.S.S.R. proper' which would be subject to atomic bombardment. The JSPC list included 'employment against the political, governmental, administrative, technical and scientific elements of the Soviet Union and against those specific targets which were considered to warrant their use in the petroleum and other target systems as shown in the analysis'.[122] Thus, unlike in the PINCHER plans, BROILER clearly outlined the more specific (although still broad) political, military, and industrial regions which were seen as core to ensuring the rapid destruction of the enemy war-making capacity. Progress was being made. In fact, the plans also outlined the specific industries which were set to be hit and the level of destruction to be achieved by atomic deployment. As BROILER stated, the bombing would result in the destruction of the:

> Soviet war-making capacity to the following extent: Airframes 98.8%, Autos & Trucks 88%, Aero Engines 100%, Tanks and Self-propelled Guns 94%, Armament 65%, Crude Oil Refineries 63.7%, Coke 67.5%, Steel 65%, Zinc 44%, Aviation Gasoline Refineries 77.8%, Submarine Const. Facilities 89%, Total Shipbuilding Facilities 45%.[123]

Of course, scholars can (and have) rightly argued that, with 20/20 hindsight, if carried out with the weapons available during the period, the BROILER plans would have resulted in widespread destruction of cities on the scale of Hiroshima and Nagasaki (at a minimum). Nevertheless, this additional list added a layer of much-needed clarity to the war plans; it was a wish list that could guide strategy and the development of technology for use in future war. What must be understood here, therefore, is that Hiroshima levels of destruction were not the *core ambition* of the JSPC, nor the JCS, when they approved such plans. As the dominant narrative of the document dictated, indiscriminate and disproportionate destruction was a contingency.

As the planners stated, they were 'devoted to ... the launching of this air offensive against the vital strategic elements of the Soviet war-making capacity'. Furthermore, the planners stated '[t]he air offensive is the primary means now available by which the Allies can deliver destructive force against those elements of national power which form the backbone of [S]oviet military power', not the civilian population.[124] Thus it was the drive for precision which was at their core. As the document concluded, '[t]he cost, scarcity, and destructive power of the atomic bomb is such that it must be employed primarily as a strategic weapon against selected targets'.[125] It was this push for the precise striking of specific targets, vital to the war-making capacity within the USSR, which continued to drive American strategic thought through 1948 and into the turbulent context of 1949–50.

OFFTACKLE (1949–50)

On 3 April 1948, a 'Soviet communication' was sent to American military authorities informing them that their hitherto '[f]ree and unrestricted use of the established corridors' into Berlin, had been 'denied'.[126] This hostile action only served to increase tensions between the Great Powers and necessitate the start of the Berlin Airlift. Such strains were further exacerbated on 23 September 1949 when the American people were informed that the Soviet Union had obtained the atomic bomb.[127] As Truman declared, 'within recent weeks an atomic explosion occurred in the U.S.S.R. ... This recent development emphasizes once again, if such emphasis were needed, the necessity for that truly effective enforceable international control of atomic energy.'[128] Quite simply, it was a turbulent time and even Truman, despite his public comments, had decided it was time to prepare for war.[129] As he stated in a private memorandum, 'I have a terrible feeling ... we are very close to war.'[130] However, though these events may have had the President contemplating future atomic warfare, they were events for which the Air Staff and JCS were prepared.[131] They had been planning for just such an atomic war for the last four years. In fact, at this initial stage, the advent of the Soviet Union's new atomic weapons only went on to galvanise the strategic utility and ambition for precision which sat at the core of their war plans.

As the historian Michael Mandelbaum explained, as a result of Arnold's reappraisal, and due to the uncertainty of the period '[b]etween 1945 and 1950

American war plans, such as they were, resembled the aerial campaigns of World War II. They called for the Air Force to try to destroy Russian industry and military support facilities.'[132] This was the case through 1949 and into early 1950. As a continuation and expansion of BROILER (which set out the need to strike discriminately the USSR's industrial, political, and military targets), the JCS and air leaders set about categorising and placing emphasis on the increasingly important atomic targets within the USSR. Such planning was pioneered by (now Chief of Staff of the United States Air Force and member of the JCS) General Vandenberg. As Fred Kaplan wrote, 'General Vandenberg and many of his aides on the Air Staff were trying to devise a targeting plan that would aim at destroying particular types of industries ... [and] the Soviet Union's atomic energy plants.'[133] Such a plan, named 'killing a nation' (and incorporated into war plan OFFTACKLE), highlighted the desire of Vandenberg and his staff within the Air Force Directorate of Intelligence to avoid actively resorting to the indiscriminate bombing of whole cities.[134]

As Kaplan stated, 'Vandenberg had no sentimental attachment to the grand dogmas surrounding the massive bombing of cities'.[135] Instead, Vandenberg and his staff sought the discriminate destruction of military and industrial targets, not civilians. As a means to achieve this they outlined a plan to categorise such targets in the USSR into predetermined target sets that could be proportionately struck through American bombardment. Specifically, they set out three target sets in total. The first, named DELTA, set about striking the Soviet Union's industry to ensure 'the disruption of the vital elements of the Soviet war-making capacity'.[136] The second, coded BRAVO, called for the destruction of enemy atomic capacity as a means of ensuring the 'blunting of Soviet capabilities to deliver an atomic offensive against the United States and its allies',[137] while the third, ROMEO, indicated the striking of specific military targets to ensure 'the retardation of Soviet advances into Western Eurasia'.[138] As such, they were DELTA-BRAVO-ROMEO (disruption, blunting, retardation) and together they were deemed the 'solar plexus' of a nation which, when struck with precision, aimed to 'kill a nation' rapidly and without the costly deployment of troops, nor the destruction of entire cities.[139] As Futrell went on to explain in detail:

> [t]he concept that atomic air power could 'kill a nation' apparently emerged in the Air Force Directorate of Intelligence ... when target planners were attempting to work up a list of industrial objectives ... In the aftermath of World War II, the United States Strategic Bombing Survey depreciated the effectiveness of Royal Air Force attacks against German population centers, thus US Air Force target

planners attempted to develop Soviet steel, oil, aluminium, aircraft engine, tank factories, and electrical power plants as air targets.[140]

Subsequently, in December 1949, it was Vandenberg and his staff's ambition for precision in targeting which formed the foundations of the final JCS-approved war plan of the decade named OFFTACKLE.[141] Within this war plan, the notions of separating industrial, military, and atomic targets into specific sets, which could be targeted through American precision atomic bombardment, epitomised the push for precision which had dominated early American atomic strategic thought. Where PINCHER had reaffirmed the ethos and BROILER had set out the targets, OFFTACKLE expanded such notions and organised them into specific groupings that, when struck with precision, would secure a rapid victory in atomic war at a reduced cost to civilian and American military life.

Thus, during the initial post-war period it was the ambition to achieve precision which made up part of American strategic thought pertaining to future atomic war. Within a context where the political elites within the Truman administration were preoccupied with notions of international control, the JCS, the Air Staff, and their war planners constructed plans, with little guidance and somewhat independently, that were based on experiences from previous wars and were in line with the long-held moral, ethical, and strategic ambitions intrinsic to American thought pertaining to bombardment.

The political and strategic context, however, soon began to change once again, and with it the belief in precision. As the next chapter highlights, as 1950 approached, hope of international control and political containment strategies continued to fade. Furthermore, perceptions of the Soviet Union as an imminent military threat took on increased importance and many at a political level became engaged in atomic war planning. It was at this point that political leaders began to question how achievable atomic precision was in reality, and how suitable it was to counter the threat of the Soviet Union.

4

Side-lining (1949–50)

Six years ago ... there was within the Soviet orbit, 180,000,000 people. Lined up on the anti-totalitarian side there were in the world at that time, roughly 1,625,000,000 people. Today, only six years later, there are 800,000,000 people under the absolute domination of Soviet Russia – an increase of over 400 percent. On our side, the figure has shrunk to around 500,000,000. In other words, in less than six years, the odds have changed from 9 to 1 in our favor to 8 to 5 against us.

Senator Joseph McCarthy (1950)[1]

Senator McCarthy's emotive language and alarming assertions epitomise a perception that had become prevalent by 1950.[2] This was the belief that American security was increasingly vulnerable in the face of the Soviet Union's growing military might and its 'parasitic' ideology.[3] Much like the high-pressure context which saw a deviation from an underachieving precision bombing doctrine in 1944, the 1950s were not seen as the time to rely on strategic ambitions with an inconsistent track record. It was a complex period, where anxiety and fear were a toxic combination.[4] At a social, political, and strategic level, perceptions of American vulnerability (in the face of the USSR's growing strength) created an atmosphere of insecurity.[5] Where 'Fortress America' and American military superiority were once secure, the Soviet Union was now perceived to be able to strike the population centres of the United States with atomic weapons. Where communism was once deemed to be contained by political means, it was now the American halls of political power which were said to have been infiltrated.[6] On top of this, as 1950 progressed, a war in Korea was underway, and far from going well for US forces.[7] Thus, as George F. Kennan aptly concluded, it was 'extreme anxiety' which defined the period leading into and including 1950.[8]

It was in this evolved context that President Truman moved away from his reliance on international control and political containment, choosing to focus on conventional and atomic military capabilities instead. With anxiety and fear prevailing, it became a growing belief that 'general military conflict' between America and the Soviet Union might occur.[9] As a result, where Truman was once detached from notions of atomic war planning, he now became engaged. Political policy and military war planning began to synchronise. This was, however, to the detriment of precision and its advocates. With the Truman administration unsure as to the state of American superiority (and increasingly worried about the threat of the Soviet Union's ground force advantage and growing atomic arsenal), atomic strategies which were deemed more 'certain' (and even more extreme) began to be condoned.[10] One document that epitomised this agenda was NSC-68.

NSC-68

The Soviet Union, unlike previous aspirants to hegemony, is animated by a new fanatic faith, antithetical to our own, and seeks to impose its absolute authority over the rest of the world.

NSC-68 (1950)[11]

While the Iran Crisis (1946), the British withdrawal from Turkey and Greece (1947), the Berlin Crisis (1948), and the first successful 'Soviet' test of the atomic bomb (1949)[12] laid the foundations for this change in US political direction, it took until 1950 for such notions to be put forward in a policy directive at the highest levels of politics. In fact, it was President Truman himself who, in reaction to the 'sense that the old policies could not cope with the increased dangers', directed that a study be undertaken into the American stance against the Soviet Union.[13] This document was NSC-68, and at the instruction of the President it was intended as a 're-examination of [American] objectives in peace and war'.[14] Whether intended or not, however, this document quickly became more than merely a 're-examination'. In fact, NSC-68 can perhaps be more accurately described as a 'position paper',[15] a document that, through a concerted effort, aimed to ensure that a political policy reorientation occurred, away from political containment and towards a focus on substantial military measures. To understand why NSC-68 became such a 'loaded' and 'directed' document we must first analyse the debates and discussion at the highest levels of American politics in 1950.

During the period preceding the directive of NSC-68 (January 1950) opinion at a political level had been torn between either continuing in the direction of political containment or proceeding towards a more military focused policy.[16] As Fred Kaplan succinctly surmised:

> [i]n the months leading up to this paper, the Truman administration was split on its policy toward the Soviet Union. Secretary of State Dean Acheson saw the Soviets as a serious threat that needed to be countered through an enormous military build-up. Secretary of Defense Louis Johnson sided with fiscal conservatives – and Truman himself – who believed that boosting the annual arms budget beyond $15 billion would wreck the economy. Acheson's powerful policy planning chief, George Kennan, though worried about the Soviets, favoured a 'containment' policy that stressed bolstering the West more through political and economic means.[17]

Opinions were at odds and division was manifest. This would all change, however, with the creation of NSC-68. This was because the author of the document sought to ensure that American policy towards the Soviet Union would become increasingly reliant on notions of military containment.

Specifically, prior to the construction of NSC-68, a substantial change had occurred at the highest levels of American policy planning. Although the above quotation by Kaplan made reference to Kennan, the staunch advocate of political containment, as being in charge of policy planning, it was no longer he who was the director of the Policy Planning Staff.[18] In early 1950, Kennan had been replaced by Paul Nitze.[19] It was Nitze, a 'close friend and bitter rival' of Kennan, who would go on to lead a committee in the creation of NSC-68.[20] Nitze was a man who believed 'recent Soviet moves reflect[ed] not only a mounting militancy but suggest[ed] a boldness that [was] essentially new– and border[ed] on recklessness'.[21] He was also concerned about the growing atomic threat and was keen for America to take a more proactive stance to counter it. As he recalled in a later interview:

> I was very much worried and so were some of my fellow workers by the fact that in the preceding year a number of adverse things had happened. One was the fact that the Russians had tested a nuclear device and therefore it was only a matter of time before our nuclear monopoly, on which we had been and were depending for our security, was going to be not a monopoly but a duopoly and maybe more, over time. And beyond that the scientists said that they had figured out a way in which you could make a thermonuclear weapon, and that was going to be at least a thousand times as powerful as the then known nuclear weapons that the Russians were working on. We knew the Russians were working on that kind of thing, and were probably ahead of us in their work on a thermonuclear device.[22]

As such, Nitze had mission and motive behind his creation of NSC-68.[23] In line with his perception of the Soviet Union as an increasing military threat, he supported a military focused form of containment. It was this position he wanted to cement in the document.[24]

Quite simply, he saw it as his job to make sure that the virtues of a military focused approach were, in no uncertain terms, made clear to those at the highest levels of political decision-making. This was a task he aimed to achieve at any cost, even if some parts of the NSC-68 had to be 'embellished'.[25] As Acheson wrote in his memoir, *Present at the Creation*, NSC-68 was 'clearer than truth',[26] its purpose was to 'so bludgeon the mass mind of "top government" that not only could the president make a decision but that the decision could be carried out'.[27] As such, the intent of NSC-68 was far from an unbiased re-examination of the facts. More accurately described, it was designed to persuade the political elites to set America in a direction of military preparedness against the Soviet Union.[28] Such intent is clear to see within NSC-68 when it is studied.

Specifically, two dominant themes can be distinguished in the document. The first is the notion that the Soviet Union was seen as an aggressive, expansionist, and distinctly untrustworthy brutal power. Such a perception of the Soviet Union was far from novel during this period. Yet Nitze most definitely stretched this perception to levels bordering on caricature. He does this as a means to create firm foundations on which to build his second theme. This is the argument for conventional military build-up and an increased reliance on the atomic military capacity (alongside a move towards a more 'suitable' and 'realistic' atomic bombardment strategy), an argument which, when placed in the context of an aggressive Soviet Union, came across as rational and palatable. Thus, it was these two narratives (the aggressive and brutal nature of the Soviet Union, followed by calls for American conventional and atomic military preparation) which Nitze used in NSC-68 as a means to convince the political elites that his position was *the* position the Truman administration should move towards as a means to ensure security. These notions were clearly identifiable from the very start of the document.

In fact, a sabre-rattling statement on the first page of analysis made both narratives clear:

> [c]onflict has ... become endemic and is waged, on the part of the Soviet Union, by violent or non-violent methods in accordance with the dictates of expediency. With the development of increasingly terrifying weapons of mass destruction, every individual faces the ever-present possibility of annihilation should the conflict enter the phase of total war.[29]

From these opening remarks it is easy to see Nitze's two clear narratives outlined above.[30] Not only was the Soviet Union represented as an overtly aggressive actor that resorted to conflict at its convenience and fancy, but as a result of this violent nature, Americans should be adequately prepared for atomic war. Such arguments became inflated as the document proceeded.

Building on these notions, the Soviet Union was frequently referred to as an aggressive and brutal actor. In fact, one of the most popular points of reference in NSC-68 was to frame the Soviet Union as akin to a slave-master or slave state that was oppressing its slave-like population. Take for instance the assertion that the population of the Soviet Union lived in 'slavery under the grim oligarchy of the Kremlin, which has come to a crisis with the polarization of power'.[31] In addition to this, it is more explicitly stated that the Soviet Union was a 'slave state',[32] consisting of 'evil men'[33] who 'enslave'[34] their own people and were driven by the desire to 'eliminate the challenge of freedom'.[35] Such deliberate wording and framing of the Soviet Union and its leadership is telling of Nitze's intentions. Specifically, by framing in this way, the document was able to create the classic American narrative of 'good versus evil' and 'freedom versus oppression'.[36] This was far from a novel narrative for the period, yet in the context of atomic weapons realising the 'evil' intent of the enemy took on increased importance.[37]

When framed in this way, America was represented as the last bastion of freedom – an actor that did not want war but should be prepared for it. This line of thought was epitomised in the document's emotive reference to the Declaration of Independence, Bill of Rights, and Divine Providence. Specifically, the document went on to state that:

> [i]n essence, the fundamental purpose is to assure the integrity and vitality of our free society, which is founded upon the dignity and worth of the individual. Three realities emerge as a consequence of this purpose: Our determination to maintain the essential elements of individual freedom, as set forth in the Constitution and Bill of Rights; our determination to create conditions under which our free and democratic system can live and prosper; and our determination to fight if necessary to defend our way of life, for which as in the Declaration of Independence, 'with a firm reliance on the protection of Divine Providence, we mutually pledge to each other our lives, our Fortunes and our sacred honor'.[38]

These comments are of course interesting in their own right.[39] Yet they also have a role to play in the justification of a more 'comprehensive' effort (and somewhat aggressive stance) in regard to American war planning, and specifically atomic war planning. In fact, it is through this emotive, patriotic, and overtly religious statement that Nitze and his planners justified the need to plan for war.

In essence, it was through the representation of the Soviet Union as an evil, oppressive slave-master, and America as a good and righteous liberator, that it was hoped Truman (and those who were undecided within his administration) would be convinced to adopt a more military focused form of containment to ensure the security of the United States. As the document made clear, to ensure American security and the security of 'the free world' America must '[d]evelop a level of military readiness which can be maintained as a long as necessary as a deterrent to Soviet aggression'.[40] Thus, it is at this point that Nitze's narratives combined. Specifically, due to the Soviet Union's increasingly aggressive stance against the free world, it was argued that America must prepare for war. This argument was made no clearer than in regard to the need for a political turn towards American preparations and planning for atomic war.[41]

As NSC-68 went on to state, '[i]n the event of a general war with the U.S.S.R., it must be anticipated that atomic weapons will be used by each side … it is hardly conceivable that, if war comes, the Soviet leaders would refrain from the use of atomic weapons'.[42] Such assertions led to an argument for a renewed political focus on American atomic war planning. As the document went on to make clear:

> [i]n the event we use atomic weapons either in retaliation for their prior use by the U.S.S.R. or because there is no alternative method by which we can attain our objectives, it is imperative that the strategic and tactical targets against which they are used be appropriate and the manner in which they are used be consistent with those objectives.[43]

Although the document failed to give a clear indication of what 'appropriate' meant or what the specific 'objectives' may have been, it is clear that it suggested that increased political engagement and direction be provided to the military planning for atomic war. The document went on to suggest some of the areas in American atomic war planning which needed attention.

Specifically, NSC-68 outlined a number of issues regarding the immediate achievability of OFFTACKLE. As NSC-68 stated, it was doubted whether current American atomic bombardment capabilities could ensure the 'complete destruction of the contemplated target systems' which were considered in the current precision-based war plans.[44] Nevertheless, specific alternatives to these precision-based target systems were not listed. Instead, the document moved to recommend that the current American atomic capacity could be used to inflict a large and 'very serious initial blow'.[45] In fact, it was this recommendation for the Truman administration to direct strategic thought towards a strategy which prioritised a 'serious blow' over a set 'target system' which defined the rest of the document.

As NSC-68 went on to state, '[a] further increase in the number and power of our atomic weapons is necessary in order to assure the effectiveness of any U.S. retaliatory blow'.[46] In fact, the document even went so far as to stress the importance of America developing a thermonuclear weapon before the Soviet Union. As it stated, '[i]f the U.S. develops a thermonuclear weapon ahead of the U.S.S.R. the U.S. should for the time being be able to bring increased pressure on the U.S.S.R.'.[47] Thus, NSC-68 clearly proposed not only a recommendation to turn away from international control and political containment towards a reliance on American military and atomic capabilities, but also the early recommendations for the political elites to condone a more destructive atomic weapon as a means to counter the brutal, aggressive, and oppressive Soviet Union.

Consequently, in NSC-68 it is clear to see how Nitze's two dominant narratives (one regarding the Soviet Union's increased aggression and the other concerning the need for American policy to turn towards the military containment of the said aggression) manifested themselves. Although overstated, such arguments undoubtedly had the desired impact on those who read the document (including the President). As Fred Kaplan wrote, NSC-68 was one of those documents in history 'that not only gave their readers cold sweats, but also changed the course of American security policy'.[48] As such, this document would help create an amenable political climate to ensure the side-lining of precision and an adoption of a comparatively more indiscriminate and disproportionate atomic strategy at a strategic level in JCS strategic thought.[49] It was not only Nitze and NSC-68, however, which persuaded the politicians of the need for this shift. In fact, the presidential approval of NSC-68 and subsequent side-lining of precision was helped, in part, by the Moscow-supported communist aggression in Korea which occurred not long after NSC-68 was first proposed.

Korea

Korea altered U.S. foreign policy by three processes. On some issues it changed the domestic political climate and so allowed statesmen to do what they wanted to do before. In other cases (often hard to distinguish from the first), it resolved ambivalences in their mind. On a few issues it altered their beliefs.

Robert Jervis (1980)[50]

Jervis's statement clearly illustrates the influence that the Korean War had on American political perceptions of the Soviet Union and the risk it posed to American security. The numerous military setbacks for the American-led coalition in Korea helped contribute towards a growing sense of anxiety and fear in 1950.[51] This broader reaction would greatly influence the direction of political policy in the United States. Not only would it see American social and political thought adjust to notions of military build-up, but it would also allow for a growing acceptance of the recommendations put forward in NSC-68. In essence, as the historian John Lewis Gaddis wrote, '[a]s it happened, NSC-68's advocates did not have to work as hard as anticipated to win support for it thanks to unexpected help from the Russians'.[52] Such 'help' was useful, if not vital, in getting NSC-68 passed in its final, somewhat extreme, form.

NSC-68 was released by Nitze in April 1950,[53] but it did not receive presidential approval until December 1950.[54] In fact, Truman initially delayed approval as he wanted further details on the financial implication of the proposal,[55] a luxury he could afford in April. Nevertheless, such delays would not last long. During the period between the release and the approval of the document, the small matter of the Korean War had arisen, and its initial outcomes were far from positive for the Truman administration. In fact, so negative were the political perceptions of the situation in Korea that they influenced the extent to which the Soviet Union and a Moscow-led world communism were considered a threat to America. As Jervis argued, '[w]ithout a sharp change in the international situation, it seems the administration would have to … avoid policies that would have increased Sino-American enmity and Sino-Soviet solidarity'.[56] Thus, alongside Nitze's powerful rhetoric, the events of the Korean War would help to shape a landscape in which NSC-68 was deemed necessary for American national security and American objectives internationally. The progression of these events and their impact on NSC-68 can be seen though a study of the Korean War.

The original agreement on Korea, set out 'at Cairo [1943] and confirmed in Yalta [1945]', planned for the unification of the American and Soviet Union divisions of Korea.[57] This was intended to be quickly followed by independence and democratic governance.[58] By January 1947, however, the Office of Reports and Estimates (ORE)[59] stated that the 'unification and eventual independence of Korea, [had] not been implemented, largely because of a disagreement between the U.S. and Soviet Union over the interpretation of … the meaning of democracy'.[60] Such comments alluded to the seemingly insurmountable ideological difference between the two powers, differences which, although political, increasingly took a militaristic form. As the report went on to declare, the 'division of Korea at the 38th parallel has become an almost impenetrable barrier between the U.S. and Soviet Zones'.[61] As such, far from unification, the two Koreas were being driven further apart. It soon became clear to the ORE, however, that mere separation and communist rule were not the long-term aims for the Soviet Union and its zone of control. Moscow had far more bellicose intentions.

By November 1947, the ORE was reporting that 'Soviet tactics in Korea ha[d] clearly demonstrated that the U.S.S.R. [was] intent on securing *all* of Korea as a satellite [emphasis added]'.[62] Specifically, it was detailed that while the American-controlled 'South Korea [was] in a state of unrest' due to 'food shortages', 'well-organized Communist opponents of the U.S. occupation [were] endeavouring to give political direction'[63] to such disorder. As a result, the ORE issued a warning that stated a 'Korean army [was] being trained in the Soviet Zone, and may be expected to intervene, probably by mass infiltration, in case U.S. forces should lose control of the situation in South Korea'.[64] Such fears were realised in 1950.

It was on 25 June 1950[65] that the North Korean People's Army (NKPA), allegedly with Stalin's approval,[66] crossed the line of division that was the 38th Parallel and entered into the South with a preponderance of force.[67] Caught off-guard and with inferior weapons, the Republic of Korea's (ROK) forces were quickly overrun.[68] As General MacArthur wrote in a letter to President Truman on 19 July, the North Korean Forces 'with overwhelming numbers and superior weapons temporarily shattered South Korean resistance'.[69] In response, sections of the American 8th Army were deployed, followed by a UN mandated coalition force (UNC – United Nations Command).[70] These forces, American-led and under the command of MacArthur, made rapid and significant gains.[71]

By October 1950 MacArthur's forces were hastily pursuing the NKPA back across the 38th Parallel.[72] In addition to this, by late October they had progressed deep into North Korea and were in the general vicinity of the Manchurian boarder with China.[73] Thus, America had quickly gained the advantage. As MacArthur wrote in a letter to Truman oh 30 October, '[o]perations in Korea are proceeding according to plan and while as we draw close to the Manchurian border enemy resistance had somewhat stiffened, I do not think this represents a strong defense'.[74] Yet, regrettably for MacArthur, such remarks could be labelled as his 'famous last words'.

Unfortunately for MacArthur the 'stiffening' to which he refers was being contributed to by the Chinese who had already crossed the border into the

North. In fact, even before his letter had been sent to Truman, unbeknown to MacArthur, Chinese People's Volunteer (CPV) forces (sent in reaction to the threat of American encroachment on Chinese territory)[75] had 'secretly cross[ed] the border into North Korea' and were making their first strikes on UNC forces.[76] Specifically, the CPV began by attacking a UN force on 25–26 October, followed by American divisions on the night of 1 November.[77] Largely successful in both attacks, it was at this point that the dynamic of the war began to change.[78]

After initially 'disappearing' after their first attack, it was on 25–26 November that the CPV launched their second-phase attack.[79] With numbers perceived to be in excess of 'twenty-six Chinese divisions … and another 200,000 … in the vicinity', the American-led coalition had most certainly lost its advantage.[80] As MacArthur reported back to the JCS in late November:

[a]ll hope of localization of the Korean conflict to enemy forces composed of North Korean troops with alien token elements can now be completely abandoned. The Chinese forces are committed in North Korea in great and ever increasing strength … We now face an entirely new war.[81]

Thus, it was in this 'new' Korean War context that the situation began to take a dramatically negative turn for the American-led coalition.

The impact of the second phase was felt on 27 November with American divisions being forced to a retreat south of the Chongchon River (a hundred miles south of the border with China) due to the sheer ferocity of the CPV surge.[82] Nevertheless, this quickly escalated. By 30 November the extent of the Chinese superiority in force meant that the retreat had expanded to all coalition forces and a 'general retreat' was ordered.[83] The call for retreat, however, did not mark the end to such chaos. Instead, the Chinese continued a rapid advance.[84] As a result, despite attempts to retreat as quickly as possible, within the first two weeks of withdrawal the American-led forces were frequently overrun by the persistent Chinese. As Adrian R. Lewis writes, it was in this retreat that '[t]housands of U.N. soldiers became casualties, prisoners of war, or went missing in action'.[85] Thus, the coalition forces were caught in a desperate and bloody retreat south. By 5 December they had abandoned the capital Pyongyang (fifty miles south of the Chongchon River) and were continuing rapidly towards the 38th Parallel.[86]

Despite this, over another hundred miles south, they managed to reach the 38th Parallel by mid-December.[87] By 15 December the coalition forces had fully managed to retreat from the North, allowing the CPV to take 'control of nearly all North Korean territory'.[88] As such, the military situation in Korea by late 1950 was bordering on the catastrophic. Within three months the American-led forces had retreated almost three hundred miles, moving from the Chinese border in the north of Korea in October south of the 38th Parallel by December.[89] Not only this, but they had incurred death, injury, and capture at the hands of the Chinese and North Korean forces. In all, they had seemingly been defeated. It was within this evolved and extreme context that notions of military build-up, a reliance on the atomic strategy, and NSC-68 took on increased importance.

Not only did Truman's initial hesitation (and funding limitations) all but disappear, but even Kennan agreed that action had to be taken to ensure the reversal of the situation.[90] As he made clear in a memorandum intended for Acheson, 'if these developments proceed in a way favourable to Soviet purposes and prestige, and unfavourable to our own, there will scarcely be any theatre of east–west conflict which will not be adversely affected thereby'.[91] With political opinion swaying towards the need for action, the proposals put forward in NSC-68 were becoming increasingly compelling.[92] Quite simply, after 'the most infamous retreat in American military history' it became difficult for even the staunchest advocates of political containment to deny that a more assertive course of action had to be taken, and NSC-68 was ready to be implemented for just such an occurrence.[93] It was in this context that Truman was finally able and willing to approve NSC-68. This he did in December 1950, alongside declaring a national emergency.[94] Such decisions would lead to a dramatic change in American atomic war plans and the role atomic weapons would play in American policy.[95]

The age of extremes

Whereas recent events in Korea and elsewhere constitute a grave threat to the peace of the world ... and

Whereas world conquest by communist imperialism is the goal of the forces of aggression that have been loosed upon the world; and

Whereas, if the goal of communist imperialism were to be achieved, the people of this country would no longer enjoy the full and rich life they have with God's help built for themselves and their children; ... and

Whereas the increasing menace of the forces of communist aggression requires that the national defense of the United States be strengthened as speedily as possible:

Now, Therefore, I, Harry S. Truman, president of the United States of America, do proclaim the existence of a national emergency, which requires that the military, naval, air, and civilian defenses of this country be strengthened as speedily as possible to the end that we may be able to repel any and all threats against our national security.

President Truman (1950)[96]

As President Truman clearly outlined in the above 'Proclamation 2914, Proclaiming the Existence of a National Emergency', by December 1950 the perceived threat posed by world communism, atomic weapons, and the situation in Korea had led to a reappraisal of American's stance towards the Soviet Union. No longer did the Truman administration base its policy directives on the foundations of political containment and international control. The stakes were too high and the threat too severe to be reliant on such notions. Instead, as outlined in NSC-68, a military approach to containment (spearheaded by atomic weapons and the advocacy of their increasingly indiscriminate deployment) was now the preferred means by which to ensure American security.[97] As Rosenberg stated, Truman had moved towards a 'reluctant acceptance of nuclear weapons as the centrepiece of American defense policy'.[98] In essence, a change in presidential thinking had taken place. It was the utilisation of America's atomic capabilities, not the restriction of it, which was now key to national security.[99] Thus, such changes in political policy towards atomic weapons proceeded to have a rapid and significant impact upon the direction of existing precision-based atomic war plans at a strategic planning level.

Where JCS atomic war planning had once been marginalised and allowed to develop in an atmosphere of uncertainty and ambiguity, it was now the case that, with Truman's approval of NSC-68, JCS precision-based plans for atomic war were placed under increased and intense political scrutiny. In essence, it was these war plans which would now be relied on as the frontline of American defence and security if (or when, as the anxiety of the period seemed to reflect) war between America and the Soviet Union were to occur. As such, precision had to be able to guarantee strategic success and American security. If it was deemed that it might not, then precision had to be side-lined and replaced.

Thus, many questions began to be asked of precision. Were the atomic precision bombardment elements of the latest war plans, such as OFFTACKLE, the most strategically appropriate way to ensure American security if atomic war were to occur in the near future? Was such an ambition even technologically achievable in reality? Could the targets be hit? And did planners even know where all the targets were? Such questions now represented the difference between security and insecurity. Thus, with the increase in volume afforded to them by changes in political direction, it was these questions that would fuel the strategic debates of the early 1950s. Quite simply, every inter-service rival and intra-service critic of the JCS level of strategic planning came out of the woodwork – a development which would mark the side-lining of precision and its replacement with a far more 'pragmatic' idea for atomic targeting and bombardment.

5

Replacement (1950–61)

Where was the need for precision bombing when SAC could destroy the evil empire all but literally?

Colin Grey (2012)[1]

Although the US Army and Navy expressed criticism during this period, most surprisingly it was from within the Air Force that the majority of objections arose.[2] Specifically, such questioning came from Strategic Air Command (SAC), now led by General Curtis E. LeMay (the architect of the firebombing of Japan during the Second World War), who did not see the logic of attempting to ensure discriminate bombardment in times of atomic war.[3] Furthermore, and perhaps most influentially, LeMay and his command did not believe it was an achievable strategy at this period in time. This was largely as a result of the Air Force's inadequate targeting intelligence data and its overstretched reconnaissance systems.[4] These lapses meant that, in reality, even if precision in targeting could be achieved (a factor which was far from a technological guarantee), the pilots in the air would not be certain as to where all vital targets were located.[5] Therefore, it was LeMay and his SAC leadership who put the Air Staff and JCS reliance on a precision-based atomic strategy under intense scrutiny.[6]

As an alternative, much like the process that led to LeMay's initial abandonment of precision bombing in the Pacific during the Second World War, he pushed for a comparatively indiscriminate targeting policy – one that would focus on the destruction of whole cities (alongside key military and scientific targets) as a means to guarantee the striking of the 'right' target and thus American victory in the event of atomic war. Such a notion, as exemplified by the directives put forward in NSC-68, was popular in certain political circles in the United States. Furthermore, at a strategic level, it is fair to say that LeMay had a compelling argument as to the flaws manifest in precision bombardment at this time, an argument to which the Air Staff and the JCS would ultimately have to concede.

Figure 5.1 Major General Curtis E. LeMay (centre) talking to General Joseph W. Stilwell

Thus, as this chapter explains, from 1950 onwards American nuclear strategy took a turn from the long-held ambition to achieve precision bombardment and adopted LeMay's 'bomb everything' mantra. Targeting lists and proposed bomb deployment numbers quickly increased from the tens to the hundreds and into the thousands. Subsequently, by 1960/61 and the acceptance of Strategic Integrated Operating Plan 62 (SIOP-62), the American military was left in a situation where, if war was to break out (or was to be perceived to be breaking out), the United States would be on a default footing to launch a pre-emptive atomic strike which would destroy the Soviet Union and devastate its satellite states many times over. In essence, precision was cast far to the side-lines during this period.

To support this argument, the chapter begins by conducting an in-depth study into LeMay's own thoughts about strategic bombardment. Following this, the justification for the deviation from precision in 1950 is analysed. In particular, LeMay's push for the control of atomic targeting is outlined alongside the arguments stated by the SAC leadership during the Air Force commanders' conference in 1950 as a means to justify such an attempt to take control.

The proceeding battle for control, and the ultimate JCS and Air Staff acceptance of SAC arguments, is detailed to highlight how precision was officially side-lined during this period. Following this, a study of the strategic changes implemented by LeMay's SAC at the end of the Truman and into the Eisenhower administration is undertaken. It is shown how LeMay and SAC took control of atomic targeting in the context of Eisenhower's policy of 'massive retaliation' and were able to implement their comparatively indiscriminate 'bomb everything' doctrine with little resistance. Next, the importance of SAC's 'bootstrapping' during this period is explained. The chapter concludes with an analysis of SIOP-62, which epitomised the change in strategic focus by allotting tens of thousands of atomic weapons to thousands of atomic targets, all to be deployed in one blunt massive retaliatory strike. Overall, the chapter highlights how and why, between 1950 and 1961, American strategic ambitions changed from being focused on the achievement of precision, to the implementation of an indiscriminate and disproportionate strategy, a strategy which aptly came to be described as 'overkill'. To begin, however, LeMay's justification for the side-lining of precision and his replacement strategic bombardment strategy is first outlined in detail.

LeMay's doctrine

[W]e should concentrate on industry itself which is located in urban areas …
[through this] a bonus will be derived from use of the bomb.
General Curtis E. LeMay (1950)[7]

The justification for LeMay and SAC contributing to debates regarding atomic strategy during the last years of the 1940s came from the fact that SAC was the subsidiary command of both the Air Force and the Department of Defense charged with the deployment of atomic weapons in the event of atomic war.[8] Due to limited funding, and as a by-product of the low priority given to atomic war planning after the Second World War, SAC spent its initial years (1946–48) in the background of strategic planning. Reflecting the ever-increasing unease during this period, and Truman's emergent reliance on the atomic option, General Curtis E. LeMay was eventually given charge of SAC in 1948 (alongside increased funding) and it was at this point that SAC began to make itself heard in debates on atomic bombardment. True to his formidable and no-nonsense reputation forged in the previous war, by 1950–51, LeMay had helped establish SAC as an accomplished, highly trained, and professional military command. As the historian David Rosenberg stated, 'LeMay instilled a spirit in his command which made SAC for a time the nation's most elite military unit.'[9] This was not, however, the only attribute LeMay instilled into SAC. During this period, he also became the 'living personification' of SAC, and in turn SAC became the organisational manifestation of his trademark 'bomb everything' approach to strategic bombardment.[10] Thus, it was as a direct result of LeMay's position in charge of SAC that the organisation took on its stance against precision.

LeMay's criticism of strategic precision bombardment was nothing new. He had never been a traditional disciple of Mitchell and was not considered an 'ACTS man' while in Alabama.[11] Instead, LeMay had risen through the ranks the hard way. He had not gone to West Point, but had instead been commissioned as a second lieutenant in the Air Corps Reserve (1929), before receiving a regular commission (1930). This meant he had the opportunity to work across fighter and bomber assignments, obtaining vital first-hand experience at an operational level.[12] During the early stages of the Second World War, LeMay organised, trained, and led the 305th Bombardment Group in the European Theatre (1942–44). As the war progressed and the fight turned to Japan, LeMay then moved to take over from General Hansell in the Pacific (1945). As a result, he understood first-hand the challenges of trying to hit the 'precise' target. Such experiences gave LeMay a differing approach to bombardment compared to many of his colleagues.

Specifically, as Chapter 2 has highlighted, during the Second World War LeMay had convinced air leaders that, in the face of an underachieving precision bombing doctrine, it was strategic area bombing, through firebombing, that was the key to victory.[13] As Kaplan stated, '[t]o LeMay, demolishing everything was how you win a war'.[14] As such, LeMay had a 'bomb everything mantra' and, in much the same way as he had done during the Second World War, he wished to instil this approach into American atomic war plans.[15] As he stated in his diary on 23 January 1950, 'we should concentrate on industry itself which is located in urban areas … [through this] a bonus will be derived from use of the bomb'.[16] Thus, for LeMay, it was far from the nature of the target that was most important. To him it was the total destruction of the enemy's cities which was the key. Through this, not only would the military and industrial targets be destroyed, but also 'bonus cost' to the population and infrastructure would occur.[17] It was with this form of bombardment in mind that LeMay and the SAC leadership 'fought for control' of atomic targeting.[18] This was a battle that saw LeMay confront the leadership of the Air Staff and challenge the existing JCS stance on atomic war plans.[19]

The push for control

[Targeting] developed considerable controversy on the Joint Staff and even within the Air Force. Should cities be the main targets, or should targeting be confined strictly to military and industrial targets?

> Major General Kenneth Nichols,[20] quoted in
> Richard Rhodes, *Dark Sun* (1996)[21]

Fortunately for LeMay, as leader of the command responsible for the deployment of atomic weapons, his opinion on such matters carried considerable weight. As Kaplan observed:

> LeMay was the one who would route the bombers to their destinations; he was the one who would be pressed to deliver; he had the bombs. And most of the Air Force officers knew that, on a tactical level anyway, LeMay pretty much did as he pleased.[22]

LeMay was deemed a legitimate and powerful voice in the debate. Quite simply, he was seen as an 'elite' military commander who 'had the ultimate clout' when it came down to how his SAC forces, and the bomb itself, would be deployed.[23] Therefore, LeMay had the right to express his doubts when it came to atomic targeting plans and their reliance on precision. It was from this position of power that he launched his challenge to the existing targeting priorities.

LeMay began his scrutiny of precision strategic bombardment by reiterating the shortcomings of the precision bombing that he had witnessed during the previous war. LeMay thought, 'strategic bombing in Europe had been handled all wrong, too much fussing with "bottleneck" targets and "precision bombing"'.[24] Thus, where Arnold had once attempted to reappraise the American Second World War experience of precision bombing, LeMay criticised its performance. To LeMay, 'the idea of separating out specific industrial sectors in some delicate and discriminating fashion was a disastrous notion'.[25] Instead, he argued that strategic success in future atomic war could be guaranteed through the 'very careful selection' of the USSR's largest and most strategically important cities.[26] As Rosenberg confirms, this form of bombardment would guarantee that 'SAC would cause maximum damage to Soviet war-making capacity'.[27] In addition, this strategy ensured that 'a' target, if not 'the' target, was struck with invaluable US atomic assets. These thoughts were in line with LeMay's own SAC Emergency War Plan 1–49 which argued that it would be most effective to 'deliver the entire stockpile of atomic bombs … in a single massive attack'.[28] Thus, from LeMay's point of view, if victory was to be secured in any future atomic war, the atomic offensive would have to be 'conducted like his air war against Japanese cities – by attacking industrial complexes, which in effect ... meant cities'.[29] LeMay knew, however, that persuasive rhetoric and compelling examples from the past would not be enough to convince the Air Staff and JCS to deviate from their (now deeply ingrained) reliance on precision. As such, he reinforced his argument by highlighting how, if precision were to continue as the foundational driving factor of American atomic war plans, failures akin to those seen in the previous war would be manifest in the next.

As a means to prove that this was the case, LeMay and the SAC leadership scrutinised the most recent targeting list in JCS war plan OFFTACKLE. Specifically, in April 1950, with political concerns about the Soviet Union increasing, LeMay and his SAC leadership presented their critique of OFFTACKLE at the Commanders Conference United States Air Force held at Ramey Air Force Base in Aguadilla, Puerto Rico.[30] Here, in the SAC presentation to Air Force commanders, it was explained how aspects of the current targeting plans were not fit for purpose.[31] In detail, the SAC presentation described how in existing targeting plans, a number of the 'discriminate' and 'delicate' targets that had been outlined in the USSR were not guaranteed to be targeted accurately if an atomic offensive was to be launched in the immediate future.[32] Put simply, the achievement of certain pivotal objectives outlined in OFFTACKLE would not be possible and an American victory, along with American security, would be compromised.[33] In support of this damning conclusion the SAC team gave two key examples.

First it was explained how a lack of targeting intelligence contributed to this strategic shortfall. In reference to the below chart, the SAC presentation stated that although '"OFFTACKLE" lists a total of 123 [targets] ... with the target material we now have, we are prepared to strike 60 of the 123 targets.'[34] As such, the SAC presentation identified that, for 51 per cent of the OFFTACKLE targets, 'pre-strike reconnaissance is required'.[35] In other words, the appropriate level of targeting intelligence to strike the target accurately was not available. With the below chart as a backdrop, they went on to reiterate and reaffirm these damning conclusions.

As a means of providing increased understanding of the severity of this situation to the Air Force commanders in attendance, the SAC presentation explained that, in reference to the above chart, the '[r]ed discs [black in the chart] indicate areas on which we now have target material, and blank discs indicate areas which will require pre-strike reconnaissance'.[36] As they went on to explain, the 'magnitude of the reconnaissance effort can be appreciated by noting the numbers of untargeted areas and their geographical spread'.[37]

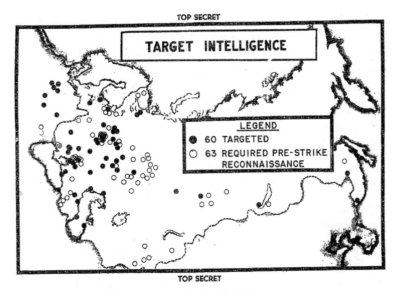

Figure 5.2 Target intelligence for war plan OFFTACKLE

Thus, the argument made by LeMay and his staff was clear: the OFFTACKLE targeting list relied too heavily on the notion that it was achievable to strike specific, unverified, and geographically spread targets with precision.[38] With the limited targeting intelligence data available, this was not a realistic strategic aim. In addition to this point, and as a means of reinforcing their argument further, the SAC leadership went on to explain why this targeting intelligence was not already available and why it would not be ready for a number of years.

The explanation they gave focused on the shortfalls in the reconnaissance capabilities available to SAC. Explicitly stating that the 'soft spot is reconnaissance',[39] they proceeded to outline the manifest equipment shortfalls. As they stated:

> the picture can be summed up briefly. Although three reconnaissance wings are presently programmed, we now have the equivalent strength of one wing, and, considering the basic equipment of this wing [is] the [older and inefficient] RB-29, we are stretching a point to assess our present strength as the equivalent of one wing.[40]

They proceeded to explain that these shortfalls were compounded by the fact that the 'total [r]econnaissance strength is 62 [aircraft]. All of these are the B-29 type. We have not yet received our first [new and more effective] RB-36 or our first RB-50'.[41] Thus, quite simply, LeMay's team made it clear to the Air Force commanders how this lack of sufficient reconnaissance equipment and aircraft translated into the fact that OFFTACKLE's precision-based target list was currently unachievable and would remain unachievable for the foreseeable future. As they went on to conclude:

> [l]ooking at the job required by OFFTACKLE, we estimate that at least four reconnaissance wings would be required on a minimum basis. The accomplishment of such essential photography as pre-strike and post-strike missions would require approximately 750 sorties. In the event of an early emergency, it would be necessary to draw heavily on the bomber forces to supplement the effort of our present reconnaissance forces. As for post-strike reconnaissance, the tactical difficulties involved in operating RB-29 aircraft during daylight hours are obvious. The RB-47 will greatly alleviate the bomb-damage assessment problem, but the airplanes will not be with us in numbers until early 1953.[42]

As such, with the evidence mounting as to the shortcoming of precision, the SAC leadership's message to the Air Force commanders was clear. The OFFTACKLE target list, in its current form, should be scrapped. For as long as the Air Staff and JCS continued to prioritise the precision targeting of specific sites, American atomic war plans remained unachievable and the chances of an American victory in an atomic war against the Soviet Union were greatly reduced.

Such conclusions were damning. It became increasingly apparent (to those sympathetic to the SAC argument at least) that efforts to achieve precision had run their course. No longer was there the luxury, or the time, to consider these seemingly moral, ethical 'humanitarian' aims. At least not while there were gaps in intel and technical deficits. A far more pragmatic approach was needed. Yet, despite these realisations, deviation from the existing targeting plans did not occur straight away. Instead, over the next six months the pressure mounted on the Air Staff and JCS from a variety of sources.[43] For instance, in August 1950 in an article for the *Reporter*, the historian and strategist Bernard Brodie expressed his criticism of the current war plans.[44] Although a believer in the need for precision in targeting, Brodie made it clear that the current lists were unachievable without further time and investment in technical advancements and equipment. In fact, it was off the back of such criticism that Brodie was brought into 'the savage jungle of nuclear war planning' to provide his own assessment of the situation.[45] As Kaplan stated, it was during this period that Brodie increased his scepticism, 'telling them [the targeting staff] that LeMay was right, they didn't know where all the ... plants were; how could they hope that such an attack would have any effect at all'.[46] Such criticism only added further credence to LeMay's conclusions and, unfortunately for those in the Air Staff and the JCS holding onto notions of precision, Brodie was not alone in these thoughts. The pressure was mounting.

Further support for LeMay's critique came from the Joint Intelligence Committee (JIC), a branch that helped construct the JCS war plans. As one JIC officer stated to the JCS, the war plan's 'condition precludes a specific appraisal of intelligence adequacy'.[47] Such 'jargon' from an intelligence officer, as Kaplan explained, 'could be translated as meaning, '[q]uit wasting your time, this mission is impossible'.[48] Consequently, in the context of pressure, fear, and escalation that defined the early 1950s, precision's place as a core ambition in American strategic thought was rapidly diminishing. Instead, it was now LeMay's belief, that 'the whole point of strategic bombing was to be massive, a campaign of holy terror', which was rising to prominence.[49] It was in the face of this mounting pressure that the JCS and the Air Staff began to consider significant changes to the foundations and ethos of American nuclear bombardment strategy.

In January 1951, LeMay finally achieved what he had been aiming for – and more. It was at this point that he met with the Air Staff Targeting Panel to discuss his concerns. This meeting was pivotal for LeMay as it was here that he could explain in detail to the Air Staff the limitations, shortfalls, and operational pressure that precision targeting with nuclear weapons would place on SAC. As he went on to declare, 'any target system picked that failed to reap the benefits derived from urban area bombing ... was wasteful'.[50] As he proposed, American atomic war plans should abandon such notions of precision and 'concentrate on industry itself which is located in urban areas'.[51] This way, he argued, if a target was missed, 'a bonus will be derived from the use of the bomb'.[52] Although these comments were, in essence, 'anti-precision', there can be little doubt that given the unique bipolar international context and the slow realisation that precision may not be technically achievable at this time, LeMay's proposals were compelling.[53] Consequently, the panel decided not only to reconsider the targeting priorities in American atomic war plans, but to 'submit such lists to SAC before sending them to the JCS for approval'.[54] In addition to this, by mid-1951 the OFFTACKLE targeting list – which LeMay and his SAC team had discredited a year earlier – was 'formally rejected' by the JCS.[55] From this point onwards the very ethos of American nuclear strategy began to change.

On being granted his new 'power' to, in effect, amend any targeting list he disapproved of, and with the rejection of the old lists, LeMay finally began to side-line any notion of precision within official American atomic targeting plans and replace it with his own 'bomb everything' doctrine. This was the case as the decade progressed. In fact, it was specifically between 1953 and 1961, with a change in presidential administrations and the implementation of 'massive retaliation', that LeMay found increased autonomy, increased funding, and increased control over the implementation and expansion of his doctrine.[56]

Consolidating control: Eisenhower's massive retaliation and LeMay's bootstrapping

General Jack D. Ripper: Mandrake, do you recall what Clemenceau once said about war?

Group Capt. Lionel Mandrake: No, I don't think I do, sir, no.

General Jack D. Ripper: He said war was too important to be left to the generals. When he said that, 50 years ago, he might have been right. But today, war is too important to be left to politicians. They have neither the time, the training, nor the inclination for strategic thought. I can no longer sit back and allow Communist infiltration, Communist indoctrination, Communist subversion and the international Communist conspiracy to sap and impurify all of our precious bodily fluids.

Dr Strangelove (1964)[57]

President Truman left office in January 1953 and subsequently his presidency has been defined by the baptism of atomic fire to which it opened. It is perhaps most fitting, however, to recognise the personal and political struggle Truman faced when attempting to define the role that atomic weapons should play in the post-Second World War world. Nevertheless, when President Eisenhower came to power, a very different approach was adopted. Arguably America's most famous general, when he came to power there was little hesitation about the military importance of nuclear weapons.

It has been argued that Eisenhower understood the political and strategic potential of nuclear weapons more than any other president before or after him. This is not to say that he did not grasp the devastating reality of these weapons. Eisenhower was 'the first NATO Supreme Allied Commander from 1950 to 1952 [and was] familiar with JCS targeting categories and priorities'.[58] He knew what the impact would be if the decision to use nuclear weapons was made, and thus such a decision would not be taken lightly. As he stated to his Cabinet in March 1953, nuclear weapons were not to be seen as 'a cheap way to solve things ... It is cold comfort for any citizen of Western Europe to be assured that – after his country is overrun and he is pushing up the daisies – someone still alive will drop a bomb on the Kremlin'.[59] Thus, Eisenhower was fully aware of the devastation that would transpire from the use of nuclear weapons. Nevertheless, this did not stop him harnessing the obvious utility of these weapons and continuing – even increasing – the reliance on nuclear weapons as part of American foreign policy.[60] In fact, it was upon this threat of massive nuclear destruction that Eisenhower's foreign policy was built.

Specifically for Eisenhower, a strategy of 'massive retaliation' became the foundation on which his foreign policy towards the Soviet Union would be built.[61] When describing the approach informally to a congressional delegation in late 1954, he stated that massive retaliation aimed to 'blow the hell out of them in a hurry if they started anything'.[62] Nevertheless, when described more formally, as Secretary of State John Foster Dulles outlined to the Council on Foreign Relations in January 1954, the doctrine depended 'primarily upon a great capacity to retaliate instantly by means and at places of our own choosing'.[63] In essence, the idea was to ensure the policy for American nuclear deployment was on a defensive footing, with use only condoned in retaliatory circumstances. If retaliation (even pre-emptive retaliation) were ever necessary, the United States would ensure it was in a position to inflict massive destruction on the USSR in a manner and on a scale never before seen.[64] For Eisenhower it was this doctrine which would act as the keystone to safeguarding American security.

By as early as October 1953 the Eisenhower administration had rapidly devised and approved presidential policy directive NSC-162/2 which set out the criteria needed to ensure massive retaliation was constructed and maintained as an achievable reality.[65] By December 1953, a three-year defence programme had been approved by the President to implement the criteria set out in NSC-162/2. This consisted of increases in the quality and quantity of nuclear weapons – such as the continued development of thermonuclear weapons –[66] and improvements in the operational effectiveness of the Air Force's intelligence gathering and strategic bombardment capacity.[67] From very early on in the Eisenhower presidency, therefore, a foreign policy based on massive nuclear bombardment had been approved and a defence programme to expand the capacity of strategic air power had been implemented. As the year progressed from 1953 and into 1954, the next step to ensuring the operational achievability of massive retaliation lay at an operational level within the JCS, the Air Force, and LeMay's Strategic Air Command. It was here that the targeting categories would be set and payloads assigned.

During the process of assigning nuclear weapons to 'appropriate' targets for massive nuclear bombardment, General LeMay found fertile ground for the increased implementation of his own preferred method of attack. As a continuation of the control over targeting lists handed to him by the Air Staff during the Truman years, LeMay was in a position where he could amend and add specific targets that he deemed most appropriate to ensure the SAC fulfilment of massive retaliation before they were sent on to the JCS for approval. Furthermore, as the leader of SAC, along with his commanders, he dictated the manner in which SAC would carry out an offensive on said targets. This gave LeMay enormous control over how massive retaliation would be conducted and achieved at an operational level.

Known as the SAC 'combined bombing offensive', LeMay's targeting lists kept within the framework of existing JCS categories – BRAVO (blunting), ROMEO (retardation), and DELTA (disruption) – but greatly expanded the number and the character of the targets in the said categories. For instance, whereas Vanderberg's 'killing a nation' had sought discriminate military and industrial sites as targets, not whole cities, LeMay's interpretation of these categories included the vast expansion of targets deemed of strategic utility. This included suspected atomic installations and airfields in the USSR and the direct nuclear bombardment and destruction of whole cities in both the USSR and China.[68] Furthermore, as a means to ensure as much destruction as possible, LeMay decided that any offensive would involve one massive and inflexible combined offensive against all targets as a means to 'minimize the time U.S. bombers would have to remain in hostile air space, maximise destruction, and reduce the need for costly follow up strikes'.[69] Thus, by March 1954, if the full SAC capability was to be deployed, the offensive would have seen a total of 735 nuclear armed strategic bombers simultaneously breaking through the threshold of enemy early warning systems and launching a 'single massive blow' on the cities and war-making capacity in the Soviet Union.[70] Although technically in line with the massive retaliation doctrine, to say such a plan was accepted with open arms by the Eisenhower administration would be an oversimplification.[71] Even Eisenhower had not envisioned destruction on this level.

In fact, it is interesting to note that President Eisenhower involved himself directly in the matter and expressly questioned the JCS on the utility of this unprecedented approach to nuclear bombardment. Eisenhower – providing retrospective clarity – stated that his vision of massive retaliation had been against military targets, not whole cities. As he declared to the JCS in June 1954: '[i]f we batter Soviet cities to pieces by bombing ... what solution do we have to take control of the situation and handle it so as to achieve the objectives for which we went to war?'[72] He went on to ask them to expand their thinking and utilise their imagination when planning 'the best way to fight the next war in order that we [the US] could attain our national objectives with the minimum cost and least dislocation to the world'.[73] Yet despite these presidential concerns, LeMay's planning continued along the same lines on which it had begun.

This was able to happen because LeMay's line of strategic thought had rapidly gained the support of the Air Force leadership who now protected and condoned his approach. Without the ability to achieve precision, LeMay's bombardment doctrine was seen as the only viable option; it would be pivotal to ensuring victory through air power in the next war. The development of thermonuclear weapons only further justified LeMay's approach to Air Force leaders, as his much lauded 'bonus damage' of cities and even whole regions could now be achieved. As Rosenberg stated, the 'possibility that SAC might be able to deliver a single war-winning blow was an irresistible temptation to Air Force planners'.[74] Economic incentives also helped guarantee support from the Air Force leadership. The perceived utility and achievability of LeMay's strategy gave an incentive to continue, even increase, funding for the Air Force. This meant that the US Air Force could grow in power compared to other branches of the US military. As a result, LeMay's line of strategic thought was encouraged. The more targets LeMay identified, the more nuclear weapons needed, and the more aircraft needed to deploy them. All of this meant more funds were obtained for the US Air Force.[75]

Known as 'bootstrapping', such a process caused considerable alarm and bitterness within the other services. As Admiral R.L. Johnson, Deputy Director of Joint Strategic Target Planning Staff (1961–63), emotively recalled in a 1980 interview, '[t]he SAC people never seemed to be satisfied that to kill once was enough. They want to kill, overkill, overkill, because all of this has built up the prestige of SAC, it created the need for more forces, for a larger budget … [T]hat's the way their thinking went.'[76] The admiral was not alone in this line of thought. In fact, many in the military saw it as an irresponsible allocation of funding. A core worry was that, ultimately, these endless funds would lead to a strategy detached from American values and American notions of warfare. As Army Chief of Staff General Ridgeway stated in October 1954:

> I consider it imperative that the Joint Chief of Staff insure that the great striking power of the Strategic Air Command be employed in accordance with the sound military principles of economy of force and in accordance with a national policy which seeks to attain national objectives without indiscriminate mass destruction of human life.[77]

Despite such concerns, however, Ridgeway retired soon after his remarks; and although his comments did initiate a Joint Staff committee review, little changed in regard to SAC's influence over the process.

In fact, as a result of the continued funding SAC had received, by 1954/55 they had installed the latest IBM 704 computer systems to advance their methods of data analysis. The IBM's ability to process vast and complex inputs helped SAC to decide which sites should be included on the nuclear target lists. This now put SAC in a position of dominance over the JCS as they had superior technology to calculate the targets deemed necessary to ensure the security of the United States. Another consequence was that the IBM 704 further isolated the other branches of the US military from the target planning process because they did not have the same advanced capabilities to check SAC calculations and intervene in the bootstrapping process. Thus, with few checks and balances left in place, it was from this point that LeMay and SAC consolidated their control over targeting and began to expand their target lists and weapons requirements in line with the SAC bombardment ethos.

To put this expansion into perspective, whereas the American atomic weapons stockpile consisted of 250 weapons in 1949, by 1961 – the year LeMay became Chief of Staff of the US Air Force and the year Single Integrated Operational Plan 62 (SIOP-62) was enshrined into policy – this had increased to 18,000 weapons[78] – weapons like the first truly thermonuclear bomb, which was successfully tested in 1954.[79] Thus, between obtaining the IBM 704 in 1954/55 and the beginning of the 1960s, the SAC leadership had embarked on a rapid expansion and implementation of their strategic doctrine. Although still obliged to submit such plans to the JCS before implementation, 'the Joint Staff had neither the time not the resources to thoroughly evaluate the finished product'.[80] Furthermore, with SAC's superior targeting computation technology, it made it hard, if not impossible, for the JCS to challenge their targeting calculations and data. As a result, SAC had increased autonomy and free rein to implement their preferred bombardment strategy. To highlight the extent to which SAC was able to exploit its dominance over the JCS and other branches of the military to implement its plans, a study into the ultimate manifestation of the SAC line of strategic thought, SIOP-62, is necessary. Through the study of this document and the process behind its construction between 1952 and 1961, we can begin to understand the extent to which American strategic thought had deviated from precision and, by the beginning of the 1960s, had become based on an indiscriminate and disproportionate strategy of the most devastating proportions.[81]

The road to SIOP-62

[i]f SAC takes over the function of the Joint Chiefs ... it is the fault of the Chiefs themselves.[82]

Secretary of Defense Gates to President Eisenhower (July 1960)

Due to the continued secrecy that has surrounded SIOP-62 over the last six decades, it has remained difficult for scholars to fully portray the extremes of this nuclear bombardment strategy and the process behind its construction. There can be little doubt that some insightful and interesting studies have been produced on the topic – many of which, such as Rosenberg (1983) and Sagan (1989), have provided scholars with the core details and statistics needed to understand the broad aims behind the first SIOP and the potential consequences of its deployment.[83] Nevertheless, such studies have been constrained by the limited material available to them. In fact, it is only in recent years that the situation has begun to change with the declassification of formerly top secret and restricted documentation. Now, through the analysis of these recently declassified documents (2007, 2011, and 2015), we can build on early scholarly work and understand SIOP-62 in greater detail. Through continued declassification attempts by scholars such as William Burr and Nate Jones at the National Security Archive, we are able to gain increased insight into the processes behind the construction of the SIOP and provide additional statistical details on the damage it would have caused.[84] Through these documents, the extent to which the first SIOP marked the ultimate deviation from any notion of precision in American nuclear strategy can be fully understood.

As the previous section has highlighted, between 1950 and 1955 SAC was able to consolidate its position of dominance in American atomic war planning. During this period LeMay had fought to ensure that SAC not only had the utmost influence on how atomic bombardment planning would be constructed, but by 1955, through a bootstrapping dynamic consolidated by astute investment in the latest technology, he had led SAC to a position where its bombardment targeting lists could be constructed, funded, and expanded with little oversight from the JCS. During this period, however, a matter which continued to irritate the SAC leadership – one which hindered their overall dominance – were the attempts made by other forces to construct their own atomic bombardment forces as a means to justify their strategic utility and to 'muscle in' on what was now purely an SAC remit. For LeMay, his SAC leaders (such as General Power), and the Air Force more generally, this could not be allowed to continue. For SAC to continue its dominance, retain funding, and maintain its bombardment ethos in official American nuclear strategy, it had to remain the dominant actor. Outlined below is the process by which SAC and the Air Force came to largely control much of American nuclear strategy development and ultimately implement the most extreme version of the LeMay and SAC's indiscriminate bombardment ethos (SIOP-62) by the start of the 1960s.

Although still the largest and most dominant force in American nuclear planning, SAC no longer had 'a virtual monopoly on the means of delivering atomic weapons'.[85] Instead, with the US Navy's announcement in 1952 that 'all of its new attack planes were capable of carrying tactical atomic bombs, and that it had on hand aircraft capable of delivering large bombs', atomic bombardment planning was no longer the purview of SAC alone.[86] Involvement from the other branches of the US military created practical problems in planning and, ultimately, a struggle for overall dominance over American nuclear strategy. As an overview of the SIOP's history now shows, this was a struggle that SAC would ultimately win.

As analysis of the *History of the Joint Strategic Target Planning Staff (JSTPS): Background and Preparation of SIOP-62* (declassified in 2007) highlights, 'coordination problems' had arisen as a result of the cross-service proliferation of nuclear 'weapons and delivery vehicles' outside of SAC control.[87] Initial attempts to resolve these issues were undertaken by the JCS from as early as 1952 with the creation of an ad hoc committee to assess the issue at hand. Concluding that problems with coordination and interference did exist, the committee recommended 'centralizing [the process] for maximum bombing effect and minimum interference between forces'.[88] Such recommendations would mark the start of the journey to the Single Integrated Operational Plan, a process which over the next nine years would be dominated by SAC. This process would ultimately allow SAC to take control of all service bombardment plans and combine them into one plan – a plan that would enshrine the LeMay and SAC bombardment ethos.

Initially, the JCS continued to maintain control over the 'centralization' process, reacting to the committee's recommendations by establishing Joint Coordination Centres (JCC). These centres, set up in Buckinghamshire (United Kingdom) and Pershing Heights (Japan), facilitated the 'receipt, compilation, display, review [and] coordination' of information regarding the planning and deployment of nuclear weapons. This information was then relayed to all commanders from the various branches of the military concerned with the deployment of atomic weapons. Such attempts aimed to provide coordinated information to all relevant commanders in these branches of the military as a means to facilitate increased dialogue and coordination planning between the different branches of the military.[89] To a limited extent this was successful, although problems persisted.

In 1954, the JCS recognised the 'requirement for pre-hostilities coordination' and instructed 'each appropriate commander to submit an atomic annex, i.e. a target list, to his war plans and to coordinate it with theatre commanders and the Commander-in-Chief Strategic Air Command (CINCSAC)'.[90] Further to this, in 1955 the JCS instructed SAC to host a conference for all 'appropriate commanders' from all services as a means to discuss said targeting plans and to ultimately 'determine a methodology or modus operandi for the defeat of communist air power'.[91] Unfortunately, not all aims were met. As the JSTPS documents made clear, although an agreement was reached to establish a yearly World-Wide Coordination Conference (WWCC) (held each year through to 1958), SAC and Air Force leaders believed the issues of 'interference' and coordination were not resolved to their satisfaction. Specifically, it was the issue of 'duplication' or 'targeting conflicts' which irritated SAC the most. As the declassified report stated:

> [t]he conferences did not solve targeting conflicts; for example, in the 1957 and 1958 meetings duplications and triplications (two or more commands delivering weapons to the same target) were not significantly reduced. Neither did they achieve mutual support or unity of strategic effort.[92]

To add further support to the SAC argument, it was noted that during JCC exercises between 1958 and 1960 there were 'over 200 time over target (TOT) conflicts', highlighting the unacceptable amount of targeting conflict between the branches of the military in the existing war plans.[93] If such conflicts were to manifest themselves in theatre, it was argued that they would have resulted in the 'needless loss of aircraft and crews', many of which may have been heading for additional targets, and therefore their destruction would have led to an overall decrease in the fulfilment of atomic bombardment aims.[94] Thus, with problems persisting, it was clear that the JCS had not been able to unite the forces under the remit of operational cooperation and dialogue. It was feared that such a failure could jeopardise the overall effectiveness of the American atomic bombardment, and national survival, if nuclear war were to occur – or at least this was the rhetoric espoused by SAC and the Air Force.

For SAC and a number of Air Force commanders, a 'common doctrine' between all branches of the military (under SAC control) was needed to ensure American victory. Anything less would have been a risk to national security.[95]

With the JCS failure to unite the branches evident, it was not long before these apparent flaws became a political issue. In fact, it was President Eisenhower himself who, with the passing of the Defense Reorganization Act of 1958, pioneered the search for more effective coordination in atomic bombardment plans. Specifically, as Eisenhower made clear while outlining his plan to Congress in 1958, it was the 'vital necessity of complete unity in our strategic planning and basic operational direction' which needed to be concentrated on.[96] Such plans proved popular with – and were overtly promoted by – the Air Force and SAC.[97] Due to their dominance in nuclear planning, they were safe in the knowledge that any integration would see them remain as the dominant and lead architect of any plans.[98] Of course, as the official history of the SIOP stated, the Army and Navy were 'less enthusiastic'.[99]

While the Air Force led the call for the creation of a unified (SAC-led) 'U.S. Strategic Command',[100] the US Navy, which was in the final stages of developing its own Polaris submarine-based nuclear missile system, and the US Army, which wanted to keep its own independent assets, were less keen on the plan, especially as it involved the 'integrating [of] all strategic weapon systems into a single command'.[101] As a means to protect new naval assets, Admiral Burke (Chief of Naval Operations) vocalised a most ardent rebuff to these plans. For Burke, there was little need for things to change. In fact, it was his belief that the continuation of planning as it was, separate, yet coordinated, and the integration of Polaris under US Navy control 'into the fleet would pose no targeting problems'.[102] In fact, in opposition to the Air Force and SAC, it was Burke's view that the creation of a single command 'would disrupt and alter the U.S. defence organisation' in a negative manner.[103] As declassified documents from the period outlined, for Burke '[a]uthority already existed in the JCS to prevent undesirable duplication in strategic targeting, planning, and weapons employment and [he] believed it should remain there'.[104] Unfortunately for Burke his protestations only exacerbated the political situation.

As a result of this disagreement 'a split decision paper' entitled SM-171-59 was presented by the commanders of the differing branches to the Secretary of Defense in 1959.[105] With the new presidential remit to take action to create an integrated plan in place, Secretary Gates (new to the position) began to take firm action. After a consultation period with all branches, and on the advice of Chairman of the JCS, General Twining, that 'endemic conceptual differences'[106] hamper the need for 'a national strategic targeting policy',[107] Gates made a decision that would influence the course of American nuclear strategy.

In what was intended as a compromise – one which endorsed neither 'the Air Force position favouring a unified command, nor the Navy position that existing JCS machinery could do the work' – Gates appointed the new CINCSAC, General Thomas S. Power, to head up a joint command made up of representatives of all military branches to construct a National Strategic Target List (NSTL) and ultimately a Single Integrated Operational Plan (SIOP).[108] It should be noted that Power had directed the first large-scale firebombing of Tokyo back in March 1945 and was a long-time ally of LeMay. In fact, when LeMay was elevated to Vice Chief of Staff of the Air Force in 1957, Power took his place as Commander-in-Chief of SAC and was promoted to four-star general. In this capacity, along with his new 'coordination role', Power was instructed to act as 'the agent of the JCS' and, from his SAC headquarters, was to collect 'a team of experts from all services to prepare a plan for all U.S. forces committed to the initial strategic strike effort'.[109] Unsurprisingly, from the very beginning such a 'compromise' played into the hands of SAC, allowing SAC commanders, at an SAC base, under CINCSAC leadership, to consolidate their power and impose their ethos over the deployment of all branches of nuclear weapons in the event of war. As the distribution of the initial SIOP and NSTL inter-service teams highlighted (see Table 5.1 below), SAC and Air Force dominance was deeply ingrained in the process from the start.

With the numbers stacked against them, the Army leadership soon realised that this was an 'inter-service process' upon which they would have little influence. Army Chief of Staff George Decker decided not to waste time sending a strong group of officers to challenge SAC dominance in the creation of the NSTL and SIOP. As Rosenberg outlined in his study on the origins of overkill, Decker 'did not believe that his planners could influence its [the SIOP's] development'.[110] Admiral Burke on the other hand, whose Navy had much more of a vested interest in the process due to the advent of the Polaris system, sent a strong team of Navy planners. Yet, ultimately, their efforts were also in vain.

Table 5.1 *Strategic Air Command. (1961).* History of the Joint Strategic Target Planning Staff and Preparation of SIOP-62 (B82767). *History and Research Division, Headquarters. p.14.*

Branches of the US military	Number of representatives on the initial SIOP NSTL staff (1960)
US Army	10 officers
US Navy (including Marine Corps)	32 officers
SAC and US Air Force	148 officers, 57 airmen and 22 civilians
Total	269

As the process progressed Burke soon realised that, outnumbered seven to one, there was little his planning staff – without the support of the Army – could do to 'curb what they perceived to be excesses in the plan' put forward by SAC.[111]

After a decade in the making, SAC had finally achieved their ultimate goal. With the other branches of the military under SAC leadership, dominance over the construction of American nuclear strategy had been attained. With this power came great opportunity. SAC could now implement, without outside interference, the most extreme version of the LeMay bombardment ethos – a plan that would come to be known as 'overkill'.

SIOP-62: The ultimate departure from precision

SIOP-62 ... deliberately designed to inflict hundreds of millions of deaths and uncounted casualties, mostly on innocent civilians in the USSR and China ... deliberately removed effective operational control from the president or any other civilian or even military commander in the event of a nuclear confrontation.

John H. Rubel (Assistant Secretary of Defense, 1961–63)[112]

The aim of SIOP-62 was simple. As official documents pertaining to its history highlighted, the objective was to achieve 'optimum targeting' and strike an 'optimum mix' of the 'best combination' of targets to ensure an American victory in the event of nuclear war.[113] What did this mean in reality? Building upon LeMay's 'bomb everything' ethos, the SAC-dominated SIOP planning team simply expanded upon the SAC 'combined bombing offensive' model first established in the early 1950s.[114] This bombardment model, which had already been ingrained (in one form or another) into JCS nuclear planning, merged BRAVO, ROMEO, and DELTA target sections and placed them into rigid single-strike Alert Force and Full Force bombardment plans.[115] Utilising the majority of their '538 B-52, 1,292 B-47, and 19 B-58' bombers (not to forget the additional twelve Atlas intercontinental ballistic missiles stationed in the United States and the sixty Thor intermediate-range ballistic *missiles* in the UK, alongside Army and Navy assets now under a single integrated command),[116] the SAC-led team planned for the deployment of 3,200 nuclear weapons in the single, blunt, Full Force attack and 1,706 nuclear weapons in the Alert Force attack.[117] The indiscriminate nature of targeting and large-scale destruction intended by this vast level of nuclear weapons deployment served to highlight SAC's success in ingraining LeMay's bombardment ethos into American nuclear strategy.

Exponentially expanded from the days of precision and 'a few dozen targets'[118] in 1948, the SIOP's 3,200 nuclear weapons were designed to be deployed en masse as a means of ensuring the total destruction of 1,060 targets in a Full Force attack.[119] Alongside this the 1,706 nuclear weapons of the Alert Force option would seek the destruction of 725 targets.[120] These target lists consisted of more traditional military objectives, such as airfields, weapons development facilities, and missile silos.[121] In addition – and to a greater extent than had ever been seen before in American nuclear strategy – the SIOP target lists also included the SAC plan to ensure the direct and deliberate destruction of entire cities and population centres.[122] As SAC documents (declassified in 2015) highlighted, such planning had been part of the SAC strategic development process since 1956, yet it was only now that they became officially incorporated in a multiservice and integrated American nuclear strategy.[123]

Based on the SAC idea of 'systematic destruction'[124] the plans set about purposefully targeting the 'population' of the enemy.[125] Scholars such as William Burr highlighted that 'targeting civilian population as such directly conflicted with the international norms of the day which prohibited attacks on people per se'.[126] As highlighted by the considerable number of population centres targeted and the proportion of casualties intended, however, this was far from an SAC concern while developing the SIOP.[127] Precision was a distant memory; their own ethos was now dominant. Through the study of Joint Chiefs of Staff reports from 1961[128] (declassified in 2011) we can begin to accurately identify the specific cities targeted, casualties intended, and the total destruction estimated by the SAC-led SIOP planners.[129]

One document that helps us understand the levels of proposed destruction is JCS report JCSM 421–61 (26 June 1961).[130] This report was created for National Security Advisor McGeorge Bundy as a means to assist him in 'answering questions posed by White House advisor and former Secretary of State Dean Acheson' pertaining to 'Berlin Contingency Planning' in light of the Berlin Crisis.[131] This detailed report provides us with fresh insight into the range of targets, the nature of these targets, and the destruction intended by SAC through the SIOP. As a continuation of targeting choices made by SAC from as early as 1954 and 1956, the report highlighted that the SIOP incorporated the targeting of strategically important cities in both China and the Soviet bloc with a population over 50,000.[132] As the 1961 JCS report clarified, this was tantamount to the maximum destruction of 199 cities (Alert Force) and 295 cities (Full Force) in the Soviet Union.[133] In addition to this, it included the striking of 49 cities (Alert Force) and 78 cities (Full Force) in 'Red China'.[134] As a point of interest, planning also included the indirect targeting of civilians across Europe.[135] It is also important to note that to ensure each city was satisfactorily destroyed, the planners estimated that 'it would take three 80 kiloton weapons to destroy a city like Nagasaki'.[136] Such estimations when, as Burr stated, 'the U.S. had actually bombed [Nagasaki] with a 22 kiloton weapon' to ensure its obliteration, highlighted the total destruction intended through the deployment of the SIOP.[137] Starting with the 199 and 295 cities in USSR, the reports detailed the estimated (and explicitly intended) destruction.

Proceeding to estimate the 'achievements' obtained by such bombardment on the Soviet Union, JCSM 421–61 stipulated that:

> [i]n the USSR, 199 cities would be struck by the Alert Force and 295 by the Full Force. By a 1959 census, there are 293 cities in the USSR of 50,000 or greater population. Assuming that at least one weapon arrives at each programmed Desired Ground Zero (DGZ), the Alert Force can be expected to inflict casualties (including fallout effects for the first seventy-two hours with a 60% shielding factor) to 56% of the urban population and 37% of the total population. The Full Force can be expected to inflict casualties to 72% of the urban population and 54% of the total population.[138]

With casualty rates reaching over 50 per cent of the total population of the USSR, the extensive death and injury is clear to see. Nevertheless, it is only when these percentages are analysed in the context of the 1959 population census data, mentioned in the report, that we can fully understand the destructive capacity of the SIOP. Specifically, it can be estimated that the SIOP (launched with Full Force) would have ensured the death of 108 million people in the Soviet Union.[139] Although shocking to modern eyes, for LeMay and SAC this level of destruction was necessary, required, and desired in the event of war. It was, in essence, the deliberate end result of a 'pragmatic and realistic' bombardment ethos that had reached its zenith by 1961. Such dominance can be further highlighted by the estimated and intended destruction planned for China.

As the 1961 report proceeded to outline, even if China was not involved in the outbreak of nuclear war, its destruction would have been neither mitigated nor avoided. The report clearly stated that:

> [i]n China, 49 cities would be struck by the Alert Force and 41% of the urban population and 10% of the total population would be expected casualties. Seventy-eight cities would be struck by the Full Force, and 53% of the urban population and 16% of the total population would be expected casualties. These figures also include the fallout effects.[140]

Again, when such percentages are calculated and compared against the census data from the period it can be concluded that 104 million men, women and children in China would have been killed if the SIOP had been deployed.[141] This, we must remember, would have taken place *whether China had been involved in the war or not*. Such casualty levels, and the overt targeting of cities in a country that the US may or may not have been at war with, once again highlight the indiscriminate destruction that was manifest in the SIOP during this period. Finally, the death and destruction intended through the bombing of satellite countries in Europe further exemplifies the dominance of SAC and its influence over the SIOP. As the 1961 JCS report expressly stated:

> [i]n the Satellite countries of Bulgaria, Czechoslovakia, East Germany, Hungary, Poland and Rumania, only military installations are scheduled to be attacked. Basically, these consist of 166 airfields. Incident to these attacks, the Alert Force would cause an expected 1,378,000 casualties and the Full Force 4,004,000. These figures equate to about 1% and 4% respectively of the European satellite populations, again including the fall out considerations mentioned earlier.[142]

Here, once again, it can be seen that even when the population centres of nations were not being targeted, the sheer scale the SIOP – and the multiple bombs per target – would have led to the death of over four million people in Europe alone. This included East Germany, although the figures did not cover the additional deaths that would have occurred in West Germany (and other parts of Western Europe) from residual atomic fires and radiation.[143]

Overall, when all data from the report presented above is collated, a shocking yet clear picture emerges. With the proposed total destruction of up to 373 cities across the Soviet Union and China, it can be understood why SIOP-62 has subsequently been described as 'overkill'.[144] In addition, when quantified as 200 million (plus) casualties across China, the USSR, and Europe it can be concluded that the SAC planners who led the construction of the SIOP ensured the acceptance of an indiscriminate LeMay and SAC ethos. Precision was now a distant memory from a bygone era. Indeed, as the early 1960s progressed and the Eisenhower administration came to an end, SIOP-62 was implemented by the JCS as the United States' Single Integrated Operational Plan in the event of nuclear war.[145]

6

Resurrection (1961–91)

[A]ny plan that kills millions of Chinese when it isn't even their war is not a good plan. This is not the American way.
General David Shoup to General Thomas Power (Pentagon Briefing, 1961)[1]

SIOP-62 was built on the foundations of a LeMay and SAC line of strategic thought. Both its excess and perceived success were a product of the social, strategic, and political context of the period. As the previous chapter described, the 1950s were an 'age of extremes'; when faced with the failure of international control and the Soviet Union obtaining the atomic bomb, consecutive presidential administrations chose to move towards massive destruction. Not only did the Truman and Eisenhower administrations rely on nuclear weapons as the bedrock of American military power and the maintenance of national security, they also supported an SAC approach that would have seen nuclear weapons deployed with increasing levels of indiscriminate force. By the time Eisenhower left office in January 1961,[2] SIOP-62 had been completed, 18,000[3] nuclear weapons had been incorporated into the American arsenal, and the path to a further decade of extremes had been laid.[4]

Perhaps surprisingly, however, such a path would ultimately not be followed. As this chapter explains, despite being a decade in the making, the LeMay bombardment ethos did not dominate American nuclear strategy through the 1960s. Instead, due to the changing security context of the period, by August 1962 a shift towards a more discriminate nuclear bombardment strategy had taken place and a precision ethos had been resurrected. In a series of events that were of great frustration to LeMay and SAC commanders, the SIOP was politically 'reappraised' by the new administration of President John F. Kennedy and his select group of novel civilian strategic thinkers from the RAND Corporation (the US Air Force think tank), who rose to the highest levels of power. Together they challenged SAC, replaced 'overkill' with a counterforce 'no cities' strategy, and implemented the complementary war plan SIOP-63.[5] An analysis of the manner in which this U-turn in strategic direction occurred, and the far-reaching legacies of precision's resurrection (from the 1960s through to the 1990s), are the focus of this chapter.

The Age of Ambition

Do you want a man for president who's seasoned through and through? But not so doggone seasoned that he won't try something new!? A man who's old enough to know, and young enough to do? Well, it's up to you, it's up to you, it's strictly up to you! But it's Kennedy, Kennedy, Kennedy, Kennedy, Kennedy, Kennedy, it's Kenn-ed-y for me! Kennedy, Kennedy, Kennedy, Kennedy!
'It's Kennedy for Me' (John F. Kennedy Campaign Song, 1960).[6]

The 1950s ideas about bombardment would not dominate the 1960s. In much the same way as events at the end of the 1940s had sparked a deviation from precision towards a more extreme line of thought, the end of the 1950s would also see the emergence of a new epoch. In November 1960, the 'young and ambitious' John F. Kennedy claimed a staggeringly close and influential victory over the incumbent Vice President Richard Nixon – a man who had built his campaign on being synonymous with the 'old guard' of the previous decade.[7] Such a victory was indicative of the changing societal context during this period.[8]

The campaign fought between these two figures was dominated by potent Cold War tensions that had reached a climatic stage by 1960. The years 1955/56 had arguably catalysed a period of instability with the Suez Crisis, the Hungarian Uprising, and increasing tension in Vietnam.[9] In 1957, the Soviet Union successfully launch Sputnik, raising fears that 'the Soviets' were 'creeping ahead' of America in missile technologies.[10] In addition to this, Cuba's alignment with the Soviet Union in 1959 placed the threat of 'world communism' geographically closer to the US. Moreover, in 1960 a perceived nuclear 'missile gap' between the US and Soviet Union in strategic nuclear capabilities (exploited by Kennedy during his campaign) contributed to public unease. Furthermore, with the campaign in full swing, American U-2 spy plane pilot Francis Gary Powers was shot down, captured, and paraded in front of the media by the Soviet leadership.[11] Such footage was publicly and politically influential. The incident led to the Moscow summit planned between Eisenhower and Khrushchev being cancelled and a reduction in cooperation and communication between the Soviet Union and US.[12] These tensions and perceived advantages for the Soviet Union led to a fearful, restless, and frustrated proportion of the American public desiring long overdue change.[13] As public opinion polls from 1960 reveal, 'more than half the American people thought war with the Soviet Union was inevitable'.[14] This discontent would lead to the 'fresh', 'vibrant', and 'progressive' John F. Kennedy prevailing over Nixon and his 'flabby Republican circles'.[15]

The Kennedy administration and SIOP-62

General Lemnitzer's briefing demonstrates the degree to which SIOP-62 was a highly inflexible plan for massive retaliation, or massive preemption, against all categories of targets within the Sino-Soviet bloc and helps explain why the Kennedy [a]dministration sought to increase the options available to the president in a crisis or war.

Scott Sagan (1987)[16]

With Kennedy's victory, a different breed of presidential administration came to power. Elected upon the platform of 'youth', 'hope', and on the promise of 'overdue change', it was in a changing American societal context that a reorientation of political and strategic ambitions could and would occur.[17] This change was epitomised by the reaction of Kennedy and his administration to a briefing received on the destructive capability of SIOP-62 on taking office in 1961.

Through the release of JCS and SAC documents pertaining to this period (declassified in 1986 and 2007) we can see what information this briefing consisted of and begin to understand their perceptions of SIOP-62's nuclear bombardment strategy. As Scott Sagan (1987) stated in his seminal article on the topic, it was on:

September 13th, 1961 [that] President John F. Kennedy received a top secret military briefing from General Lyman L. Lemnitzer, Chairman of the Joint Chiefs of Staff, on the U.S. plan for nuclear war. Also present at the White House meeting were Secretary of Defense Robert McNamara, Military Representative to the President General Maxwell Taylor and Deputy Special Assistant to the President for National Security Affairs Walt W. Rostow.[18]

It was in this meeting that Kennedy and his closest advisors were told of SIOP-62 and its massive destructive capability.[19] JCS 2056/281 documented this meeting and outlined the details General Lemnitzer revealed to the new administration. As the document stated, Lemnitzer explained in great detail the aims, objectives, and designated outcomes of the SIOP, which had entered into effect just a few months prior on 15 April 1961.[20] Lemnitzer highlighted the military and civilian sites set for destruction, and stated that 'the very great majority of targets now covered by the SIOP are military in nature. For example, of about 1000 DGZs [Designated Ground Zeroes] covered by the plan, some 800 are military targets. Further, atomic weapons are relatively non-discriminating, particularly with respect to fallout.'[21] In addition to this, Lemnitzer made the 'flexibility' (or lack thereof) abundantly clear to the group. He highlighted that:

> [a] fundamental characteristic of the current SIOP is that it provides for attack of an Optimum-Mix Target System. This follows the conclusions and the presidential decision relative to Study No. 2009 that an optimum-mix of both military and urban-industrial targets must be successfully attacked in order for the US ultimately to prevail. Consequently, the SIOP is designed for the accomplishment of this total essential task ... Thus, basically, the SIOP is designed for execution as a whole.[22]

Here it can be seen that Lemnitzer informed the administration that the SIOP was designed to be deployed in its massive retaliatory entirety, not with options for discriminate, proportionate, or precision targeting of the enemy. The inflexibility and destructive capability of the SIOP were brought home to the administration by Lemnitzer's concluding remarks. As he made clear, such was the destruction planned by the SIOP, that even if attempts were made to withhold the targeting of civilian/urban areas, such measures would make little difference to the overall death toll. He stated:

> there is considerable question that the Soviets would be able to distinguish between total attack and an attack of military targets only even if US authorities indicated that the US attack had been limited to attack military targets ... because of fallout from attack of military targets and co-location of many military targets with urban-industrial targets, the casualties would be many millions in number. Thus, limiting attack to military targets has little practical meaning as a humanitarian measure.[23]

In essence, Kennedy and his team were informed that, due to the sheer number of weapons and the location of the chosen targets, even if an attempt was made to avoid civilian centres, it would make little difference to the level of indiscriminate destruction and costs to civilian life. These revelatory details about the SIOP were impactful.[24] Kennedy and his administration's subsequent reaction to this frank and forthright briefing, and to the strategy of massive retaliation more broadly would, over the coming months and years, dramatically change the strategic ambitions at the heart of American nuclear strategy.

Put simply, the reaction of the Kennedy administration to massive retaliation and SIOP-62 was a mixture of moral discomfort, strategic unease, and a desire for rapid change.[25] President Kennedy was strongly averse to the indiscriminate, inflexible, imprecise, and disproportionate bombardment plans which he had inherited from Eisenhower.[26] As one witness stated, Kennedy left the briefing 'thoroughly persuaded that there was insufficient capability for the President to exercise discrimination and control should nuclear conflict come'.[27] Kennedy's inner circle was of a similar opinion and reaffirmed their support for a more flexible and controlled alternative, believing that the SIOP in its current form was 'too rigidly geared to a massive retaliation surprise attack'.[28] Thus, Kennedy and his administration began to unstitch a decade of LeMay's 'bomb everything' ethos and Eisenhower's massive retaliation. Their aim was to usher in a new and ambitious strategy, one centred on control, discrimination, and flexibility, not rigid and indiscriminate imprecision.

The man charged with turning this public and political demand into a strategic reality was Secretary of Defense Robert S. McNamara, who was equally as incensed by the SIOP. McNamara had been briefed on some of the SIOP's details in February 1961 and again (in more detail) in September.[29] Both times he had been appalled by its inflexibility and blunt destructive capacity.[30] McNamara was no stranger to indiscriminate bombardment; during the Second World War he had served under LeMay, running part of his logistical and statistical analysis during the Army Air Forces bombardment of Japan.[31] He was also no stranger to massive reform, having joined the Ford Motor Company post-war, overhauling its uneconomical systems and bringing the company back into the black.[32] He was President of Ford by the age of 44. Just ten weeks into his tenure, however, Kennedy approached McNamara and – impressed by his outstanding record – urged him to become his Secretary of Defense, a position he accepted.[33] When faced with the uneconomical, morally questionable, and strategically flawed SIOP, McNamara's experience and track record were to prove useful.[34] In the face of such a 'macabre, shallow and horrifying' plan for nuclear war his primary task was to 'find some way not only to control the Joint Chiefs' appetite for more nuclear weapons [but to also] control the pace and scope of a nuclear war'.[35] This task would dominate much of McNamara's initial period in office. Yet in this effort, he would not be alone. A small team of civilian 'defence intellectuals' from the RAND Corporation would come to work closely with McNamara to devise a 'new' line of strategic thought.[36]

RAND and the return of a precision ethos

[W]hen Robert S. McNamara met the RAND Corporation, the effect was like love at first sight.

Fred Kaplan, Wizards of Armageddon (1983)[37]

The RAND Corporation (previously Project RAND) was a product of the Second World War.[38] Spearheaded by General Arnold in 1946, the aim was to continue to harness the relationship between civilian scientists, civilian academics, and the military which had proven vitally important and productive as the conflict progressed.[39] LeMay was also a cofounder of RAND, however, and as this book will go on to show, he soon grew tired of the meddling by civilian researchers. For Arnold, however, the continuation of this civil–military relationship post-war was essential for the maintenance of American national security and the progression of American military capacity and effectiveness.[40] As Arnold declared:

> [d]uring this war the Army, Army Air Forces, and the Navy have made unprecedented use of scientific and industrial resources. The conclusion is inescapable that we have not yet established the balance necessary to insure the continuance of teamwork among the military, other government agencies, industry, and the universities. Scientific planning must be years in advance of the actual research and development work.[41]

Thus, it was out of Arnold's drive for continued research and development cooperation that RAND (standing for *R*esearch *and* *D*evelopment) was born.[42]

Initial RAND projects were in line with Arnold's long-held passion for the achievement of precision missile and pilotless technologies.[43] As previous chapters have highlighted, Arnold had long sought to implement a bombardment ethos based on the idea of precision bombing and had also been involved in developing the early 'drone' known as the Kettering Bug.[44] Unsuccessful during the Second World War, precision was an ambition that he continued to strive for in the initial post-war nuclear age.[45] During this period, Arnold promoted a nuclear bombardment strategy based on city avoidance and the discriminate targeting of enemy military targets, not civilians.[46] As has already been explained, however, such a line of strategic thought was deemed unachievable in 1949/50, largely due to a lack of technological progress in the scientific achievement of accurate, long-distance precision missiles and bombardment technologies.[47] Thus, by 1950 precision had been side-lined. Instead, with the increasing nuclear threat of the Soviet Union and the Korean War deteriorating, it was General LeMay's extreme bombardment ethos that became dominant. Yet, the ambition to achieve precision did not disappear. Although Arnold died in 1950, the establishment of RAND was his legacy. A $10,000,000 endowment from the US Air Force budget, personally approved and allocated by Arnold, meant that the quest for precision would continue and develop outside the realms of official American nuclear war planning. As Arnold's long-time colleague (and Secretary of War for Air during the Second World War) Robert Lovett revealed, Arnold wanted to secure 'sources of brain power for the future' and 'in his typical, impetuous way ran with the ball'.[48]

In an attempt to make sure precision would one day be achievable, one of RAND's first major projects concerned a 'comparison of ramjets and rockets ... as offensive weapons'.[49] This work on the strategic utility of missiles included and increasingly focused on precision guidance and ballistic missiles.[50] These technical projects dominated much of RAND's early scientific research and laid the foundations for developments in the achievability of precision strikes. As Bruno Augenstein, one of the fathers of the precision missile[51] and an employee at RAND for 46 years, stated:

> [RAND] offered a synthesis of insights on high-yield weapons, precision guidance, reentry techniques, rocket technologies, and strategic reconnaissance and outlined a program that would provide the United States with a new level of strategic power.[52]

Thus, research into precision formed one of RAND's foundational pillars. Initially, RAND continued to focus on technical research, 'attracting top-notch scientists and mathematicians' to work on these pioneering projects.[53] Yet RAND's research quickly branched out to incorporate economics and social science modes of thought in regard to nuclear strategy and the utility of precision.

Such an interdisciplinary research base had always been a core intention behind RAND.[54] The think tank was not just established to conduct research into the technical and engineering side of warfare; the social sciences, economics, and research into strategy more broadly were also important. As RAND's 1946 charter outlined:

> Project RAND is a continuing program of scientific study and research on the broad subject of air warfare with the object of recommending to the Air Force preferred methods, techniques and instrumentalities for this purpose.[55]

Thus, technical engineering research was but one strand of RAND. Identifying a growing need to understand and critique the technical military research RAND was undertaking, RAND mathematician Olaf Helmer and RAND's head of mathematics John Williams capitalised on RAND's broader remit and soon set about establishing social science and economics departments.[56] As Fred Kaplan highlighted, for RAND '[m]ilitary problems, after all, were not just engineering or mathematical or physics problems'.[57] By 1947, the two departments had been approved and incorporated into the existing RAND structure: it was at this point that recruitment began.[58]

Specifically, RAND held an interview day in August 1947 and a RAND conference was held at the New York Economics Club the following month.[59] The New York conference was held as means to bring together the great and the good in strategic thought, and thus to identify prospective candidates.[60] The conference opening address was delivered by Warren Weaver (Director of Natural Sciences at the Rockefeller Foundation, mathematician, and RAND associate).[61] In his address, Weaver alluded to the kinds of research RAND was looking to undertake and the type of person RAND wanted to recruit.[62] He stated that RAND was interested in 'military worth ... to what extent is it possible to have useful quantitative indices for a gadget, a tactic or a strategy, so that one can compare it with available alternatives and guide decision by analysis'.[63] Put simply, Weaver outlined to the delegates that RAND was expanding to include analysis of 'military worth' as a means to understand the utility of technological developments, critique existing strategy, and develop alternative lines of tactical and strategic thought. Yet what sort of people would be required at RAND to conduct such work? In relation to this, Weaver proceeded to allude to the sort of team RAND was looking to build. As he outlined:

> [t]here's a curious assortment of individuals in this room at the present time – I didn't say an assortment of curious individuals, but a curious assortment of individuals ... I assume that every person in this room is fundamentally interested in and devoted to what can broadly be called the rational life ... He believes fundamentally that there is something to this business of having some knowledge ... and some analysis of problems, as compared with living in a state of ignorance, superstition and drifting-into-what-ever-may-come.[64]

The characteristics Weaver described would soon be classified as RAND characteristics. A curious mix of people, considerate of military worth, set on developing alternative strategy and pursuing the 'rational life' – these elements would come to define those hired by RAND over the coming weeks, months, and years. In their turn the team of like-minded individuals hired within the new social science, economic, and broader multidisciplinary 'Military Worth Section' would come to define 'the RAND way' (and ultimately the official American way under Kennedy and McNamara) of thinking about nuclear strategy.[65]

Hans Speier – the famed German-American sociologist specialising in the sociological history of war – was the first to be recruited, and was chosen to direct the social sciences division (a position he held for fifteen years).[66]

Soon after, Charles Hitch was recruited from the University of Oxford to head the economics division and add expertise on the economics of defence.[67] Although very different in their approach to the analysis of warfare, one quantitative and one qualitative, both sections embraced the ethos of 'knowledge in pursuit of rationality' as outlined by Weaver. Each section sought and analysed knowledge in a unique way, yet with complimentary and overlapping conclusions about what 'rationality' should look like.[68] This was specifically the case when it came to their early work at RAND, where they were charged with critiquing elements of massive retaliation, overkill, and making recommendations for a more rational American nuclear strategy.

During the 1950s both schools of analysis at RAND came to abhor the massive retaliation doctrine put forward by Eisenhower and Dulles and the inflexible SIOP devised by LeMay to fulfil it.[69] In reaction to this, each section conducted both individual and collaborative research into the strategic utility and achievability of discriminate city/civilian avoidance, flexible response, force protection, second strike capabilities, precision strikes, and ultimately notions of 'counterforce' (not to be confused with 'countervalue').[70] These notions were not only in line with RAND's precision origins, but were also deemed to be far more economically, strategically, and morally rational than those proposed in SIOP-62. At RAND, in a similar vein to the early strategic thought of RAND founder General Arnold, these characteristics would come to epitomise a 'rational nuclear strategy' – one far more in keeping with traditional American bombardment values.[71]

There were prominent figures in the economics section, including the charismatic and confident 'cavaliero' Albert Wohlstetter – a 'mathematical logician, concerned with … the logic of science'[72] – and his team consisting of Henry S. Rowen, Alain C. Enthoven, and Fred Hoffman (among others).[73] The noted defence intellectual and historian, Roberta Wohlstetter, who helped her husband Albert get a job at RAND in 1951, was also heavily involved in the research and critique of SAC strategy.[74] The 'Wohlstetter Team' provided the initial contributions to this new rationality by working on early RAND projects concerned with reappraising SAC force protection and SAC strategic thought.[75]

Wohlstetter and his team would, in time, highlight to the Air Force the dramatic vulnerability of the large SAC bomber forces to surprise attack by the Soviet Union and the rational need for below-ground concrete bunkers to maintain nuclear force protection and ensure a second strike capacity was viable and maintained in the event of nuclear war.[76] Later work would push for the use of intercontinental ballistic missiles, which lent themselves to underground silo storage, and the submarine-based Polaris systems, which allowed for decreased vulnerability hidden and on the move in the world's oceans.[77] In the social science section, scholars such as Bernard Brodie (recruited by RAND full time after his unsuccessful stint advising General Vandenberg in 1951 and critiquing Air Force targeting plans) helped to develop these projects while also bringing their social science methodology and self-proclaimed rational desire for city avoidance into the study and critique of SAC's doctrine.[78]

During this early period, it was Brodie's scholarship that was perhaps most influential in laying the foundations for RAND's rational approach to nuclear strategy.[79] Like others in the social sciences section at RAND,[80] Brodie's strategic thought was 'derived from his historical studies'.[81] Since 1950 he had evolved his line of strategic thought to increasingly focus on the idea of avoiding the direct targeting of cities when it came down to nuclear bombardment. His justifications for this were based on both strategic and moral reasons. Much like General Arnold had concluded from his analysis of the previous war, Brodie's historical studies had helped him reach the conclusion that 'the biggest single factor in delaying useful results [during the Second World War] was the effort devoted to "area" or urban bombing – which simply did not pay off militarily'.[82] Instead, for Brodie it was the precise nature of the target which had been, and should continue to be, the most important factor in American bombardment strategy, especially with atomic weapons.[83] Although Brodie did not provide a comprehensive list of what should be targeted with nuclear weapons, what he did conclude was that '[t]he atomic bomb in its various forms may well weaken our incentive to choose targets shrewdly and carefully ... But such an event would argue a military failure as well as a moral one'.[84] In his later work he expanded on his strategic and moral motivations for city avoidance.[85] Again in a similar vein to General Arnold's recommendations, for Brodie the idea of being proportionate and discriminate in striking the enemy allowed for a reduced risk to American cities from retaliatory attacks and reduced the cost to American and enemy life. In an age where the Soviet Union had the bomb, such thoughts became increasingly important. As Brodie explained in his seminal text, *Strategy in the Missile Age* (1959), '[o]ur hitting at enemy cities would simply force the destruction of our own'.[86] Instead, for Brodie, it was worth, for moral and strategic reasons, considering 'destruction to cities an evil to be avoided, at least at the outset'.[87] During the 1950s and early 1960s this 'rational' line of thought became the firm foundation on which RAND scholars would build.[88]

William Kaufmann was arguably the most influential strategic thinker at RAND to take up this mantel.[89] Like Brodie, Kaufmann was not a trained economist; instead, as a product of his tutelage under Brodie at Yale and Princeton, Kaufmann was, as Brodie described, primarily 'a political scientist in international relations'.[90] In essence, Kaufmann was Brodie's protégé, something which Kaufmann openly acknowledged: 'I shall always want it to be known how indebted I am to you for friendship, knowledge, and advice.'[91] Their similarities were exemplified by their shared moral and strategic ideas on city avoidance and their desire for more flexibility in American nuclear strategy. Kaufmann expressed his moral aversion to city bombing quite clearly. He stated, 'if you believe in the more traditional views of warfare, civilians should not be considered as targets ... there are certain laws of war which say, don't attack civilians which we have subscribed to'.[92] Kaufmann espoused his strategic doubts about city bombing with equal clarity. Like Brodie, Kaufmann saw little strategic worth in the premise of city destruction and the destruction of a whole society. He understood that for the notion of 'deterrence' to be achieved from a nuclear strategy, one had to be willing to 'make good' on said strategy and ultimately 'accept the consequences of its deployment'.[93] In the face of Dulles's 1954 massive retaliation speech, Kaufmann saw flaws in both the 'making good' and the 'consequences' of these actions. As he recalled in 1964:

> [t]he threat to destroy all or some portion of an enemy's society wore the appearance of a powerful deterrent. But what if the strategic exchange started accidentally? Indeed, what if the enemy's first strike were confined to military targets, or the United States itself were required to retaliate with its strategic forces for an attack on Western Europe? Did it remain desirable, in all these circumstances, to launch the offensive capabilities against the urban-industrial targets of the enemy, or would the United States really be interested in destroying the hostile nuclear forces, striving to limit damage to itself and its allies, and attempting to end the war on terms acceptable to the West?[94]

Thus, for Kauffman, like Brodie, the rigid reliance on massive retaliation and the targeting of cities was neither the best means by which to achieve the ends of an effective deterrence, nor the most effective and morally justifiable bombardment plan to 'win' a nuclear war if one was to occur. In essence, massive retaliation's inflexibility and indiscriminate destructive capacity were its shortfall, not its strength. In reaction to this, Kaufmann outlined his own thoughts on deterrence, bombardment targeting, and nuclear strategy in *Requirements of Defence* (1954, 1956, 1958).[95] It was from this document that Kaufmann's famous 'counterforce' strategy was born.

Counterforce was largely a continuation and conflation of critique and scholarship at RAND during the early 1950s.[96] Nevertheless, it expanded upon the
established foundations in one important way. Where Brodie did not stipu-
late what exact targets should be precisely struck in the event of nuclear war,
Kaufmann did.[97] Kaufmann believed – much like RAND founder General
Arnold and the pioneers of precision Gorrell and Mitchell – that it should be
the proportionate and discriminate targeting of specific enemy military targets,
not civilian centres, which should be the primary target of American bombardment in the event of war. As Kaufmann stated:

> there are many targets in any country. They're not just cities. There are counter-
> force targets, if you will, i.e. military targets, and there are strategic nuclear forces
> that one can target ... there's a very large array of targets that can be broken
> down, classified and given our improving intelligence identified very explicitly.[98]

Over time Kaufmann built on this line of thought, providing firm strategic justifications for counterforce, framed within moral, ethical, and strategic debates
around deterrence.

Kaufmann's counterforce strategy came to be known as his 'no cities' attack
plan[99]. In practice, if the Soviet Union was to move ground forces into and
invade Western Europe, Kaufmann's strategy would see the US deploy a 'small
number of nuclear weapons on [the Soviet Union's] strategic military targets
(bomber bases, nuclear-missile sites, submarine pens, and so forth)' instead of
launching a massive blunt attack as stipulated by LeMay's overall bombardment plan.[100] At this point the President would tell the Kremlin to 'halt their
aggression'.[101] If the aggression was not halted, Kaufmann then allowed, as a
last resort, for a second strike nuclear 'reserve force' – protected from attack
by underground concrete bunkers and silos as put forward by Wohlstetter – to
'pick off their cities'.[102] For Kaufmann, this was the ultimate 'deterrence'. As he
stated in *The Evolution of Deterrence* (1958):

> [deterrence] consists of essentially two basic components: first, the expressed
> intention to defend a certain interest; secondly, the demonstrated capability actu-
> ally to achieve the defense of the interest in question, or to inflict such a cost on
> the attacker that, even if he should be able to gain his end, it would not seem
> worth the effort to him.[103]

In this scenario, the US would have had to express its intention to defend its
interests (in this case Western Europe) without the destruction of an entire society and its population (as was planned in SIOP-62). It also left the Soviet Union
with little option – in theory – but to halt its activities. As Kaplan explained,

'[a] few of the Soviet's nuclear bombers might survive our counterforce strike, but – the logic went – they wouldn't dare attack our cities, for fear that we would fire our remaining [fully functioning and protected] weapons against theirs'.[104] There can be little doubt that creating the circumstances for a 'winnable' nuclear war, alongside the reliance on the rationality of one's enemy, was a great risk. Yet for Kaufmann and many other thinkers at RAND, it provided a more strategically credible, morally justifiable, and rational deterrence than massive retaliation. As Kaufmann concluded, although allowing for the possibility of nuclear war, 'a world which has suffered 10 million fatalities is still a better world than one that has suffered 200 million fatalities'.[105] Thus Kaufmann's strategy offered an alternative to massive retaliation and overkill. When Secretary of Defense McNamara heard about the notion it was quickly adopted.[106] It was, in essence, the far less 'horrifying' alternative McNamara had been looking for and allowed for part of the 'control, flexibility [and] choice' that Kennedy had desired.[107]

The McNamara-Kaufmann 'no cities' policy

One wonders how many of the words that Kaufmann quotes from McNamara are originally out of Kaufmann.

Bernard Brodie (1965)[108]

It is worth reiterating that McNamara's first briefing on the Eisenhower administration's SIOP 'left him shaken' and 'appalled'.[109] Not only was the SIOP irrational, uneconomical and illogical, in McNamara eyes, it also only allowed for limited flexibility. As a result, in the event of nuclear war, the President would have had very little choice but to launch a massive retaliatory strike, with, at its core, the aim of destroying Soviet society and killing millions of civilians across Europe, the USSR, and China. So by the time McNamara returned to Washington he was, as Lepgold argued, particularly 'receptive' to new ideas.[110] It was in this context that Kaufmann's counterforce strategy offered a solution to his strategic, economic, and moral dilemma.

As a concept, although new to McNamara, counterforce was not new to the Air Force. As has been outlined above, counterforce had been devised at RAND in reaction to Dulles's massive retaliation speech in 1954; by 1958, however, the strategy had already been reviewed and, in due course, rejected by the Air Force.[111] Initially supported by General Parish (a 1930s ACTS graduate) through the funding of a major project at RAND, at the final stages of deliberation counterforce was unsurprisingly cast aside by LeMay disciple and

CINCSAC General Power.[112] As Kaufmann recalled, the initial support for the comparatively discriminate and proportionate strategy had 'led to a big study at RAND which sort of fell apart'.[113] This affair, he added, meant that many people involved in the promotion of counterforce 'went off mad'.[114] As Power famously quipped to Kaufmann after his briefing on counterforce in December 1960, '[r]estraint? Why are you so concerned with saving their lives? The whole idea is to kill the bastards. At the end of the war if there are two Americans and one Russian left alive, we win!'[115] Kaufmann replied, '[w]ell, you better make sure that they're a man and a woman'.[116] Yet this SAC resistance would not mark the end of the road for counterforce.

The relationship between 'the RAND way of thinking' and Kennedy had been maturing since at least 1960 (arguably earlier). It had been recommended by Senator Henry 'Scoop' Jackson (who became Chair of the Democratic National Committee in July 1960), that the young Democratic hopeful – then Senator Kennedy – should look into harnessing the intellectual power of the RAND researchers during his run for the White House. Jackson had been working with RAND since 1959.[117] He had been in correspondence with Bernard Brodie and William Kaufmann,[118] seeking feedback and advice on speeches, and by January 1960 was in discussions with RAND Director Frank Collbohm about visiting Santa Monica to take part in discussions on 'formulating and executing national policy in the contest with world communism'.[119] As such, Jackson was well aware of what RAND could offer. Kennedy, of course, would ultimately become the nominee for president, and it was felt that RAND's intellectual power, and knowledge of Eisenhower-Nixon era shortfalls, could be helpful to the Democratic hopeful. In fact, Kennedy personally directed the head of his 'Brain Trust', Professor Archibald Cox, and Kennedy's researcher Deirdre Henderson, to investigate a possible relationship.[120] Kennedy's Brain Trust was in essence his own think tank, and it was Henderson who would be sent to Santa Monica, to RAND, to judge their intellectual worth. As she explained to me, the opportunity for this research trip came about from her ambition to expand her role within the JFK team:

> I walked out with Senator Kennedy and told him I wanted to ask him a favour. I told him I wasn't learning enough about politics and therefore could I attend the Democratic National Convention in Los Angeles. It took him a second to answer and say yes, if I spent half of my time helping different members of his campaign staff and the other half of my time with the members of the RAND Corporation.[121]

As such, Deirdre Henderson became the link person – a bridge builder – between RAND and the Kennedy team, and in 1960 she set off for the RAND HQ in Santa Monica. Her time there was deeply influential, and she discovered just exactly what was being researched and how useful the work could be to Kennedy's election campaign. The rest, as they say, is history.[122]

The RAND researchers embraced Deirdre and the interest of Kennedy. Disheartened by being persistently rebuffed by the SAC commanders during the Eisenhower-Nixon years, many of them would advise on the Kennedy presidential campaign, with Henderson ringing them up on a regular basis on her return to the East Coast.[123] When it came to drawing up a list of people who should be employed by Kennedy on his ascent to power, Henderson suggested a number of RAND researchers, such as Enthoven and Hitch, but also Albert Wohlstetter.[124] Wohlstetter would politely decline, preferring an advisory role to the administration. As Henderson explained, Wohlstetter was the 'Kingpin of the group'; his place was at RAND, not under the management of the White House.[125] Yet he would encourage his team to fill up the ranks, allowing channels of influence.[126] Enthoven would become Kennedy's Deputy Assistant Secretary of Defense and Charles Hitch would rise to Assistant Secretary of Defense.[127] In fact, it is here that we can see how Kaufmann also became involved in the Kennedy administration. On the urging of the two former RAND analysts, Kaufmann was invited to the White House to brief McNamara on his 'no cities' and 'restraint'-based strategy.[128]

The briefing took place on 10 February 1961.[129] As Kaufmann recalled, 'I was asked to present this story to Mr. McNamara ... I was scheduled to talk with him, I think, it was for about half an hour.'[130] But the meeting did not last for half an hour, and three hours later the discussion was still in progress.[131] McNamara was captivated and excited by the briefing. Not only did it offer a rational alternative to massive retaliation, it also provided the flexibility, control, and multiple options that Kennedy had publicly called for. As Kaufmann stated:

> I started showing [the charts] to Mr. McNamara and it was just obvious from the outset that he understood these in a flash ... he was very animated and asking questions as we went along ... when we finished he said, let's sit down and start thrashing out some of the issues that I still have. And we must have spent another hour or two going over the various issues that he wanted to discuss in more detail. But I frankly don't recall anybody ever having sort of learned this thing so fast. It was ... a very impressive performance on his part.[132]

Although McNamara continued to quiz Kaufmann on aspects of diminishing returns and the specifics of force adequacy, McNamara accepted the core ethos of the counterforce argument.[133] As Kaufmann outlined, 'he [McNamara] accepted the main arguments. Not necessarily all of them, but ... from the standpoint of changes in the force structure, yes, as far as I know, he did, and changes were subsequently made.'[134] Shortly after, Kaufmann would become Special Assistant to McNamara, a position he would maintain in one form or another under the next six defence secretaries (from the Kennedy years to the Carter administration). Kaufmann's assumptions regarding the impact of his briefing to McNamara are confirmed by analysis of declassified documents from McNamara to President Kennedy.

In a 1961 memorandum entitled 'Memorandum for the President: Recommended Long Range Nuclear Delivery Forces 1963–1967', it is clear to see that McNamara was greatly influenced by the core ethos of the Kaufmann counterforce strategy. Specifically, McNamara directly recommended to President Kennedy that '[w]e should reject the "minimum deterrence" extreme'.[135] Instead, due to the fact that '[d]eterrence may fail, or war may break out for accidental or unintended reasons', McNamara recommended to the President that shifting towards 'a capability to counter-attack against high-priority Soviet military targets' would be preferable.[136] McNamara concluded that this change in targeting policy towards the precise striking of counterforce targets could 'make a major contribution to the objective of limiting damage and terminating the war on acceptable terms'.[137] Thus, for McNamara, in the shadow of massive retaliation, it was Kaufmann's (and of course RAND's) comparatively proportionate, discriminate, and flexible counterforce city/civilian avoidance line of strategic thought that were deemed the logical, rational, and morally acceptable direction for American nuclear strategy to proceed.[138]

Little time was wasted by McNamara and his team of RAND (or former RAND) strategic thinkers in implementing and finalising counterforce changes to the existing war plans. Thirteen days after the Kaufmann briefing, on 23 February 1961, McNamara hawkishly declared to the House Armed Service Committee that '[s]o long as the adversaries of freedom continue to expand their stockpile of massive destruction weapons ... the United States has no alternative but to ensure that at all times and under all circumstances it has the capability to deter their use'.[139] Yet, as he continued, there was now an important distinction that had to be made within American nuclear strategy under the Kennedy administration. As he explained, unlike under Eisenhower, American forces must now 'be of a character which will permit [their] use, in the event of attack, in a cool and deliberated fashion and always under the complete control of the constituted authority'.[140] These remarks were the initial steps taken by McNamara towards outlining and implementing counterforce.

Unsurprisingly, LeMay was not convinced by McNamara's changes in policy and posture. Not only had McNamara worked under LeMay as an Army Air Force statistician during the Second World War, but the two were from very different worlds. Post-war, McNamara had become a highly paid executive and the youngest President of the Ford Motor Company. LeMay, on the other hand, had stayed in the fight, becoming an experienced Cold War warrior. Tensions between the two built over the years, with LeMay resenting civilian staff (such as those from RAND) knowing more about the administration's plans then he did. This state of affairs was not helped when LeMay was left in the dark about the botched Bay of Pigs fiasco in 1961. In addition, when it came to Kennedy and McNamara's dealings with Cuba and the Soviet Union during the Cuban Missile Crisis in 1962, LeMay believed the men to be cowards. As LeMay argued at one briefing during the crisis: 'the Russian bear has always been eager to stick his paw in Latin American waters. Now we've got him in a trap, let's take his leg off right up to his testicles. On second thought, let's take off his testicles, too.'[141] This was entirely against the Kennedy-McNamara view and their more restrained, flexible, rational approach. Indeed, LeMay's response did not surprise McNamara. As he revealed in an oral history interview published in 1989, 'LeMay talked openly about a first strike against the Soviet Union if the Russians ever backed us into a corner.'[142] Such a stance highlighted the fundamental differences in the approaches adopted by the two men and the chasm that had opened up in their working relationship.[143] As LeMay's biographer, Warren Kozak, argued, 'it was not a match made in heaven'.[144] Nevertheless, McNamara pushed forwards.

Over the coming months, the counterforce strategy was built upon and implemented into official American plans for nuclear war. Only one month after the Kaufmann briefing, in March 1961, progress had been made at the war planning level with McNamara instructing the JCS to begin work on a new SIOP (SIOP-63) and to 'review the organization and planning of JSTPS'.[145] This process lasted until the latter half of 1962 and saw the core ambitions at the heart of American nuclear strategy change dramatically. These changes are most accurately highlighted though the analysis of declassified SAC documents pertaining to SIOP-63's development (declassified in 2007) and by outlining McNamara's Ann Arbor speech (July 1962) which, near the end of the process, publicly declared the core tenets of the new approach. When combined they provide an interesting insight into the process of change that occurred in American nuclear war planning.

The declassified document that gives us most insight is the 'History of the Joint Strategic Target Planning Staff: Preparation of SIOP-63, DOD 5200.10' (the declassified SAC history of SIOP-63). Written in 1964, this document clearly explained how it was now necessary for American nuclear forces to:

> destroy or neutralize the military capabilities of the enemy, whilst retaining ready, effective and controlled U.S. strategic capabilities adequate to assure, to the maximum extent possible, retention of U.S. military superiority to the enemy, or any potential enemies, at any point during or after the war.[146]

As the document continued, '[e]very effort would be made in this task to minimize damage to people and industry ... includ[ing] the capability to withhold attacks to China and any other communist satellites'.[147] With reference to the explicit targeting of military capabilities and the minimising of damage to people, it is clear to see that an obvious change in the strategic footing of American nuclear war plans had occurred. Quite simply, as a result of the adoption of counterforce, the targeting of enemy cities and their civilian populations was no longer a primary focus.[148]

By 20 July 1962, SIOP-63 had been approved by the JCS and McNamara, with it officially becoming effective as American nuclear strategy on 1 August.[149] Ultimately, these plans were made public by McNamara in his Ann Arbor speech at the University of Michigan.[150] As McNamara outlined:

> [t]he U.S. has come to the conclusion that to the extent feasible, basic military strategy in a possible general nuclear war should be approached in much the same way that more *conventional military operations have been regarded in the past* [emphasis added]. That is to say, principal military objectives, in the event of a nuclear war stemming from a major attack on the Alliance, should be the destruction of the enemy's forces, not of his civilian population.[151]

With reference to 'conventional' operations in the 'past' and the 'no civilians' targeting policy, McNamara's Ann Arbor speech once again highlighted the core tenets of a traditional American precision-based bombardment ethos. These long-held ideas were now enshrined in counterforce, and so were at the heart of American nuclear strategy. In addition, the public nature of the speech provides us with useful insight into the perceived public applicability of the approach.[152] In essence, the speech marked the point at which the characteristics of a more rational strategy, in line with public and political demands for 'restraint', 'control', and 'overdue change', became incorporated in the official American stance on nuclear war.

Thus, as the above analysis has shown, the move towards counterforce had been made. It was facilitated by an American societal demand for a new approach to nuclear policy, the subsequent election of Kennedy and, consequently, the ambitions of the Kennedy administration to overhaul the horrors of massive retaliation. American war plans were now akin to a more traditional precision-based bombardment ethos. This proportionate, discriminate, and rational line of strategic thought was built upon by a pioneering group of defence intellectuals who began life at Arnold's RAND Corporation. These RAND intellectuals, as a continuation of a long line of American strategic thinkers who had sought to achieve such ambitions, had ensured the resurrection of this ethos and had overseen its reincorporation, through a counterforce strategy, into official American war plans.[153] As Enthoven confirmed to me, '[w]e were trying to move back toward the traditional principles of the just war, including discriminating between combatants and non-combatants, and avoiding deliberate attacks on civilians'.[154] Now precision had been resurrected, however, counterforce was just the first step in the proliferation of a precision ethos and its rise to dominance within American strategy.

The legacies of counterforce

> By promoting the development of technologies and systems that stressed precision, control, and information, Wohlstetter would help the United States to reject MAD-inspired threats against noncombatants, and instead to field a new generation of more discriminate and less destructive non-nuclear capabilities that, in turn, would substantially reduce America's reliance on nuclear weapons.
>
> Robert Zarate (2009)[155]

For Albert Wohlstetter – the RAND analyst, counterforce contributor and 'high priest of nuclear strategy' – the moral and strategic foundations of counterforce were the logical approach by which to proceed with nuclear and, in time, conventional American war planning.[156] In fact, it was from renewed notions of counterforce that a shift towards conventional precision warfare and conventional precision weapons would occur. Like many defence intellectuals at RAND during the 1960s, Wohlstetter believed that 1950s notions of massive retaliation lacked rationality and credibility as viable nuclear deterrence. When commenting on McNamara's 'no cities' speech (1962), Wohlstetter stated, 'let me just say, the statement that we were going to try to confine damage to military targets seemed to me to be right'.[157] As he explained, it is 'the only prudent thing to do … I think also it's the only moral thing to do. I don't believe that you should ever attack cities … there's no excuse for that.'[158] Thus, for Wohlstetter, the idea of precisely striking enemy military targets, not civilians, made considerable strategic and moral sense. As the final section of this chapter explains, for Wohlstetter, the strategic and technological ability to ensure the controlled, discriminate, limited, and precise deployment of force against enemy military targets, not civilians, was the key to ensuring long-term American security. It would be these core notions that ultimately contributed to the 'Wohlstetter School' of strategic thought. In time, this school would provide the foundational underpinning for American nuclear strategy and, in due course, it's 'graduates' (protégés of Wohlstetter) would drive a shift in American warfare towards conventional precision strikes, precision missiles, and a reliance on 'pinpoint precise' drone technologies.[159] The Wohlstetter School's rise did, however, have to endure and overcome a contested and contentious period during the mid-to-late-1960s where counterforce would be subject to considerable pressure, and, as declaratory policy at least, be replaced by the concept of mutual assured destruction (MAD).[160]

The core premise of MAD was outlined by McNamara during his 1967 'assured destruction' speech.[161] For McNamara, counterforce, and its reliance on the discriminate striking of enemy military targets, was no longer fit to remain at the forefront of *declaratory* American nuclear strategy. As he avowed to an audience of journalists and publishers in San Francisco, it was now 'important to understand that assured destruction is the very essence of the whole deterrence concept'.[162]. This concept, McNamara explained, meant that the US must ensure 'a highly reliable ability to inflict *unacceptable* damage upon any single aggressor or combination of aggressors at any time during the course of a strategic nuclear exchange, even after absorbing a surprise first strike [emphasis added]'.[163] As he concluded, 'if the United States is to deter a nuclear attack in itself or its allies, it must possess an actual and a credible assured-destruction capability'.[164] To many (including Wohlstetter) this blunt 'unacceptable' assured destruction resonated with the seemingly similar idea of massive retaliation which McNamara had attempted to avoid.[165] Although the possibility for massive destruction had always been a part – albeit a secondary part – of the counterforce deterrent factor, it had not been the declaratory and public focus. Yet for McNamara this shift towards MAD was of vital importance, especially due to the unforeseen consequences of counterforce and the trying context of the mid-1960s.

The frustrations of the mid-1960s were succinctly explained by Wohlstetter, who, when asked about the progression of the counterforce ethos at the heart of McNamara's 'no cities' speech, simply stated, 'I believe that it should have led to some things which unfortunately were delayed by intervening events.'[166] These 'intervening events' were relatively straightforward in their reasoning, yet damning in terms of their implications for counterforce as declaratory American nuclear strategy.[167] Although McNamara had initially been keen to maintain focus on the concept, he was faced with a problematic paradox.[168] For as long as he pushed the Air Force to shift their strategic planning towards the discriminate destruction of enemy military targets (of which there was a fluid and seemingly endless amount), the Air Force (which was headed by LeMay as Chief of Staff between 1961 and 1965) would be able to justify substantial increases in the procurement of nuclear capabilities and weapons technologies in order to fulfil their 'boundless' remit.[169] As one of McNamara's closest advisors, Alain Enthoven, explained, 'McNamara's thinking on "no cities and counterforce" evolved to an emphasis on "Mutual Assured Destruction" (as a criterion for force adequacy, not necessarily as a targeting policy) because talk about "no cities and counterforce" was serving as the basis for [increased] military requirements.'[170] It was, in part, as a result of this reasoning that a change was made in declaratory policy and MAD was adopted. A secondary, yet related, reason also influenced McNamara's decision-making.

In addition to the force adequacy implications of Air Force demands (aka the growing cost of buying military systems to strike the endless list of counterforce military targets), McNamara was concerned that interpretations of counterforce which chose to focus on obtaining a large and viable 'war-winning' capacity would, if achieved, lead to increased tensions with the USSR. As Enthoven explained, not only was the increased procurement of nuclear weapons contrary to the limitations on force levels which McNamara had been aiming to achieve – he had discussed this with Kaufmann in the very first briefing on counterforce – but it also posed the possibility that such an increase in nuclear weaponry 'would lead to an open-ended arms race' leading to amplified nuclear tensions and instability.[171] These Air Force demands, Enthoven concluded, undermined McNamara's primary aim to effectively deter nuclear war. Indeed, McNamara's core principle may have been that 'nobody wins a nuclear war, that we could not fight and win a nuclear war', but to the outside world, this may have looked like he was building for just such a war.[172] When combined, these flaws contributed towards McNamara's new public stance – one that would see counterforce replaced by the seemingly indiscriminate and blunt notion of MAD as declaratory nuclear policy. Yet this did not mean the end of counterforce. On the contrary, there was more to MAD than McNamara had publicly let on.

Although MAD has often been mistakenly merged with LeMay's massive retaliation (as it was by some at the time), the two served very different purposes. Whereas massive retaliation was blunt, setting a disproportionate nuclear response to a wide range of potential 'aggressions' committed by the Soviet Union, MAD was part of a multilayered nuclear strategy. At an overarching level, MAD was intended to deter the use of nuclear weapons by the Soviet Union against the US and its Western European allies.[173] It was for this reason that, to fulfil the amended American declaratory policy, the objective of acquiring *enough* of a nuclear capacity to ensure the destruction of 20 to 25 per cent of Soviet society was set by McNamara.[174] This facilitated McNamara's aim of capping force procurement levels (saving money), while also ensuring the achievability, and thus the logic and credibility, of the overarching MAD deterrence factor.[175] At an operational level – that is the way any nuclear strike would have been deployed in reality – the focus on counterforce remained.

In a potentially confusing twist to MAD, SIOP-63 – and thus the discriminate 'no cities' targeting flexibility of the counterforce ethos – remained the official foundations of American nuclear war plans, despite the conversion to MAD. Although this decision is seemingly odd and in contrast to MAD, it can be explained through a simple clarification. As McNamara's Director of Defence Research and Engineering, Harold Brown (also formerly of RAND) stated, the SIOP-63 'war plan remained directed at military targets with the ability to withhold, if it was so decided at the time by the president, attacks on cities'.[176] This not only gave the President the option to withhold and limit attacks on the USSR, but if the USSR was to launch a nuclear attack on a 'lesser' US priority, a controlled response, much reduced from 'unacceptable' assured destruction could, in theory, be chosen. As McNamara explained when recalling the strategy:

> [if] we're talking an exchange of nuclear weapons with respect to Europe and under those circumstances I want absolute certainty in the Soviet mind that if they launch a nuclear attack on Western Europe or North America they will be destroyed. I don't want any uncertainty there. Now, in the case of use of one nuclear weapon by the Soviets against Turkey ... I want them to feel certain that they're going to get more than they gave.[177]

Thus, it is clear to see that, despite public posturing, MAD was but one option in the American nuclear playbook. A flexible response was available to the President under SIOP-63 and its counterforce ethos. The SIOP-63 counterforce war plan was itself, however, not the only option below the overarching MAD declaratory policy that was made available to the President by McNamara in the event of Soviet aggression.

Below the 'nuclear option' the choice for 'limited' conventional warfare was posited as a viable (if not preferred) alternative.[178] This option was in line with McNamara's attempts to avoid nuclear exchange and thus explained the reasoning behind its prioritisation. As we can see from the analysis of a declassified memorandum between McNamara and President Kennedy, by late 1962 McNamara had already advised the President that a first-strike capability was 'neither necessary or particularly useful'.[179] By the late 1960s, McNamara's thoughts on nuclear war had progressed even further, to the point where he was, he stated, advising the President, 'there should never be the launch of a nuclear weapon unless you know what you're hoping to achieve by doing so'.[180] He continued, 'I think we can agree that there's no way to limit a nuclear war. Once you start a nuclear war, your society is going to be destroyed.'[181] Therefore, for McNamara, the avoidance of, not preparation for, nuclear war became an increased focus.[182] The shift towards limited conventional forces appeared to fulfil this goal.[183] As Enthoven explained, the reasoning behind the shift was simple: 'by building up our conventional forces [we aimed] to make nuclear war less and less likely'.[184] Thus, along with the overarching MAD declaratory policy and the counterforce options intrinsic to SIOP-63, these 'limited warfare' options provided McNamara with the justifications he needed to avoid the exponential build-up of nuclear capabilities and provide the President with differing, yet viable, options as a means to overcome the aggressions and threats of the 1960s. Despite initial protestations, this approach obtained broad support from across the political spectrum (including prominent Republican Barry Goldwater) and prospered during the mid- to late 1960s.[185] Yet not everyone was convinced by McNamara's amended strategy, especially Albert Wohlstetter.

Wohlstetter agreed with McNamara on two core issues. First, he felt that the move towards an increased reliance on conventional forces was a positive one.[186] Second, he believed that the flexibility and discriminate city avoidance of the counterforce ethos within SIOP-63 should remain as the American war plan in the event of nuclear hostilities.[187] What Wohlstetter did not approve of, however, was McNamara's deviation from counterforce as declaratory nuclear policy. As Wohlstetter bluntly put it, 'I think that Bob McNamara made a mistake.'[188] Wohlstetter's reasoning behind this declaration was simple; he felt that by having a declaratory strategy (MAD) proposed publicly, which differed

Figure 6.1 Albert and Roberta Wohlstetter with Paul Nitze, receiving the Presidential Medal of Freedom from Ronald Reagan in 1985

from the war plan (SIOP-63's and counterforce), one would inevitably be left in a situation where the Air Force would purchase and advance weapons for the indiscriminate former, even though the latter strategy, which required discriminate precision weapons, was the only 'real' option if deterrence were to fail.[189] Thus, Wohlstetter asked, 'Why do you have a criterion on what you'd buy [that] is … irrelevant to how you'd use it?'[190] As he continued, 'if deterrence failed [we would] actually attack military forces'.[191] Wohlstetter, found this entire situation rather 'curious' as it 'took attention away from the real … changes [in weapons technology and procurement] that the policy required'.[192] As he concluded, 'we're talking about responding in a way that's proportionate'. The aim was 'to confine damage more selectively to things that we wanted to eliminate. And try to keep it from just innocent bystanders whose destruction only endangered our own innocent bystanders by making the whole thing get out of control.'[193] For Wohlstetter, it was the investment in and purchase of precision technologies, like precision missiles, that would be the key to ensuring the achievement of these moral and strategic American aims, both in the short and the longer term.

Counterforce remained, and arguably continues to remain, as the foundational underpinning of American nuclear war plans today.[194] In addition, the MAD verses counterforce issue continues to be a core topic of contention within debate regarding American declaratory nuclear policy.[195] As Wohlstetter recalled in 1986, 'no one has been able to get away from that [counterforce] completely and you had Under Secretary Laird, and then Schlesinger and Rumsfeld and then under Harold Brown, a return in this sort of thing'.[196] As the decades progressed thereafter, however, the legacies of the precision ambitions at the heart of counterforce would cast influential shadows across the American strategic landscape. Wohlstetter's thoughts on the moral and strategic utility of precision capabilities would emerge out of the nuclear Cold War period and filter into the post-Cold War era of conventional force and precision strikes.

It was the moral and strategic ambition to secure American interests through conventional precision strikes that would become a defining feature of Wohlstetter's later work. As the Boston Globe stated in 2003, '[s]trategy guru Albert Wohlstetter spent decades arguing for military flexibility and pre-cision targeting'.[197] Furthermore, as historian Andrew Bacevich has written, 'Wohlstetter was touting the potential of an "expanding family of precision guided munitions" to permit the "much more effective and discriminating application of force in an increasingly wider variety of political and opera-tion circumstances".'[198] Such thoughts became the topic of Wohlstetter's influ-ential policy reports in 1967, 1975 and 1988, and would go on to influence a generation of influential 'Wohlstetter protégés', including Richard Perle,[199] Paul Wolfowitz,[200] and Zalmay Khalilzad.[201] Together, these reports and Wohlstetter's disciples paved the way for the precision warfare of the 1990s and into the twenty-first century.

Wohlstetter – along with many of his fellow RAND researchers – had first alluded to the potential utility of accurate missiles during the 1950s; by the end of the 1960s, however, he had begun to see substantial advancements in the technologies that, he believed, could make his moral and strategic ambitions a reality.[202] Wohlstetter's 1968 work '*Strength, Interest and New Technologies*' was writ-ten in the context of the MAD versus counterforce debate and outlined the 'most immediately significant' of these technological advancements.[203] In the report he focused on the worth of computer information technologies, control tech-nologies, and their relationship to precision technologies.[204] Wohlstetter argued that, due to the '*Receding Technological Plateau* [emphasis added]', advancements in computer data gathering and transmission, missile range, multiple inde-pendently targetable re-entry vehicles (MIRVs), and 'improvements in offen-sive accuracies and reliability', a revolution in technology was underway.[205] This revolution, he believed, would combine to greatly enhance American long-range precision capabilities and transform the American ability 'to project strength to distant places'.[206] Put succinctly, Wohlstetter saw the emergence of a new, achievable, precision strike capacity that would allow force to not only be directed to the right target, but due to advancements in reliability and accuracy could actually strike the targets discriminately and proportionately. The consequences of this were clear to Wohlstetter: they would allow for the achievement of counterforce at a nuclear level, but could also allow for a new, conventional, deterrence capability.

Wohlstetter's research on conventional precision came to maturity with the 1975 'Summary Report of the Long Range Research and Development Planning Program' (declassified 1983) – a Defence Advanced Research Project Agency (DARPA) and Defence Nuclear Agency's (DNA) co-sponsored report, of which Wohlstetter was a primary author.[207] His research on conventional precision was them implemented into policy recommendations in his 1988 report, *Discriminate Deterrence: Report of the Commission on Integrated Long-Term Strategy*, co-authored with Fred Iklé (President Reagan's Under Secretary of Defense for Policy).[208] In the 1975 report (henceforth called the 'LRRDPP report'), we not only see the legacies of RAND's counterforce, but a continuation of a precision ethos. The LRRDPP report was carried out as a means to find 'alternatives to massive nuclear destruction' – the core recommendation of which was precision at a conventional level.[209] As the report explained, '[t]he strongest technology incentive to emerge from the program are those related to precise delivery of munitions'.[210] Specifically, the LRRDPP report recommended the implementation of precision munitions at a conventional level as a means to provide a more reliable deterrence factor than MAD, one that operated below the threshold of nuclear war. As the report stated, '[b]ased on the analysis it appears that non-nuclear weapons with near zero miss may be technically feasible and militarily effective'.[211] These advancements, according to the report, were of pivotal importance to the future of deterrence and American power projection as 'such non-nuclear weapons, under some circumstances, might satisfy the current United States and allied damage requirements that now require the use of nuclear weapons'.[212] Therefore, '[n]ear zero miss non-nuclear weapons', the report concluded, 'could provide the National Command Authority with a variety of strategic response options as alternatives to massive nuclear destruction'.[213] In simple terms this was because reliable pinpoint precision strikes could guarantee the destruction of a designated target. As such, if the US military could deploy a powerful (high-yield) conventional precision missile against a hardened Soviet nuclear silo – and if they could strike that target with a direct hit – they would achieve the same end result as sending multiple inaccurate nuclear missiles at the target in the vain hope of hitting it by chance or destroying it with residual blast effect (as LeMay's bomb everything ethos had once hoped). Such recommendations were pioneering for the advancement of conventional precision strike capabilities in American warfare and continued to dominate the development of policy (and Wohlstetter's own thoughts) into the late 1980s and early 1990s.

As the 1988 *Discriminate Deterrence* report highlighted, just prior to the Gulf War (1991), although still focused on conventional precision as a form of deterrence, the ambition of striking the enemy with precision in order to ensure the rapid achievement of American strategic aims, but in a proportionate, discriminate, and low-cost manner, was now at the heart of American strategic thought. As Wohlstetter's report stated, '[t]he precision associated with the new technologies will enable us to use conventional weapons for many of the missions once assigned to nuclear weapons'.[214] As the report continued:

> [w]e must diversify and strengthen our ability to bring discriminating, non-nuclear force to bear where needed in time to defeat aggression. To this end, we and our allies need to exploit emerging technologies of precision, control, and intelligence that can provide our conventional forces with more selective and more effective capabilities for destroying military targets.[215]

Wohlstetter's recommendations were clearly fuelled by his long-held ambition for precision crafted out of the RAND 'rational' way of thinking. As the report explained, the advancements make 'possible more discriminate attacks on enemy troops and reduced civilian casualties'.[216] The report concluded, 'we will want to use smart missiles that can apply force in a discriminate fashion and avoid collateral damage to civilians'.[217] These notions would be familiar to those well versed in the strategic ambitions and rhetoric of Desert Storm during the Gulf War, the Kosovo Campaign, or the characteristics of American and allied drone warfare in the 2010s and 2020s. In fact, as the 1988 report stated, '[o]ur strategy must be designed for the long term'.[218]

Epilogue: The legacies of precision

'what allowed the success of Desert Storm, and what happened there, is that technology had enabled the theories that our forefathers had anticipated, and it became a reality'.

Lieutenant General (ret.) David Deptula (2021)[1]

The Gulf War marked a new era in American Warfare. When Iraq's President Saddam Hussein invaded his oil rich neighbour Kuwait in August 1990, he promised that the American people would face 'the mother of all battles' – a war for which he believed there was little public appetite or political will from President George H.W. Bush.[2] What Saddam had not planned for, however, was the vast technological transformation that had taken place in the US military during the latter decades of the Cold War. As a result of advances in all the systems Wohlstetter had been highlighting since the 1960s, a Revolution in Military Affairs (RMA) had taken place.[3] The defining features of this RMA are still hotly debated, but needless to say it involved the advancement of computer data gathering and transmission, missile range and yield, and improvements in offensive accuracies and reliability.[4] As a result, by the time the Gulf War began the US military had grown to control the most technologically sophisticated conventional precision strike force in the world.

From cruise missiles reportedly turning left at traffic lights, F-117s launching 2,000-pound laser-guided 'smart' bombs on bunkers in Baghdad, and Saddam's forces ultimately surrendering to new Pioneer surveillance drones, the air war above the Gulf would become known as 'the most successful war of the 20th Century'.[5] In a feat that Gorrell or Mitchell, Hansell or Arnold could only have dreamed of, US airpower enacted the most precise war in history. As the *New York Times* reported in February 1991, '[f]or the first time in history, precision-guided bombs and missiles have played a decisive role in war, paving the way for the invasion of Kuwait and Iraq. With their help, the United States and its

Figure 7.1 An F-117 conducts a live exercise bombing run using GBU-27 laser-guided bombs

allies critically weakened the fourth-largest army in the world while suffering surprisingly light casualties'.[6] After a 38-day air war and 100-hour ground campaign, victory against Saddam was secured.

This is not to say that the war was 'perfect' and waged without mistake. The estimated 2,300 civilian fatalities, 100,000+ Iraqi military fatalities, and the 247 coalition battle deaths,[7] show that this war – like all wars – resulted in significant loss of human life.[8] In addition, the infamous 'Highway of Death',[9] 'Al Firdos Bunker Strike',[10] and 'Bulldozer Assault'[11] exemplify the imprecision and reputational damage of the war. Nevertheless, it is undeniable that the war marked a new epoch in the successful deployment of precision technologies and precision-based strategies.[12] In fact, what is interesting to note is that the strategy itself was intellectually inspired by the early American airpower thinkers who had persevered with precision bombing during the first half of the twentieth century.

This was revealed to me during an interview with Lieutenant General (ret.) David Deptula. We met at his office in Washington, DC where he explained how it was the writings of Major General Haywood S. Hansell Jr. that had been at the forefront of his mind when planning the air campaign in the Gulf. Hansell was a precision pioneer and one of the chief architects of precision bombing during the Second World War. It was he who had been abruptly replaced by LeMay as Commander of XXI Bomber Command in 1945 – a move which marked the dramatic shift from precision bombing to area bombing and the start of the firebombing of Japan. As such, Hansell's influence on Deptula bares great historical significance. This is because Deptula was the principal attack planner for the air campaign in the Gulf and the ghostwriter of the underpinning US Air Force White Paper on the Air Force and US National Security titled 'Global Reach – Global Power'.[13] I also spoke with Deptula about this same issue on my Warfare podcast where he went into greater detail about his inspiration.[14] To be specific, Deptula detailed how in the summer of 1990 he had 'read two books, both by retired General Hayward Hansell'. The first one, he explained, 'was *The Air Plan That Defeated Hitler* and it was about how Hansell and some of the early planners had put together Air War Planning Document 1 (AWPD-1)'.[15] AWPD-1 was a founding document of US airpower doctrine and focused on the strategic utility of Industrial Web Theory. Reading about this history 'entranced' Deptula to the point where he picked up Hansell's second book, which was the *Strategic Air War Against Germany and Japan*.[16] As Deptula recalled:

> it was sort of fortuitous that I'd read both of those books that yielded some first-hand insight into how one of the key planners of World War Two thought about, from both a theoretical and a practical perspective, the take down of these two nation states. And while I was familiar with strategic bombing theory before that, it sort of refreshed and gave me insights that I'd never really had before.[17]

All books possess the power to pass on lessons through history, and in this case there can be little doubt that Deptula admired, identified with, and adopted the ambitions of those early air power thinkers. As Deptula recounted, 'what the planners had done in World War Two, in retrospect, the theory, was pretty similar [to what] we were trying to apply when you move forward to Desert Storm'.[18] As Deptula clarified, the key difference 'was that the technology of the times in World War Two simply had not advanced to be able to accomplish what they wanted to do ... there was not a lot of precision involved in World War Two precision bombing, but what had happened now, by the time you got to Desert Storm, I could target one bomb one target'.[19] Deptula's detailed explanation highlights the considerable influence Hansell's work had on him and ultimately on how the Gulf War was fought and won. As Deptula concluded:

> I had the virtue of technology that had advanced to catch up with the theories that Hansell ... and Arnold had talked about and discussed. At a very very

macro-level, what allowed the success of Desert Storm, and what happened there, is that technology had enabled the theories that our forefathers had anticipated, and it became a reality.[20]

Such realities had a monumental impact on how American warfare would be fought through the 1990s. The Gulf War, and its rapid victory, set the blueprint for the future of American warfare in a post-Cold War world. Thanks, in part, to Wohlstetter's pioneering of precise conventional weapons and precision strategies during the Cold War, and Deptula's harnessing of Hansell's theories, precision was now the spearhead of American force deployment.

Precision after the Gulf War

'It [Kosovo] was the first war in history, where, as General Clark has remarked, couples walked along the Danube and dined at sidewalk cafes while the bombardment went on around them.'

Admiral William J. Crowe (2003)[21]

There were, of course, many other factors that contributed to the rise of precision strike technologies and strategies during the 1990s. Beyond the Wohlstetter, Hansell, Deptula connection, historians can (and have) looked at how tactical bombing, laser guided munitions, and the use of Lightning Bug drones during the Vietnam War impacted future US military investment in precision missile and drone systems.[22] In addition, satellite control, microprocessing, and CIA experiments with various drone initiatives – including attempts to assassinate Libyan leader Colonel Muammar Gaddafi – all influenced the effectiveness, reliability, and readiness of precision weapons by the 1990s.[23] Additionally, and worthy of specific mention, is the impact of Israeli engineering innovations and the work of Abraham Karem – known as the father of drones – who laid the design and engineering foundations for the first mass-produced and armed American medium-altitude long-endurance drone, known as the Predator.[24] When combined – and considered alongside the broader technological and strategic trajectory of the America precision ethos outlined in this book– it is clear to see how precision became the underpinning strategic concept of American war planning during the 1990s (and beyond).[25]

In fact, it is hard to find an example of American warfare during the 1990s that was not greatly influenced by precision strike technologies and the underpinning American precision ethos. As the Soviet Union crumbled and former communist nations descended into internal conflict, the new administration of President Bill Clinton (1993–2001) chose to continue where the administration

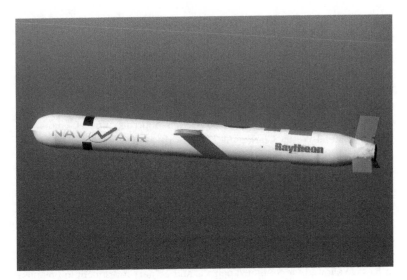

Figure 7.2 Tomahawk cruise missile during a flight test

of President George H.W. Bush had left off during the Gulf War. Noting the seemingly war winning capabilities of precision technologies, the Clinton administration chose to intervene in a limited fashion, where needed, but at arm's length and with distancing weapons of conventional precision.

It would take a second volume to provide the in-depth analysis needed to fully understand the political and strategic motivations behind the Clinton administration's reliance on precision weapons. But even a cursory glance at US-led conflicts during this period highlights the continued importance of precision strike technologies and precision strategies. When Milošević's forces perpetrated the Bosnian Genocide (1992–95), President Clinton turned to conventional precision strikes to halt the killings. As Albert Wohlstetter stated at the time, '[p]recision and discriminate air power can help disarm the Serbian military forces that are slaughtering civilians and can reduce any unintended harm by the coalition'.[26] Although it took many months, Clinton did finally choose to follow a precision-based strategy to end the bloodshed. As former US Air Force Historian, Richard P. Hallion, explained, 'the vast majority of NATO munitions employed in the Bosnian conflict were precision ones: in fact, over 98 per cent of those used by American forces' were precision munitions.[27] For Hallion, and indeed Clinton officials, this was yet another example of what precision could achieve – a war winning and alluring technology that enabled a rapid and low-cost victory.[28] In fact, when Milošević once again enacted violent attacks against minority populations (this time in Kosovo, 1998–99), it was precision airpower that was relied on to end the killing.

Referred to as the 'perfect war', due to the fact that the conflict ended with zero NATO combat fatalities,[29] the 78-day air campaign that comprised Operation Allied Force involved 7,000 NATO attack sorties, 'most of which entailed [the] use of precision weapons'.[30] As Supreme Allied Commander Europe General Wesley Clark remarked after the conflict, such were the levels of precision deployed during the operation that 'couples walked along the Danube and dined at sidewalk cafes while the bombardment went on around them' safe in the knowledge that NATO strikes would hit military, not civilian targets.[31] Academic studies continue to challenge this narrative of infallible precision, with the accidental bombing of the Chinese Embassy in Belgrade and the documented 528 civilian casualties dispelling the myth that precision can ever 'perfect' war.[32] However, the US framing of a sanitized and clean war in Kosovo allowed for continued political and military investment in precision technologies and strategies. As a result, just over two years later, when al-Qaeda attacked the US homeland on 11 September 2001, it was precision airpower that was relied on to spearhead a new War on Terror.[33]

Precision and the War on Terror

'On September the 11th, enemies of freedom committed an act of war against our country. Americans have known wars – but for the past 136 years, they have been wars on foreign soil, except for one Sunday in 1941.'
President George W. Bush, Address to a Joint Session of Congress and the American People, 20 September 2001

On Sunday 7 December 1941, at 07:55 local time, the US Pacific Fleet was attacked by the Imperial Japanese Navy Air Service as it sat in dock at Pearl Harbor in Hawaii. As Roberta Wohlstetter wrote in her analysis of the attack, it was 'achieved with complete and overwhelming surprise' maximising the death and destruction.[34] As President Roosevelt stated, such a day would 'live in infamy'.[35] Just four days after the attack, the US would officially join the Second World War.

In that war, precision airpower played a leading role. As Chapter 2 explained, for better or worse, it was precision bombing – pioneered by Gorrell and Mitchell and built upon by their intellectual disciples, like Arnold – that provided the moral and strategic underpinning for American strategic bombardment against the Axis powers. Interestingly, however, during the initial period after the 11September attacks of 2001, an arguably comparable path to retribution was followed. History, as they say, doesn't repeat itself, but it rhymes. Not only was Roberta Wohlstetter's work cited by the 9/11 Commission, influencing the final report on the al-Qaeda surprise attack, but Albert's quest for ever greater precision in war – fostered with colleagues during the Cold War in the fertile environment of Arnold's RAND Corporation – would go on influence the Bush administration's response to 9/11.[36]

Although Albert would pass away in January 1997 (and Roberta almost exactly ten years later in January 2007), select graduates of the Wohlstetter School would be elevated to the Bush administration, influencing the highest levels of national security and defence policy. Richard Perle is but one key example. As a high school friend of the Wohlstetter's daughter Joan, Perle was mentored by the Wohlstetter's and would go on to work for Senator Henry 'Scoop' Jackson as his principal aide in Congress.[37] Under President Bush, Perle would become Chairman of the Defense Policy Board (a Department of Defense advisory group that provided informed advice and opinions concerning matters of defence policy to the Deputy Secretary of Defense and Secretary of Defense).[38] As reported by the *New Yorker*, he was also 'one of the most outspoken and influential American advocates of war with Iraq'.[39] Next is Zalmay Khalilzad. A student of Albert Wohlstetter's and a former RAND researcher, Khalilzad would go on to be US Ambassador to Afghanistan (2003–05), Ambassador to Iraq (2005–07), and Ambassador to the UN (2007–09).[40] Khalilzad was also US Special Representative for Afghanistan Reconciliation from September 2018 to October 2021, helping to finalise the controversial Doha Agreement with the Taliban.[41] Finally, and perhaps most influentially for the purposes of our journey through the history of precision, is Paul Wolfowitz.

Wolfowitz was Albert Wohlstetter's PhD student and he had also worked with Senator Jackson in 1969 while devising a report on ballistic missile defence with Richard Perle.[42] He also served as Director of Policy Planning at the State Department under President Reagan, and Under Secretary of Defense for Policy (1989–93) under President George H.W. Bush during the Gulf War.[43] Under President George W. Bush, however, Wolfowitz would rise to Deputy Secretary of Defense (2001–05). He would later become President of the World Bank (2005–07).[44] When I interviewed Wolfowitz back in 2016, he explained to me how important Albert was to the advancement of precision technologies and strategies in the US and to his own understanding of precision's strategic and political utility during the Bush years.[45] Wohlstetter, he stated in an earlier interview, was one of the 'most influential people to understand what a dramatic difference it would make to have accurate weapons'.[46] As he elaborated, there were two core components of Wohlstetter's thought that resonated with him most: '[n]umber one' was the ambition 'to be able to use conventional weapons in ways that people [thought] that only nuclear weapons could be used, to be able to get out of the nuclear mindset ... But secondly, and importantly, to be able to avoid unnecessary loss of innocent life in war'.[47] Such ambitions were important to Wolfowitz during his time in power. Not only did Wolfowitz bolster US stocks of precision weapons by replacing the old Crusader artillery system with precision artillery systems, but at a strategic level he became a vocal public advocate of precision strategies.[48]

This can be evidenced through Wolfowitz's interviews and public declarations during his time as Deputy Secretary of Defense. During the opening stages of the War on Terror, it could be said that precision was paramount to Wolfowitz. As he made clear in a statement to the House of Representatives Armed Services Committee in 2003, 'U.S. military forces will rely on speed and precision weaponry to win future conflicts, such as the ones in Iraq and Afghanistan, and battles in the War on Terror.'[49] Indeed, Wolfowitz went on to inform the committee that 'the use of precision munitions, and full use of information technology ... are all key lessons taken from the conflicts in Afghanistan and Iraq'.[50] It is, of course, almost impossible to look back on the highly destructive and controversial War on Terror as a war of precision. The war cost thousands of US and coalition lives and hundreds of thousands of civilian lives. The American precision ethos was pioneered to avoid such risks to American life and to reduce unintended costs to civilians. There is, however, an argument to be made that during Wolfowitz's tenure, in the early years of the War on Terror, there were initial attempts to keep in line with the 'precise' lessons of the Gulf, Bosnia, and Kosovo.

Between 2001 and 2003 the precision airpower components deployed during the early stages of the War on Terror were frequently represented as war winning successes. As the historian Rebecca Grant argued in 2003:

> as foreshadowed in Operation Allied Force and in Enduring Freedom, coalition airpower attained a new level of precision and persistence ... The early total for precision in Iraqi Freedom was 68 percent. With all fighters and bombers capable of precision attack, and with most able to plug into an enhanced ISR network, the value of each sortie rose exponentially'.[51]

Afghanistan was a markedly different war, however. As Wolfowitz's boss, Secretary of Defense Donald Rumsfeld, stated, there were 'not a lot of high value targets' in the country and thus less reason to launch a full-scale strategic precision air campaign.[52] This does not mean precision airpower was absent from Afghanistan. On the contrary, as Grant explained, 'the role of strategic airpower was to work with special operations forces on the ground and carry out swift strikes that stayed in step with constantly shifting command priorities – for example, hitting leadership targets'.[53] This meant that after the initial 'short, sharp air campaign' that opened the war in Afghanistan, precision airpower would be used to provide close air support to those on the ground and to hunt down and kill the perpetrators of 9/11.[54] This was aided by the fact that by 2001 the pinpoint accuracy of the conventional precision missile had been combined with the loitering capacity and near real-time video link up of the surveillance drone to form the Predator, and so a revolutionary precision technology was born. The administration of President George W. Bush would be the first in US history to deploy such weapons in active conflict, paving the way for an exponential increase in the use of drones.

The first drone strike

'The Predator is a good example. This unmanned aerial vehicle is able to circle over enemy forces, gather intelligence, transmit information instantly back to commanders, then fire on targets with extreme accuracy. Before the war, the Predator had sceptics because it did not fit the old ways. Now it is clear the military does not have enough unmanned vehicles.'

President George W. Bush, 12 December 2001[55]

The first drone strike took place on the opening night of the War on Terror, 7 October 2001.[56] It was a strike that Deptula, and his boss Lieutenant General Chuck Wald, were closely involved in as they orchestrated 'air operations over Afghanistan during the period of decisive combat'.[57] As Deptula explained in a 2015 interview, it was Mullah Omar, the head of the Taliban, who was the target of the strike. Omar had been spotted by a newly armed Predator drone as he neared 'his facility in an entourage', just outside the southern city of Kandahar.[58] This 'entourage' was believed to be made up of key members of Omar's Taliban leadership. Less than a month after the 9/11 attacks, such a decisive 'decapitation strike' (a strike which removes the leadership of a hostile organisation) may well have led to a very different history of the war in Afghanistan. Yet it did not go to plan.

Due to complications in the chain of command – which involved a confusing mix of the CIA, CENTCOM (United States Central Command), and the

Figure 7.3 MQ-1 Predator drone, 2012

Air Force – an order was given to strike an empty truck outside the compound Omar had entered.[59] The details are still contested, but it appears Omar and his team had left his home in a convoy of vehicles, which was then tracked by the Predator as it drove to another compound across the city. Here, Omar and his team moved inside one of the buildings. With this in mind, the aim of the strike that followed was likely an attempt to lure Omar out and get a more precise strike without broader harm to unidentified people (possibly civilians). All the strike did, however, was unintentionally hand Omar an opportunity to flee. As Wald explained, 'whether out of malice or incompetence I still don't know … The first I knew the Predator was [engaged] was when I heard an unknown voice on my radio say, "You are cleared to fire".'[60] As a result, the first drone strike was a failure, kicking up a giant cloud of dust, smoke (and confusion), which allowed Omar to make his escape. He would remain on the run for over a decade until his death from 'health problems' (suspected tuberculosis) in 2013.[61]

Still, such tactical failures did not stop US political and military officials from recognising the broader allure of 'war by remote control'.[62] The ability to hunt down, loiter, and kill suspected terrorists and insurgents with precision missiles launched by robotic drones, all controlled from distant safety in Ground Control Stations (GCS) back in the continental United States, was an appealing prospect – one the Bush administration would exploit.[63] There were around fifty known drone strikes during the Bush years, a slow ramping up of the US Air Force and CIA drone programmes that ultimately laid the foundations for a growing reliance on armed drones in American warfare.[64] It would not be until the Obama era began in 2009, however, that the deployment of armed drones would really 'take off'.

The Drone President

'So this is a just war – a war waged proportionally, in last resort, and in self-defense.'
President Barack Obama, 23 May 2013[65]

The controversies and inconsistences of the Obama administration's relationship with armed military drones have been outlined in the Prologue. Nevertheless, it is important to note that it was Obama's obsession with precision strikes and drones – and his declaration of 'precise' and 'just wars' – that first inspired our journey through the history of American precision. As we reflect on this history, it is clear to see how, when Obama came to power, he saw drones as a way to overcome an age-old American problem: to reduce the costs of war while remaining decisively effective in the deployment of military force. As Chapter 1 explained, during the First World War, when American casualties began to mount and the public's appetite for large expeditionary ground campaigns faded, early precision pioneers, like Arnold, experimented with the Kettering Bug and Norden bombsight to reduce the costs of war and increase the effectiveness of military airpower. In 2009, when Obama came to power, he turned to the drone.

Obama's reliance on drones would see him anointed 'The Drone President'. It has never been easy to ascertain the true number of strikes Obama approved, but his title is reflective of the 1,878 estimated strikes that took place during his eight years in office.[66] It used to be said that there were 'only' 540 drone strikes launched during this period – a ten-fold increase on the Bush era – yet this number is limited to strikes deployed outside active war zones (for example in Somalia, Yemen, or Pakistan).[67] Due to the top secret character of the CIA drone programme, which is operated separately to the US Air Force programme and in a covert manner, and the ongoing uncertainty of the data, it will likely be many decades before we know the true extent of the administration's drone use and the deaths caused. What we do know, however, is that drones gave Obama – a constitutional law professor turned president – the perceived moral and legal justification he and his administration needed to carry out as many drone strikes as they believed were necessary to keep the amorphous threat of terrorism at bay.[68] As the President declared in 2013, 'conventional air power or missiles are far less precise than drones and are likely to cause more civilian casualties and more local outrage'; they are, he stated, part of a 'just war – a war waged proportionally, in last resort, and in self-defense'.[69] Such claims are contested, and it will be up to future historians to pass judgement on Obama's successes and failures as the files are declassified. Nevertheless, what he was trying to achieve was akin to the long-held, unique, and often illusory American ambition for precision in warfare.

In truth, as has often been the case with the pursuit of precision over the last century, mistakes were made during the Obama era and innocent people were killed.[70] Precision, after all, is only as precise as the intelligence at hand, and if the intelligence is flawed, all precision really means is guaranteed death and destruction for the unintended victims. Despite Obama's claims to White House staff that he had become 'really good at killing' – and that he had waged 'the most precise air campaign in history' – his administration's own estimates stated that between 64–116 civilians had been accidently killed during his time in office.[71] These numbers continue to be hotly disputed, with separate investigations by the Bureau of Investigative Journalism, the *New York Times*, and Airwars frequently putting the true number of civilian casualties into the hundreds, if not thousands. Nevertheless, this collateral damage did not stop those who came after Obama from continuing, and even expanding, the drone programme. Due to the fact that drones delivered many political and military successes for Obama, such as the death of up to 2,581 suspected terrorists and insurgents, the drone's allure remained.[72]

In the years directly after the Obama administration, President Trump doubled down on the use of drones, broadening and widening the remit for lethal strikes. It was the Trump administration's expansion of the drone programme, the reduction of controls designed to protect civilians, and the loosening of the criteria under which a drone strike could be undertaken, which paved the way for a number of contentious deployments.[73] These changes were carried out alongside modifications to the required reporting on drone strikes, which reduced transparency, oversight, and democratic accountability.[74] This simply meant that when drone strikes went wrong, or caused international incidents, there was a veil of secrecy that kept the American public in the dark and the Trump administration safe from scrutiny.[75]

Perhaps the most controversial example of a Trump era drone strike was the killing of General Qasem Soleimani in January 2020.[76] There can be little

Epilogue

doubt that Soleimani, an Iranian official who headed the elite Quds Force of the Islamic Revolutionary Guard Corps, was an enemy of the United States.[77] Yet his death by US drone strike – ordered directly by President Trump – was a watershed moment in international security.[78] Setting a worrying example to the world about what was acceptable in terms of the use of armed drones, it marked the first time the weapons had been used to assassinate a state representative, in a third-party country (Iraq), without that country's permission.[79] Although only in power for one term, the Trump administration certainly highlighted to both state and non-state actors around the world how drones could be used and misused inside and outside the bounds of international law.[80]

It was for this reason that, when President Biden came to power in 2021, a review was launched into the US drone programme.[81] This review mainly reintroduced the Obama era polices on drone strikes that had been amended or removed during the Trump years.[82] This included 'curtailing the use of armed drones outside of war zones as part of a new counterterrorism strategy that place[d] a greater priority on protecting civilian lives'.[83] As White House Homeland Security Advisor Elizabeth Sherwood-Randall stated in 2022, the President's new guidance required 'that U.S. counterterrorism operations meet the highest standards of precision and rigor, including for identifying appropriate targets and minimizing civilian casualties'.[84] Yet despite this declaratory policy of reintroducing 'precision' as an ambition in the drone programme, the flaws and shortfalls remained.

Global events overwhelmed Biden era restraints on the use of drones. For example, the Time Sensitive Strike (TSS) by an armed US drone in Kabul in 2021 exemplified the continuation of drone controversies.[85] During the botched withdrawal from Afghanistan, which saw a suicide bomber kill 170 civilians and 13 US troops at Hamid Karzai International Airport, the TSS was launched to stop a suspected repeat attack.[86] Unfortunately, due to intelligence failures and confirmation bias, the drone hit the wrong target, killing 10 civilians, including 7 children.[87] This is not to say that Biden has had zero 'precision successes' during his time in power. Ayman al-Zawahiri, Osama bin Laden's number two and an architect of 9/11, was killed by a CIA drone's Hellfire R9X 'ninja' missile (which releases blades from its sides as it hurtles to earth) as he stood on his balcony in Kabul.[88] As Biden stated at the time, this was 'justice' delivered.[89] 'No matter where you hide', he declared, 'if you are a threat to our people, the U.S. will find you and take you out.'[90] Yet despite these lauded precision strikes, the truth is that Biden's drone policy was altered more by an international climate of Great Power tensions and less by the preplanned and intended designs of the administration.

Russia's offensive war in Ukraine (2022), alongside growing tensions with China over Taiwan, led to a swift reprioritising and expansion of drones as a key weapon for deployment and export. The expedited export of American military drone technologies and precision missiles to key allies around the world (specifically to Ukraine and Taiwan) highlighted the growing importance of precision in the face of mounting threats around the world.[91] This fact was not lost on China and Russia who, in turn, started accelerating their own drone development, procurement, and export programmes, including with autonomous systems controlled by artificial intelligence.[92] As a result, the early 2020s saw the start of 'The Second Drone Age', a world where precision strike technologies left the custodianship of the United States and spread around the world. It is here that we return to Albert Wohlstetter one final time.[93]

The proliferation of precision

'high tech is not an American monopoly'
Fred Iklé and Albert Wohlstetter, *Discriminate Deterrence* (1988)[94]

By highlighting the innovative thinkers of the First World War, the experimental technologies of the Second World War, and the surprising Cold War nuclear strategies that made precision the dominant feature it is today, this book has explored and explained how precision evolved as a moral and strategic ambition in American warfare throughout the twentieth century and into the twenty-first. Yet the impact of this long-held ambition to achieve precision does not end with American warfare. As Albert Wohlstetter and Fred Iklé warned back in 1988, '[i]n the years ahead, weapons production will be much more widely diffused, and the superpowers will have less control over transfers of advanced systems'.[95] In fact, what they explicitly warned of was 'the worldwide diffusion of advanced weapons'.[96]

While Wohlstetter and Iklé were keenly aware of the utility of conventional precision strikes for the United States, they also understood that high-tech precision weapons systems are 'not an American monopoly' and would one day pose a threat to the US and its allies.[97] According to the Center for the Study of the Drone, in 2010 the proliferation of drones had progressed to the point where sixty states had a military drone programme.[98] As of 2022, 113 states had obtained or were developing military drones. This was an increase of 88.3 per cent in twelve years.[99] This proliferation of precision was not limited to

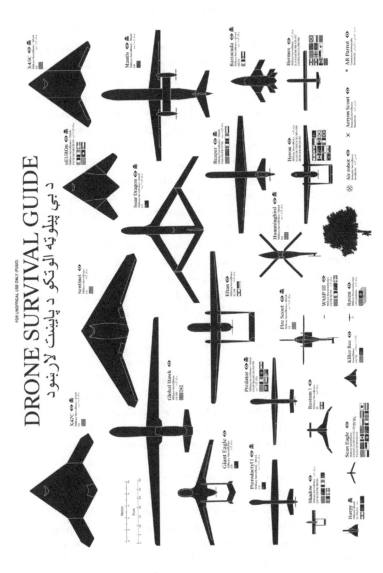

Figure 7.4 Drone Survival Guide

nation states. As of 2023,at least sixty-five non-state actors had access to weaponised drone systems, a conservative figure based on limited data meaning that the number of non-state actors with drones is likely to be much higher.[100]

In some cases, commercial technologies had been adapted for nefarious use, and in other cases states supplied non-state actors with advanced precision weapons systems so that they could do their bidding for them.[101] Drones were also created in a rudimentary, but effective, manner, by combining military grade designs with commercial technologies to provide terrorist organisations with their own indigenous long-range precision strike capacity.[102] The Houthi terrorist group in Yemen, for example, reportedly obtained an arsenal of drones from state and commercial sources that facilitated strikes on targets over 1,500 km away.[103] These were used in attacks on the Aramco oil processing sites in Saudi Arabia in 2019, the commercial tanker *Mercer Street* in 2021, and Abu Dhabi international airport in 2022.[104] As a result, vital energy infrastructure, international shipping, international airports, and the civilian centres of capital cities were all targeted by hostile precision strikes during this period.

The range and precision of these weapons systems will increase over the coming years, with key allied military and diplomatic sites around the world (and even mainland Europe or the US homeland) under threat from ever more advanced and longer-range precision and drone systems.[105] As Chairman of the Joint Chiefs of Staff, General Mark Milley, told graduating cadets at the United States Military Academy West Point in 2022, '[w]hatever overmatch we enjoyed militarily for the last 70 years is closing quickly, and the United States will be – in fact, we already are – challenged in every domain of warfare'.[106] Indeed, as Milley specifically warned the next generation of US military leaders, '[w]e've witnessed a revolution in lethality and precision munitions; what was once the exclusive province of the United States military is now available to most nation states with the money and will to acquire them'.[107] This is undoubtably a disquieting prospect, but it is a future better faced with an understanding of the history of precision.

What is it that we can learn from precision's past to help us understand modern precision warfare and the uncontrolled proliferation of precision strike technologies around the world? Well, as we look to the future, each nation will, if they so wish, develop or acquire their own precision weapons, drones, and military cultures of precision warfare. What the history has shown us, however, is that this quest for precision involves agonising technological shortfalls, unforeseen strategic mistakes, and the deliberate misuse of precision weapons in extreme ways that their inventors and pioneers never intended.

Perhaps most important of all, however, is that the history has shown us how precision can also be decisive and effective in war. It is now these same precision technologies – pioneered by the US – that have fallen, or have been placed, into the hands of hostile state and non-state actors around the world. As a result, far from a panacea to the costs and risk of war, drones and precision strike technologies are now among the greatest threats to state security.

Abbreviations

ACTS	Air Corps Tactical School
AEF	American Expeditionary Force
AWPD	Air War Planning Document
CENTCOM	United States Central Command
CIA	Central Intelligence Agency
CINCSAC	Commander-in-Chief Strategic Air Command
CPV	Chinese People's Volunteer
DARPA	Defence Advanced Research Project Agency
DNA	Defence Nuclear Agency
GCS	Ground Control Stations
ISTAR	Intelligence, Surveillance, Target Acquisition, and Reconnaissance
JCC	Joint Coordination Centres
JCS	Joint Chiefs of Staff
JIC	Joint Intelligence Committee
JSPC	Joint Strategic Plans Committee
JSTPS	Joint Strategic Target Planning Staff
JWPC	Joint War Plans Committee
LRRDPP	Long Range Research and Development Planning Program
MAD	mutual assured destruction
MIRVs	multiple independently targetable re-entry vehicles
NKPA	North Korean People's Army
NSC	National Security Council
NSTL	National Strategic Target List
ORE	Office of Reports and Estimates
RAF	Royal Air Force
RMA	Revolution in Military Affairs

Abbreviations

ROK	Republic of Korea
SAC	Strategic Air Command
SALT	Strategic Arms Limitation Talks
SIOP	Single Integrated Operational Plan
SOC	Strategic Objectives Committee
TOT	time over target
TSS	Time Sensitive Strike
UNC	United Nations Command
USAAF	United States Army Air Forces
USAF	United States Air Force
USSBS	United States Strategic Bombing Survey
VBIED	Vehicle-Borne Improvised Explosive Device
WESG	Weapons System Evaluation Group
WWCC	World-Wide Coordination Conference

Notes

Prologue

1 P. Meilinger (2009). A Matter of Precision: Why Air Power may be More Humane than Sanctions, *Foreign Policy*, 18 November. Retrieved from: http://foreignpolicy. com/2009/11/18/a-matter-of-precision/. Accessed: 21 February 2023.

2 R.G. Collingwood (2006). Outlines of a Philosophy in History. In J. van der Dussen (ed.), *R.G. Collingwood: Philosophical Texts* (pp. 427–497), Charlottesville, VA: InteLex Corporation; R.G. Collingwood (1994). *The Idea of History*, Oxford: Oxford University Press; J. Connelly (2006). Postmodern Scepticism, Truth and History. In A. L. Macfie (ed.), *The Philosophy of History: Talks given at the IHR London, 2006–2009* (pp. 186–201), Basingstoke: Palgrave.

3 Tami Biddle. Personal interview. 23 December 2015. For a detailed analysis of American values and the foundations of American foreign policy (especially regarding the foreign policy implications of the Constitution adopted in 1789) see A. Quinn and M. Cox, (2007). For Better, for Worse: How America's Foreign Policy became Wedded to Liberal Universalism, *Global Society*. Vol. 21 (4), pp. 499–519.

4 See T. Davis Biddle (2002). *Rhetoric and Reality in Air Warfare: The Evolution of British and American Ideas About Strategic Bombing, 1914–1945*, Woodstock: Princeton University Press; M. Clodfelter (2010). *Beneficial Bombing: The Progressive Foundations of American Air Power, 1917–1945*, Lincoln: University of Nebraska Press; C.C. Crane (1993). *Bombs, Cities and Civilians: American Airpower Strategy in World War II*, Lawrence: University of Kansas Press; M. Gladwell (2021). *The Bomber Mafia: Dream, a Temptation, and the Longest Night of the Second World War*, London: Little Brown; P.G. Thornhill (2012). *'Over not Through': The Search for a Strong, Unified Culture for America's Airmen*, Santa Monica, CA: RAND; P.G. Gillespie (2006). *Weapons of Choice: The Development of Precision Guided Munitions*, Tuscaloosa: University of Alabama Press; M.S. Sherry (1987). *The Rise of American Air Power: The Creation of Armageddon*, London: Yale University Press; S.L. McFarland (1995). *America's Pursuit of Precision Bombing: 1910–1945*, London: Smithsonian Institution Press; S.A. Bourque (2018). *Beyond the Beach: The Allied War Against France*. Annapolis, MD: Naval Institute Press; P. Haun (2020). *Lectures of the Air Corps Tactical School and American Strategic Bombing in World War II*, Lexington: University Press of Kentucky; R.P. O'Mara (2022). *Rise of the War Machines: The Birth of Precision Bombing in World War II*, Annapolis, MD: Naval Institute Press.

Notes

5   R.P. Hallion (1995). *Precision Guided Munitions and the New Era of Warfare*, APSC Paper No. 53, Fairbairn, Australia: Air Power Studies Centre. Retrieved from: www.fas.org/man/dod-101/sys/smart/docs/paper53.htm. Accessed: 26 July 2022.

6   M. Ignatieff (2001). *Virtual War: Kosovo and Beyond*, London: Vintage, p. 215; J. Der Derian (2009). *Virtuous War: Mapping the Military–Industrial Media-Entertainment Network*, Abingdon: Routledge; R.P. Hallion (1992). *Storm Over Iraq: Air Power and the Gulf War*, London: Smithsonian Institution Press; S.D. Wrage (2003). *Immaculate Warfare*, Westport, CT: Praeger; B. Lambeth (2001). *NATO's Air War for Kosovo*, Santa Monica, CA: RAND.

7   S. Carvin and M.J. Williams (2015). *Law, Science, Liberalism and the American Way of Warfare: The Quest for Humanity in Conflict*, Cambridge: Cambridge University Press; K.A. Grieco and J.W. Hutto (2021). Can Drones Coerce? The Effects of Remote Aerial Coercion in Counterterrorism, *International Politics*. Online first. https://doi.org/10.1057/s41311-021-00320-5; S. Kreps (2016). *Drones: What Everyone Needs to Know*. Oxford: Oxford University Press; C. Fuller (2017). *See It/Shoot It: The Secret History of the CIA's Lethal Drone Programme*, New Haven and London: Yale University Press; H. Gusterson (2016). *Drone: Remote Control Warfare*, Cambridge, MA: MIT Press; A. Khan (forthcoming). *Precision Strike*, London: Penguin Random House; M. Benjamin (2013). *Drone Warfare: Killing by Remote Control*, London: Verso; M.J. Boyle (2020). *The Drone Age: How Drone Technology Will Change War and Peace*, Oxford: Oxford University Press; G. Chamayou (2015). *Drone Theory*, London: Penguin; K. Chandler (2020). *Unmanning: How Humans, Machines and Media Perform Drone Warfare*, New Brunswick, NJ: Rutgers University Press; T.G. Mahnken (2011). Weapons: The Growth & Spread of the Precision-Strike Regime, *Daedalus*. Vol. 140 (3), pp. 45–57; C. Woods (2015). *Sudden Justice: America's Secret Drone Wars*, Oxford: Oxford University Press; C. Kennedy-Pipe, J.I. Rogers and T. Waldman (2015). *Drone Chic, Remote Control*, London: Oxford Research Group; M.P. Kreuzer (2016). *Drones and the Future of Air Warfare: The Evolution of Remotely Piloted Aircraft*, Abingdon: Routledge; J.L. Hazelton (2013). Drones: What are they Good For?, *Parameters*. Vol. 43 (1), pp. 29–33; D. Brunstetter and M. Braun (2011). The Implications of Drones on the Just War Tradition, *Ethics & International Affairs*, Vol. 25 (3), pp. 337–358; T. Farooq, S. Lucas and S. Wolff (2019). Predators and Peace: Explaining the Failure of the Pakistani Conflict Settlement Process in 2013–4, *Civil Wars*. Vol. 22 (1), pp. 26–63.

8   B. Obama (2013). Obama's Speech on US Drone Policy [transcript], *New York Times*, 23 May. Retrieved from: www.nytimes.com/2013/05/24/us/politics/transcript-of-obamas-speech-on-drone-policy.html?pagewanted=all. Accessed: 1 July 2022.

9   Ibid.

10 Talk to the Nation (2012). John Brennan Delivers Speech On Drone Ethics, *NPR*, 1 May. Retrieved from: www.npr.org/2012/05/01/151778804/john-brennan-delivers-speech-on-drone-ethics. Accessed: 10 January 2020.

11 R. Gates (2015). *Duty: Memoirs of a Secretary at War*, New York: Vintage, p. 591.

12 The university-based casualty monitoring organisation, Airwars, estimated that at least 7,500 civilians died in US-led Coalition actions against ISIS between 2014 and 2019 alone. See Airwars (2022). Airwars Investigations, *Airwars*. Retrieved from: https://airwars.org/investigations. Accessed: 2 July 2023.

13 N. Lahoud. Interview with James Rogers for the Warfare podcast (2022). The Real Bin Laden, *Warfare* podcast. Retrieved from: https://podcasts.apple.com/dk/podcast/warfare/id1526490428?i=1000570251536. Accessed: 18 February 2023.

14 N. Lahoud (2022). *The Bin Laden Papers: How the Abbottabad Raid Revealed the Truth about al-Qaeda, Its Leader and His Family*, London: Yale University Press, p. 6.

Notes

15 J. Rogers (2017). Drone Warfare: The Death of Precision, *Bulletin of the Atomic Scientists*, 12 May. Retrieved from: https://thebulletin.org/2017/05/drone-warfare-the-death-of-precision/. Accessed: 24 March 2023.

16 J. Rogers and D. Goxho (2022). Light Footprint – Heavy Destabilising Impact in Niger: Why the Western Understanding of Remote Warfare Needs to be Reconsidered, *International Politics*. Online first. https://doi.org/10.1057/s41311-021-00362-9.

17 L. Kahn and M.C. Horowitz (2021). Who Gets Smart: Explaining How Precision Bombs Proliferate, *SSRN*, 24 February. Online first. http://dx.doi.org/10.2139/ssrn.3792071; U.E. Franke (2018). Military Robots and Drones. In D.J. Galbreath and J.R. Deni (eds), *The Routledge Handbook of Defence Studies* (pp. 338–348), Abingdon: Routledge; D. Gettinger and A.H. Michel (2020). *The Drone Databook (Update)*, Annandale-On-Hudson: Bard College; Z. Kallenborn and P.C. Bleek (2018). Swarming Destruction: Drone Swarms and Chemical, Biological, Radiological, and Nuclear Weapons, *Nonproliferation Review*. Vol. 25 (5–6), pp. 523–543; A. Callamard and J. Rogers (2020). We Need a New International Accord to Control Drone Proliferation, *Bulletin of the Atomic Scientists*. Retrieved from: https://thebulletin.org/2020/12/we-need-a-new-international-accord-to-control-drone-proliferation/#post-heading. Accessed: 23 July 2022; P. Lushenko, S. Bose and W. Maley (eds) (2021). *Drones and Global Order: Implications of Remote Warfare for International Society*, Abingdon: Routledge; S. Bendett (2022). To Robot or Not to Robot? Past Analysis of Russian Military Robotics and Today's War in Ukraine, *War on the Rocks*. Retrieved from: https://warontherocks.com/2022/06/to-robot-or-not-to-robot-past-analysis-of-russian-military-robotics-and-todays-war-in-ukraine. Accessed: 26 July 2022; A. Rossiter and B.J. Cannon (2022). Turkey's Rise as a Drone Power: Trial by Fire, *Defense & Security Analysis*. Vol. 38 (2), pp. 210–229; M. Horowitz, J.A. Schwartz and M. Fuhrmann (2022). Who's Prone to Drone? A Global Time-Series Analysis of Armed Uninhabited Aerial Vehicle Proliferation, *Conflict Management and Peace Science*. Vol. 39 (2), pp. 119–142; K. Chávez and O. Swed (2021). The Proliferation of Drones to Violent Nonstate Actors, *Defence Studies*, Vol. 21 (1), pp. 1–24.

18 J. Rogers (2021). Future Threats: Military UAS, Terrorist Drones, and the Dangers of the Second Drone Age. In A. Haider (ed.), *A Comprehensive Approach to Countering Unmanned Aircraft Systems* (pp. 481–509). Kalkar: NATO Joint Air Power Competence Centre; E. Archambault and Y. Veilleux-Lepage (2020). Drone Imagery in Islamic State Propaganda: Flying like a State, *International Affairs*, Vol. 96 (4), pp. 955–973; Rogers and Goxho, Light Footprint.

19 J. Rogers (2021). Iran and Turkey have become Drone Powers, *Washington Post*, 28 January. Retrieved from: www.washingtonpost.com/politics/2021/01/28/iran-turkey-have-become-drone-powers/. Accessed: 18 June 2022; J. Rogers (2022). Arria-Formula Meeting on Transnational Terrorist Threats [Address to UN Security Council Arria-Formula: video]. *UNSC*, 31 August. Retrieved from: https://media.un.org/en/asset/k1q/k1qcqls4bg. Accessed: 17 February 2023.

20 D. Gettinger (2020). *The Drone Databook*, Annandale-On-Hudson: Center for the Study of the Drone.

21 A. Callamard and UN Human Rights Council (2020). *Use of Armed Drones for Targeted Killings: Report of the Special Rapporteur on Extrajudicial, Summary or Arbitrary Executions*, A/HRC/44/38, Geneva: UNGA. Retrieved from: www.ohchr.org/en/documents/the matic-reports/ahrc4438-use-armed-drones-targeted-killings-report-special-rapporteur. Accessed: 2 July 2023.

22 Rogers and Goxho, Light Footprint.

Notes

23 J. Rogers (2023). Arctic Drones: A New Security Dilemma?, *Geographical Journal*. Early view.

24 J. Rogers and D. Kunertova (2022). *The Vulnerabilities of the Drone Age: Established Threats and Emerging Issues out to 2035*, NATO SPS/CSS/CWS. Zurich: ETH Zurich. Retrieved from: www.research-collection.ethz.ch/handle/20.500.11850/556165. Accessed: 24 April 2024; Rogers and Goxho, Light Footprint.

25 Rogers, Iran and Turkey have become Drone Powers; Rogers, Arria-Formula Meeting on Transnational Terrorist Threats.

26 Chris Woods, quoted in M. Farooq (2019). The Second Drone Age: How Turkey Defied the US and Became a Killer Drone Power, *Intercept*. Retrieved from: https://theinter cept.com/2019/05/14/turkey-second-drone-age/. Accessed: 14 July 2022.

27 B. Ziarnick (2021). *To Rule the Skies: General Thomas S. Power and the Rise of Strategic Air Command in the Cold War*, Annapolis, MD: Naval Institute Press; J.A. Olsen (2023). *Airpower Pioneers: From Billy Mitchell to Dave Deptula*, Annapolis, MD: Naval Institute Press; F. Kaplan (1983). *The Wizards of Armageddon*, Stanford, CA: Stanford University Press; S.M. Pavelec (2010). *The Jet Race and the Second World War*, Annapolis, MD: Naval Institute Press; E. Kaplan (2015). *To Kill Nations: American Strategy in the Air-Atomic Age and the Rise of Mutually Assured Destruction*, Ithaca, NY: Cornell University Press; S. Budainsky (2005). *Air Power: The Men, Machines, and Ideas that Revolutionized War, From Kitty Hawk to Iraq*, London: Penguin; P.W. Singer (2010). *Wired for War: The Robotics Revolution and Conflict in the 21st Century*, New York: Penguin; D. Axe (2021). *Drone War Vietnam*, Annapolis, MD: Naval Institute Press; D.A. Rosenberg (1984). The Origins of Overkill: Nuclear Weapons and American Strategy, 1945–1960. In S. Miller (ed.), *Strategy and Nuclear Deterrence: An International Security Reader* (pp. 133–183). Princeton, NJ: Princeton University Press; M. Zehfuss (2011). Targeting: Precision and the Production of Ethics, *European Journal of International Relations*, Vol. 17 (3), pp. 543–566; M. Evangelista and H. Shue (2014). *The American Way of Bombing: Changing Ethical and Legal Norms, from Flying Fortresses to Drones*, London: Cornell University Press; S.D. Sagan (1989). *Moving Targets: Nuclear Strategy and National Security*, Princeton, NJ: Princeton University Press; R.A. Pape (1996). *Bombing to Win: Air Power and Coercion in War*, New York: Cornell University Press; D. Mackenzie (1990). *Inventing Accuracy: A Historical Sociology of Nuclear Missile Guidance*, London: MIT Press.

Chapter 1

1 According to Mark Van Wienen, 'I Didn't Raise my Boy to be a Solider' sold 650,000 copies during its first three months and became one of 1915's top-selling songs in the United States. See M.W. Van Wienen, (2002). *Rendezvous with Death: American Poems of the Great War*. Champaign: University of Illinois Press, p. 80. For song lyrics see A. Bryan (1915). 'I Didn't Raise My Boy to Be a Soldier' [sheet music], Historic Sheet Music Collection, 1642, Connecticut College. Retrieved from: https://digitalcommons.con ncoll.edu/sheetmusic/1642. Accessed: 23 July 2022.

2 As RAND's Paula G. Thornhill argued, it was the ethos of 'over not through' which defined American strategic thought during this period. No longer was going 'through' the battlefield and incurring the heavy costs of war acceptable. It was time to achieve victory by going 'over' the battlefield and bombing the enemy industry through precision air power. Paula, G. Thornhill. Personal interview. 11 December 2015.

3 Alan, J. Vick. Personal interview. 10 December 2015.

Notes

4 W. Millis (1986). *Arms and Men: A Study in American Military History*, New Brunswick, NJ: Rutgers University Press, p. 259.

5 C.C. Crane (1993). *Bombs, Cities and Civilians: American Airpower Strategy in World War II*, Lawrence: University of Kansas Press, p. 1.

6 The term 'Old World' denotes an American perception of Europe and often refers to the brutal perpetual cycle of warfare between European nations. From its very foundation this was not to be the new 'American way'. As Cox and Quinn stated, 'the United States was created as a way of furthering liberal ideals at home, while averting the creation of a European-style state system in North America, which realist-type thinking led the founders to believe would inexorably generate power balancing and war'. A. Quinn and M. Cox, (2007). For Better, for Worse: How America's Foreign Policy became Wedded to Liberal Universalism, *Global Society*. Vol. 21 (4), pp. 499–519. Also see D. Bönker (2012). *Militarism in a Global Age: Naval Ambitions in Germany and the United States before World War I*, New York: Cornell University Press, p. 188.

7 A. Leland and M.J. Oboroceanu (2010). *American War and Military Operations Casualties: Lists and Statistics*, Washington, DC: Congressional Research Service, p. 2.

8 A. Kramer (2007). *Dynamic of Destruction: Culture and Mass Killing in the First World War*, Oxford: Oxford University Press, p. 2.

9 Crane, *Bombs, Cities and Civilians*, p. 19.

10 D.A. Pisano (2011). General William 'Billy' Mitchell and the Sinking of the Ostfriesland: A Consideration, *Smithsonian National Air and Space Museum Airspace Blog*. Retrieved from: https://airandspace.si.edu/stories/editorial/general-william-%E2%80%9Cbilly%E2%80%9D-mitchell-and-sinking-ostfriesland-considerationoL. Accessed: 10 October 2013. Also see Dominick Pisano. Personal interview. 10 June 2014.

11 J. Virden (2008). *Americans and the Wars of the Twentieth Century*, Basingstoke: Palgrave Macmillan, p. 41.

12 S.L. McFarland (1995). *America's Pursuit of Precision Bombing: 1910–1945*, London: Smithsonian Institution Press, p. 3.

13 M. Clodfelter (2010). *Beneficial Bombing: The Progressive Foundations of American Air Power, 1917–1945*, Lincoln: University of Nebraska Press, p. 3.

14 E.S. Gorrell (1941). What! No Airplanes. Edgar S. Gorrell Collection, National Air and Space Museum, Washington, DC, Archives Division. Accession No. XXXX-0057, Box 4, Folder 11.

15 For early discussion on the utility of air power see the Senate Committee on Military Affairs debate on aircraft production during the 65th Congress 2nd Session, 1918. See US Congress Senate Committee on Military Affairs (1918). *Aircraft Production, Vol. II. 65th Cong., 2nd Sess.*, Edgar S. Gorrell Collection, National Air and Space Museum, Washington, DC, Archives Division. Accession No. XXXX-0057, Box 1, Folder 7.

16 Gorrell, What! No Airplanes.

17 E.S. Gorrell (1919). History of the Air Service, AEF. Excerpts reprinted in M. Maurer (ed.), *The US Air Service in World War I: Vol. II* (pp. 141–159). Washington, DC: Office of Air Force History, 1978.

18 Ibid.

19 E.S. Gorrell (1917). Strategical Bombardment. Reprinted in M. Maurer (ed.), *The US Air Service in World War I: Vol. II* (pp. 141–159). Washington, DC: Office of Air Force History, 1978. See also Clodfelter, *Beneficial Bombing*, p. 33.

20 E.S. Gorrell (1919). *History of the American Expeditionary Forces Air Service, 1917–1919*. Library of Congress, Washington, DC, MF, Shelf 22,664, Vol. XI, Reel 16.

Notes

21 Gorrell, Strategical Bombardment. See also Clodfelter, *Beneficial Bombing*, p. 33.

22 Gorrell, Strategical Bombardment.

23 Ibid.

24 Crane, *Bombs, Cities and Civilians*, p. 12.

25 Gorrell, History of the Air Service.

26 Ibid.

27 Clodfelter, *Beneficial Bombing*, p. 33.

28 Other air power strategists were influential in the development of American air power strategy over the inter-war period. The Marshal of the Royal Air Force, Hugh 'Boom' Trenchard, and the Russian/American air power strategist, Major Alexander P. de Seversky, are key examples. See A.P. de Seversky (1942). *Victory Through Air Power*, New York: Simon & Schuster.

29 B. Heuser (2014). *The Bomb: Nuclear Weapons in their Historical, Strategic and Ethical Context*, London: Routledge, p. 48.

30 Crane, *Bombs, Cities and Civilians*, p. 16.

31 Mitchell believed the striking of cities was important, but it was the striking of the 'sources of raw materials, his manufactories, his food, his products, his means of transportation and his railway and steamship lines', not the civilians, that were to be considered priorities. W. Mitchell (1960). *Memoirs of World War I: From Start to Finish of Our Greatest War*, New York: Random House, p. 3.

32 W. Mitchell (2009). *Winged Defence: The Development and Possibilities of Modern Air Power – Economic and Military*, Tuscaloosa: University of Alabama Press, p. 127.

33 Ibid.

34 W. Mitchell (1930). *Skyways: A Book on Modern Aeronautics*, Philadelphia, PA: J.B. Lippincott, pp. 262–263.

35 For more on the utility of American air power during the inter-war period see W. Mitchell (1928). America, Airpower, and the Pacific. General William Mitchell Papers, Library of Congress, Washington, DC, Manuscript Division, Box 24.

36 J. Tate (1998). *The Army and its Air Corps: Army Policy toward Aviation, 1919–1941*, Alabama: Air University Press, p. 2.

37 See A.F. Hurley (1975). *Billy Mitchell: Crusader for Air Power*, Bloomington: Indiana University Press, p. 47. See also R.F. Futrell (1989). *Ideas, Concepts, Doctrine: Basic Thinking in the United States Air Force 1907–1960*, Vol. 1, Alabama: Air University Press, p. 34.

38 J. Whiteclay Chambers (ed.) (1999). *The Oxford Companion to American Military History*, Oxford: Oxford University Press, p. 23.

39 J.J. Cooke (2002). *Billy Mitchell*, Boulder, CO: Lynne Rienner, p. 115.

40 Tate, *The Army and its Air Corps*, p. 3.

41 Ibid.

42 Futrell, *Ideas, Concepts, Doctrine*, p. 33.

43 R.E. McClendon (1954). *Autonomy of the Air Arm*, Alabama: Air University Press, p. 16.

44 Futrell, *Ideas, Concepts, Doctrine*, p. 33.

45 A.P. de Seversky, perf. (1943) *Victory Through Air Power*. Walt Disney. Retrieved from: www.youtube.com/watch?v=tUeKeN9bXSE. Accessed: 2 July 2023.

46 W.J. Boyne (2005). *The Influence of Air Power Upon History*, Barnsley: Pen and Sword Aviation, pp. 143–145.

47 Stephen Bourque. Personal interview. 5 February 2014.

48 Futrell, *Ideas, Concepts, Doctrine*, p. 51.

Notes

49 W. Mitchell (1921). *Our Air Force: The Keystone of National Defense*, New York: E.P. Dutton & Company, p. 67.

50 Ibid., p. 66.

51 Ibid.

52 Ibid., p. 121.

53 W.J. Boyne (1996). The Spirit of Billy Mitchell. *Air Force Magazine*, June. Retrieved from: www.airforcemag.com/MagazineArchive/Pages/1996/June%201996/0696billy.aspx. Accessed: 8 August 2016.

54 Ibid.

55 Tate, *The Army and its Air Corps*, p. 16.

56 A.H. Wagner and L.E. Braxton (2012). *Birth of a Legend: The Bomber Mafia and the Y1B-17*, Bloomington, IN: Trafford Publishing, p. 87.

57 Boyne, The Spirit of Billy Mitchell.

58 Cooke, *Billy Mitchell*, p. 126.

59 Wagner and Braxton, *Birth of a Legend*, p. 86.

60 Ibid.

61 Boyne, *The Influence of Air Power Upon History*, p. 126.

62 Wagner, and Braxton, *Birth of a Legend*, p. 88.

63 Boyne, *The Influence of Air Power Upon History*, p. 146.

64 J.T. Correll (2008). Billy Mitchell and the Battleships. *Air Force Magazine*, June, pp. 62–68.

65 Wagner and Braxton, *Birth of a Legend*, p. 89.

66 S. Budiansky (2004). *Air Power: The Men, Machines, and Ideas that Revolutionized War, from Kitty Hawk to Iraq*, New York: Penguin, p. 149.

67 Tate, *The Army and its Air Corps*, p. 16.

68 Ibid.

69 Ibid., p. 17.

70 D.E. Johnson (1998). *Fast Tanks and Heavy Bombers: Innovation in the US Army, 1917–1945*, New York: Cornell University Press, p. 83.

71 Ibid.

72 R.P. Hallion (1996). Preface. In R.E. McClendon, *Autonomy of the Air Arm* (pp. v–vi). Alabama: Air University Press, p. v.

73 Of course, Mitchell would only have been truly happy after his death when the National Security Act of 1947 created the independent Department of the Air Force. See US Senate Select Committee on Intelligence (1947). *The National Security Act 1947*. Retrieved from: www.intelligence.senate.gov/nsact1947.pdf. Accessed: 11 November 2013.

74 Boyne, *The Influence of Air Power Upon History*, p. 147.

75 Tate, *The Army and its Air Corps*, p. 3.

76 Boyne, *The Influence of Air Power Upon History*, p. 147.

77 D. Davis (1967). *The Billy Mitchell Affair*, New York: Random House, p. 285.

78 L.J. Matthews (1998). The Speech Rights of Air Professionals, *Airpower Journal*. Vol. XII (3), pp. 19–30.

79 Davis, *The Billy Mitchell Affair*, p. 247.

80 Boyne, The Spirit of Billy Mitchell.

81 As Spaatz, the future first Chief of Staff of an autonomous United States Air Force, stated in support of Mitchell's arguments, 'the next war would start in the air and … the United Stated lacked preparedness for such a war'. See Futrell, *Ideas, Concepts, Doctrine*, p. 44.

Notes

82 R.W. Harper (1948). Editorial, *Air University Quarterly Review*. Vol. 2 (3), p. 76.

83 Boyne, The Spirit of Billy Mitchell.

84 ACTS was first established at Langley Field, Virginia, in 1920. For more on ACTS see D. Mets (2009). *Airpower and Technology: Smart and Unmanned Weapons*, London: Praeger Security International, pp. 23–25.

85 See J.R. Cody (1996). *AWPD-42 to Instant Thunder: Consistent Evolutionary Thought or Revolutionary Change*, Alabama: Air University Press.

86 Arnold defended Mitchell at his court martial; they had been passionate proponents of air power from its conception within American strategic thought. It is interesting to note that Arnold was one of the first two pilots trained in the US military. He was trained by the pioneers of the airplane, the Wright brothers. Peter Jakub. Personal interview. 12 December 2015.

87 R.A. Pape (1996). *Bombing to Win: Air Power and Coercion in War*, New York: Cornell University Press, pp. 258–259.

88 M.S. Sherry (1987). *The Rise of American Air Power: The Creation of Armageddon*, London: Yale University Press, p. 58.

89 Crane, *Bombs, Cities and Civilians*, p. 19.

90 Pape, *Bombing to Win*, p. 62.

91 Crane, *Bombs, Cities and Civilians*, p. 26.

92 Devised at the newly established Air War Plans Division in Washington headed by Lieutenant Colonel George.

93 Crane, *Bombs, Cities and Civilians*, p. 26.

94 Wagner and Braxton, *Birth of a Legend*, p. 86.

95 Air Force Systems Command Aeronautical Systems Division (1961). *Development of Airborne Armament 1910–1961*, Washington, DC: Office of Information, p. 10.

96 See P.W. Singer (2010). *Wired for War: The Robotics Revolution and Conflict in the 21st Century*, New York: Penguin, p. 50. See also J. Lea Cate (1959). Development of United States Air Doctrine: 1917–41. In E.M. Emme (ed.), *The Impact of Air Power* (pp. 186–192). New York: Van Nostrand.

97 Air Force Systems Command Aeronautical Systems Division (1961). *Development of Airborne Armament*, p. 11.

98 Ibid.

99 Ibid.

100 Singer, *Wired for War*, p. 50.

101 Air Force Systems Command Aeronautical Systems Division (1961). *Development of Airborne Armament*, p. 10.

102 McFarland, *America's Pursuit of Precision Bombing*, p. 5.

103 As Charles J. 'Chuck' Richardson, who flew in B-17Gs over Europe as part of the 390th Bomb Group (H), 571st Squadron, revealed to me in an interview: 'We bombed the best we could … We could do very well at our bombing ranges in Texas where the skies were clear and we weren't being shot at. But you get over a target and there are planes shooting at you and anti-aircraft shooting at you, and weather conditions are not good. It's amazing that we hit the target at all.' C. Richardson. Personal interview. 4 November 2021. Also see C.J. Richardson (2019). *35 Missions to Hell and Back: A Mighty 8th Air Force, 390th Bomb Group (H) History*, Conneaut Lake, PA: Page Publishing.

104 T. Davis Biddle (2002). *Rhetoric and Reality in Air Warfare: The Evolution of British and American Ideas About Strategic Bombing, 1914–1945*, Woodstock: Princeton University Press, p. 161.

Notes

105 As Heuser writes, '[t]echnology made possible emphasis on the sort of precision bombing which William Mitchell had dreamed of, and on the avoidance of collateral damage and civilian casualties'. Heuser, *The Bomb*, p. 71.

Chapter 2

1 F.D. Roosevelt (September 1, 1939). An Appeal to Great Britain, France, Italy, Germany, and Poland to Refrain from Air Bombing of Civilians. *The American Presidency Project*. Retrieved from: www.presidency.ucsb.edu/documents/appeal-great-britain-france-italy-germany-and-poland-refrain-from-air-bombing-civilians. Accessed: 2 July 2023.

2 Ibid.

3 The precision bombing raid was conducted by the Halverson Detachment. It took place on 11–12 June 1942 and targeted the Ploesti oil fields in Romania. In short, this precision bombing raid 'fell far short of expectations', with only minimal damage caused. More details of this raid are outlined in the following paragraphs on the Ploesti Raid of 1 August 1943. For quotation see E. Cruickshank (1944). *US Air Force Historical Study No. 103; The Ploesti Mission of 1st August 1943*, Washington, DC: Intelligence Historical Division, p. 16.

4 Ibid.

5 W.F. Craven and J.L. Cate (eds) (1983). *The Army Air Force in World War II: Plans & Early Operations January 1939 to August 1942*, Vol. I, Washington, DC: Office of Air Force History, p. 663.

6 Ibid.

7 R.G. Davis (1993). *Carl A. Spaatz and the Air War in Europe*, Washington, DC: Center for Air Force History, p. 98.

8 J.C. Fredriksen (2011). *The United States Air Force: A Chronology*, Santa Barbara, CA: ABC-CLIO, p. 83.

9 Ibid.

10 Stephen Bourque. Personal interview. 5 February 2014.

11 Col. Armstrong (1942). Eaker Gets Silver Star, *New York Times*, 23 August. Retrieved from: http://query.nytimes.com/gst/abstract.html?res=9505EEDE1E3CE33BBC4C5 1DFBE668389659EDE&legacy=true. Accessed: 7 July 2016.

12 F.L. Kluckhohn (1942). Flying Fortresses Bomb Rouen in First All-US Blow at Nazis, *New York Times*, 18 August. Retrieved from: http://query.nytimes.com/gst/abstract. html?res=9E04E7D91239E33BBC4052DFBE668389659EDE&legacy=true. Accessed: 8 August 2016.

13 Ibid.

14 D.L. Miller (2007). *Masters of the Air: America's Bomber Boys Who Fought the Air War Against Nazi Germany*, New York: Simon & Schuster, p. 31.

15 Kluckhohn, Flying Fortresses Bomb Rouen.

16 It is also interesting to note that in 1942 the author John Steinbeck was invited to speak with President Roosevelt and General Arnold. Steinbeck said that they 'personally talked him into writing' a propagandist book highlighting the positive impact of air power and precision. Although against it at first, according to Steinbeck, during the meeting the President stated: 'Now John, you are going to do what I want you to do.' This is yet another example of how important it was for US airpower and precision

to been seen in a positive light by the US public. See J.J. Benson (1990). *John Steinbeck, Writer: A Biography*, London: Penguin, pp. 507–509. See also J. Steinbeck (2009). *Bombs Away: The Story of a Bomber Team*, London: Penguin.

17 Richard. P. Hallion. Personal interview. 22 June 2014.

18 Ibid.

19 P. Fussell (1989). *Wartime: Understanding and Behaviour in the Second World War*, Oxford: Oxford University Press, p. 14.

20 S.L. McFarland (1995). *America's Pursuit of Precision Bombing: 1910–1945*, London: Smithsonian Institution Press, p. 5.

21 C.G. Hearn (2008). *Air Force: An Illustrated History*, London: Compendium Publishing, p. 59.

22 Craven and Cate, *The Army Air Force in World War II*, p. 663.

23 E. Florentin and C. Archambault (1997). *Quand Les Alliés Bombardaient La France*, Paris: Perrin, p. 64.

24 Stephen Bourque. Personal interview. 5 February 2014. For more information on the attacks from a French perspective see P. Le Trevier (2005). *17 août 1942: Objectif-ROUEN*, Le Mesnil: Comever – De Rameau Publishing.

25 P.W. Singer (2010). *Wired for War: The Robotics Revolution and Conflict in the 21st Century*, New York: Penguin, p. 50.

26 Air Force Systems Command Aeronautical Systems Division (1961). *Development of Airborne Armament 1910–1961*, Washington, DC: Office of Information, pp. 12–13.

27 Ibid.

28 G. Butzata (ed.) (2004). *A History of Romanian Oil*, Vol. II, Bucharest: Mica Valahie Publishing House, p. 249.

29 Cruickshank, *US Air Force Historical Study No. 103*, p. 12.

30 Ibid.

31 Ibid., p. 11.

32 Ibid., p. 16.

33 Ibid., p. 17.

34 Ibid.

35 J. Parton (1986). *Air Force Spoken Here: General Ira Eaker and the Command of the Air*, Bethesda, MD: Adler & Adler, p. 264.

36 R.J. Modrovsky (1999). *1 August 1943 – Today's Target is Ploesti: A Departure From Doctrine*, Montgomery: Air University, p. 19.

37 Cruickshank, *US Air Force Historical Study No. 103*, p. 17.

38 D. Martin (2006). Gen. Jacob E. Smart, Ploesti Raid Strategist, Dies at 97, *New York Times*, 16 November. Retrieved from: www.nytimes.com/2006/11/16/obituaries/16smart. html. Accessed: 10 July 2016.

39 Cruickshank, *US Air Force Historical Study No. 103*, p. 29.

40 In regard to the raid intending to be low-cost the author understands Arnold and Smart 'recognized [the mission] as being extremely hazardous' but felt that 'a single such attack might in the long run be even more economical than numerous attacks at high altitude'. As such, comparatively, zero-altitude precision was seen as a means to keep American casualties to a minimum in the long run. See Cruickshank, *US Air Force Historical Study No. 103*, pp. 22–29.

41 M. Hill (1993). *Black Sunday: Ploesti*, Atglen: Schiffer, pp. 14–16.

42 Modrovsky, *1 August 1943*, p. 25.

43 Ibid.

Notes

44 L. Wolff (1960). *Low Level Mission*, London: Panther, p. 128.

45 Ibid.

46 J.Dugan and C. Stewart (2002). *Ploesti: The Great Ground–Air Battle of 1 August 1943*, Dulles: Potomac Books, pp. 86–90.

47 Fussell, *Wartime*, p. 14.

48 Hill, *Black Sunday*.

49 180 were set for the mission, but 'eleven planes in all aborted' for various mechanical reasons before reaching the target. Wolff, *Low Level Mission*, p. 131.

50 *Gaumont British News* (1943). The Ploesti Raid: Liberators' Great Flight to Rumanian Oilfields, *Gaumont British News*, August. Retrieved from: http://bufvc.ac.uk/newson screen/search/index.php/story/63828. Accessed: 10 July 2016.

51 A.R. Silvers (2011). Obituary: Thomas A. Hoff, *Journal Sentinel*, 16 August. Retrieved from: www.legacy.com/us/obituaries/jsonline/name/thomas-hoff-obituary?id=332 4212. Accessed: 2 July 2023.

52 Dugan and Stewart, *Ploesti*, p. 244.

53 R. Miller (2013). Operation Tidalwave: The Low-Level Bombing of the Ploesti Oil Refineries, *Air Force Historical Studies Office*. Retrieved from: www.afhistory.af.mil/FAQs/Fact-Sheets/Article/459003/1943-operation-tidalwave-the-low-level-bombing-of-the-ploesti-oil-refineries-1/. Accessed: 2 July 2013.

54 J. McClain (2013). Tidal Wave Recollections, *Quarterly Magazine of the Air Force Museum Foundation, Friends Journal*, Summer. Retrieved from: www.afhso.af.mil/shared/media/document/AFD-130805-031.pdf. Accessed: 10 July 2016 (no longer available).

55 The loss of aircraft figures was disputed. The *New York Times* stated that 54 of 177 planes were lost in action. See Martin, Gen. Jacob E. Smart, Ploesti Raid Strategist, Dies at 97.

56 Miller, Operation Tidalwave.

57 Enemy Oil Committee (1943). *Western Axis Subcommittee Report: Estimated Refinery Output in Axis Europe, 1943*, Washington, DC: Foreign Economic Administration, pp. 1–21.

58 The USAAF leadership repeatedly had to justify precision bombing to the British who were sceptical as to its effectiveness and wanted the Americans to join them in area bombing.

59 *Gaumont British News*, The Ploesti Raid.

60 Cruickshank, *US Air Force Historical Study No. 103*, p. 1.

61 N. Hamilton (1984). *Master of the Battlefield: Monty's War Years, 1942–1944*, New York: McGraw-Hill, p. 287.

62 H.S. Wolk (2003). Decision at Casablanca, *Air Force Magazine*. Retrieved from: www.airforcemag.com/MagazineArchive/Pages/2003/January%202003/0103casa.aspx. Accessed: 8 August 2016.

63 H.S. Hansell (1986). *The Strategic Air War Against Germany and Japan: A Memoir*, Washington, DC: Office of Air Force History, p. 211.

64 For Arnold see B. Yenne (2013). *Hap Arnold: The General Who Invented the US Air Force*, Washington, DC: Regnery History, pp. 126–127.

65 Wolk, Decision at Casablanca.

66 For Eaker quotation see ibid.

67 Hansell, *The Strategic Air War Against Germany and Japan*, p. 168.

68 Ibid., p. 52. For more on Hansell see H. Venable (2020). Rescuing a General: General Haywood 'Possum' Hansell and the Burden of Command, *Journal of Military History*. Vol. 84 (2), pp. 487–509.

Notes

69 W.F. Craven and J.L. Cate (eds) (1966). *The Army Air Forces in World War II: The Pacific: Matterhorn to Nagasaki June 1944 to August 1945*, Vol. V, London: University of Chicago Press, pp. 565–566.

70 Ibid., p. 565.

71 Ibid., p. 564.

72 Hansell, *The Strategic Air War Against Germany and Japan*, p. 228.

73 For a detailed breakdown of this history see M. Gladwell (2021). *The Bomber Mafia: Dream, a Temptation, and the Longest Night of the Second World War*, London: Little Brown.

74 Hansell, *The Strategic Air War Against Germany and Japan*, pp. 227–228.

75 Hansell went on to blame consistently heavy cloud cover and a lack of availability for newer precision technologies, such as the APQ-7 Radar, as reasons for the failure of precision bombing in these final few months. See Hansell, *The Strategic Air War Against Germany and Japan*, p. 228.

76 T.R. Searle (2002). 'It Made a Lot of Sense to Kill Skilled Workers': The Firebombing of Tokyo in March 1945, *Journal of Military History*. Vol. 66 (1), pp. 103–133.

77 Roosevelt, An Appeal to Great Britain, France, Italy, Germany, and Poland.

78 A.T. Harris (1947). *Bomber Offensive*, New York: Macmillan, p. 147.

79 Searle, 'It Made a Lot of Sense to Kill Skilled Workers', pp. 103–133.

80 R.M. Neer (2013). *Napalm: An American Biography*, London: Harvard University Press, p. 83.

81 Hansell, *The Strategic Air War Against Germany and Japan*, p. 217.

82 Craven and Cate, *The Army Air Forces in World War II: Vol. V*, p. 610.

83 With the release of the Magic files in 1978, the author of *Downfall* wrote: 'we learned there were only 3 or 4 messages suggesting the possibility of a compromised peace, while no fewer than 13 affirmed that Japan fully intended to fight to the bitter end … after all, the official Japanese position, adopted in an Imperial Conference in June 1945 with the emperor's sanction, was a fight to the finish'. R.B. Frank (2005). Why Truman Dropped the Bomb. *The Weekly Standard*, 8 August. Retrieved from: www.washingtonexaminer.com/weekly-standard/why-truman-dropped-the-bomb. Accessed: 2 July 2023. Also see M. McFate (2005). Anthropology and Counterinsurgency: The Strange Story of their Curious Relationship, *Military Review*. Vol. 85 (2), pp. 24–38, at p. 31.

84 Furthermore, the US had known from as early as the 1920s that Japanese housing was predominately close together and made of wood and paper. Thus, by using incendiary and cluster bombs, the US could successfully conduct the firebombing of the 'inflammable residential construction' and ultimately coerce the Japanese into unconditional surrender. See Craven and Cate, *The Army Air Forces in World War II: Vol. V*, p. 610. See also United States Strategic Bombing Survey (1946). *Summary Report Pacific War*, Washington, DC: Government Printing Office.

85 Ibid., p. 17.

86 Ibid.

87 Ibid.

88 K. Spitzer (2012). A Forgotten Horror: The Great Tokyo Air Raid. *Time*, 27 March. Retrieved from: nation.time.com/2012/03/27/a-forgotten-horror-the-great-tokyo-air-raid. Accessed: 20 February 2014.

89 F. Gibney (ed.) (2007). *SENSŌ: The Japanese Remember the Pacific War: Letters to the Editor of the Asahi Shimbun*, New York: M.E. Sharpe, p. 205.

90 For the figure of 185,000 see United States Strategic Bombing Survey, *Summary Report Pacific War*, p. 20. For the figure of 130,000 see M.S. Sherry (1987). *The Rise of American Air Power: The Creation of Armageddon*, London: Yale University Press, p. 413.

Notes

91 C.C. Crane (1993). *Bombs, Cities and Civilians: American Airpower Strategy in World War II*, Lawrence: University of Kansas Press, p. 9.

92 Crane, *Bombs, Cities and Civilians*, p. 10.

93 United States Strategic Bombing Survey, *Summary Report Pacific War*, p. 17.

94 For a comprehensive list of secondary cities targeted and the square miles destroyed see Craven and Cate, *The Army Air Forces in World War II: Vol. V*, pp. 674–675.

95 Sherry, *The Rise of American Air Power*, p. 413.

96 As Crane stated, 'A quick and overwhelming victory served both purposes'. See Crane, *Bombs, Cities and Civilians*, p. 9.

97 Hansell, *The Strategic Air War Against Germany and Japan*, p. 252.

98 United States Strategic Bombing Survey, *Summary Report Pacific War*, p. 17.

99 Much has been written about the likelihood of Japanese surrender occurring before such a ground invasion became necessary. In August 1945, however, plans for a cost-heavy ground invasion, with firebombing support, were in the latter stages of planning and were perceived as the realistic next step for the US in an attempt to ensure victory. For further study of this debate see G. Alperovitz (1995). *The Decision to Use the Atomic Bomb and the Architecture of an American Myth*, New York: Alfred A Knopf.

100 H.L. Stimson (1947). The Decision to use the Atomic Bomb. *Harper's Magazine*, February. Retrieved from: http://harpers.org/archive/1947/02/the-decision-to-use-the-atomic-bomb/. Accessed: 16 April 2016.

101 Ibid.

102 'I asked General Marshall what it would cost in lives to land on the Tokio plain and other places in Japan. It was his opinion that such an invasion would cost at a minimum one quarter of a million casualties, and might cost as much as a million, on the American side alone, with equal number of the enemy. The other military and naval men present agreed.' Craven and Cate, *The Army Air Forces in World War II: Vol. V*, p. 712.

103 This was alongside the continued blockade of the nation. This was a similar strategy to that used by the British in the blockade of Germany during the First World War and is commonly held to be responsible for the death of 763,000 civilians. *The Times* (1919). Through German Eyes: The Blockade, 18 January, p. 7.

104 R.B. Frank (2001). *Downfall: The End of the Imperial Japanese Empire*, London: Penguin, p. 350.

105 Ibid.

106 Ibid.

107 Ibid.

108 Just before the above quote, Stimson stated to the gathered Interim Committee of generals, policymakers, and scientists (such as Fermi and Oppenheimer), that the administration 'did not regard it [the atomic bomb] as a new weapon, merely but as a revolutionary change in the relations of man to the universe…'. H.L. Stimson (1945). Diary Entry, 31 May. Henry Lewis Stimson Papers, Sterling Memorial Library, Yale University, New Haven, Manuscripts and Archives. Box No. 77, Folder No. 51, p. 146.

109 The USS *Augusta* was the presidential flagship and in this capacity was carrying President Truman from the Potsdam Conference in Germany where the ultimatum of Japanese unconditional surrender was agreed. This was subsequently rejected by Japan, at which point the President gave his orders. See H.S. Truman (1952). Letter to James L. Cate, 6 December. President's Secretary's File, Truman Papers, The Harry S. Truman Library and Museum, Independence. Box 1, Folder 7. Also see Craven and Cate, *The Army Air Forces in World War II: Vol.V*, pp. 713–716.

Notes

110 As Walker argued, Truman had 'wanted his advisers to consider carefully the need for using the bomb against Japan and to spell out the options available to him'. S.J. Walker (2004). *Prompt and Utter Destruction: Truman and the Use of Atomic Bombs Against Japan*, Chapel Hill: University of North Carolina Press, pp. 1–5. For dates see Craven and Cate, *The Army Air Forces in World War II: Vol. V*, p. 714.

111 Ibid., pp. 720–725.

112 Keiko Ogura. Personal interview for the Warfare Podcast (2022). Hiroshima: A Survivor's Story, *Warfare* podcast. Retrieved from: https://podcasts.apple.com/us/podcast/hiroshima-a-survivors-story/id1526490428?i=1000575076426. Accessed: 26 February 2022.

113 For more on the closing stages of the war see L. Freedman (2003). *The Evolution of Nuclear Strategy*, Basingstoke: Palgrave, pp. 19–20.

114 This study focuses on the following authors: Freedman, *The Evolution of Nuclear Strategy*; Alperovitz, *The Decision to Use the Atomic Bomb*; Frank, *Downfall*; P. Fussell (1981). Thank God for the Atom Bomb. *The New Republic*, August. Retrieved from: www.uio.no/studier/emner/hf/iakh/HIS1300MET/v12/undervisningsmateriale/Fussel%20-%20thank%20god%20for%20the%20atom%20bomb.pdf. Accessed: 8 August 2016.

115 It should be noted that the accuracy of Truman's diary is contested. For more on this issue see Alperovitz, *The Decision to Use the Atomic Bomb*. For quotation see H.S. Truman (1945). Harry S. Truman, Personal diary, 25 July 1945. Retrieved from: https://web.mit.edu/21h.102/www/Primary%20source%20collections/World%20War%20II/Truman,%20Diary.html. Accessed: 2 July 2023.

116 Stimson confirmed this in his 'Memorandum for the President' on 2 July 1945 when he stated: 'Our own bombing should be confined to military objectives as far as possible.' H.L. Stimson (1945). Diary Entry, 31 May. Henry Lewis Stimson Papers, Sterling Memorial Library, Yale University, New Haven, Manuscripts and Archives. Box No. 77, Folder No. 51, p. 146. For Truman quote see H.S. Truman (1945). Harry S. Truman, Personal diary, 25 July 1945. Retrieved from: https://web.mit.edu/21h.102/www/Primary%20source%20collections/World%20War%20II/Truman,%20Diary.html. Accessed: 2 July 2023.

117 Craven and Cate, *The Army Air Forces in World War II: Vol. V*, p. 715.

118 Stimson gave a second reason, saying he 'was fearful that before we could get ready the Air Force might have Japan so thoroughly bombed out that the new weapon would not have a fair background to show its strength', to which Truman 'laughed and said he understood'. As stated, this shows the complex and contradictory factors motivating the bomb's deployment on Japan. H.L. Stimson (1945). Diary Entry, 31 May. Henry Lewis Stimson Papers, Sterling Memorial Library, Yale University, New Haven, Manuscripts and Archives. Box No. 77, Folder No. 51, p. 146.

119 Stimson, The Decision to use the Atomic Bomb.

120 Ibid.

121 H.S. Truman (1945). Radio Report to the American People on the Potsdam Conference, 9 August. Truman Papers, The Harry S. Truman Presidential Library and Museum, Independence. Retrieved from: www.trumanlibrary.gov/soundrecording-records/sr61-37-radio-report-american-people-potsdam-conference. Accessed: 2 July 2023.

122 L.R. Groves (1962). *Now It Can Be Told: The Story of the Manhattan Project*, Harper: New York, pp. 313–315.

123 This was stated by Lt. Gen. Leslie R. Groves Jr., who oversaw the Manhattan Project. He writes that Tibbets 'was a superb pilot of heavy planes, with years of military flying

experience, and was probably as familiar with the B-29 as anyone in the service'. Groves, *Now It Can Be Told*, p. 314. For more information see R. Goldstein (2007). Paul W. Tibbets Jr., Pilot of Enola Gay, Dies at 92, *New York Times*, 2 November. Retrieved from: www.nytimes.com/2007/11/02/obituaries/02tibbets.html. Accessed: 2 July 2023.

124 Craven and Cate, *The Army Air Forces in World War II: Vol. V*, p. 708.

125 Ibid., p. 697.

126 As Paul Ham stressed, 'Hiroshima, Kokura and Nagasaki' were the three cities intended to be bombed. One factor that led to Hiroshima being bombing was the good weather forecast over the city on the day of the bombing. See P. Ham (2013). *Hiroshima, Nagasaki: The Real Story of the Atomic Bombings and their Aftermath*, London: Doubleday, p. 289. For more details and the in-text quotation see Craven and Cate, *The Army Air Forces in World War II: Vol. V*, p. 716.

127 Report obtained from weather planes. See Craven and Cate, *The Army Air Forces in World War II: Vol. V*, pp. 715–716.

128 Ibid., pp. 719–720.

129 Ibid., pp. 720–725.

130 Ibid.

131 Ibid.

132 For more on the targeting of the bridge see P. Coffey (2014). *American Arsenal: A Century of Weapon Technology and Strategy*, Oxford: Oxford University Press, p. 140. For targeting accuracy statistics see Craven and Cate, *The Army Air Forces in World War II: Vol. V*, pp. 720–725.

133 Ibid.

134 Ibid.

135 Ibid., p. 721.

136 Stimson, H.L. (1945). Diary Entry, 1 June. Henry Lewis Stimson Papers, Sterling Memorial Library, Yale University, New Haven, Manuscripts and Archives. Box No. 77, Folder No. 51, p. 149.

137 Ibid.

138 Coffey, *American Arsenal*, p. 129.

139 Ibid., p. 106.

140 One point to consider here, however, is that there is always a difference between ambition and reality. It is important to note that 24,816 ft of damage is far more (almost 400 per cent more) damage and destruction than the 7,500 ft intended by the planners. Thus the damage may have been barbaric, but was it their intent to cause such destruction? Such questions should rightly be pondered. Craven and Cate, *The Army Air Forces in World War II: Vol. V*, p. 721.

141 M. Sherry (2014). The 'Unintended Consequences' of America's Arsenal, *Los Angeles Reviews of Books*, 13 February. Retrieved from: https://lareviewofbooks.org/review/unintended-consequences-americas-arsenal. Accessed: 17 April 2016. Also see Sherry, *The Rise of American Air Power*, p. 303.

142 Alperovitz, *The Decision to Use the Atomic Bomb*, p. 5.

143 Ibid.

144 William D. Leahy quoted in ibid., p. 5.

145 Eisenhower's 1947 statement on the use of the atomic bomb, in ibid., p. 5.

146 Alperovitz, *The Decision to Use the Atomic Bomb*, p. 5.

147 Ibid., p. 6.

148 Coffey, *American Arsenal*, p. 107.

149 Ibid., p. 108.

150 Freedman, *The Evolution of Nuclear Strategy*, pp. 18–19.

151 Ibid.

152 Ibid., p. 18.

153 Ibid., pp. 18–19.

154 Fussell, *Wartime*.

155 Fussell, Thank God for the Atom Bomb.

156 Ibid., p. 303.

157 Coffey, *American Arsenal*, p. 108.

158 M. Kato (1946). *The Lost War: A Japanese Reporter's Inside Story*, New York: A. Knopf.

159 Craven and Cate, *The Army Air Forces in World War II: Vol. V*, pp. 720–725.

160 Ibid.

161 R. McNamara (2009). Apocalypse Soon, *Foreign Policy*, 21 October. Retrieved from: http://foreignpolicy.com/2009/10/21/apocalypse-soon/. Accessed: 8 August 2016.

162 S. Hatsumi (1952). The Atomic Bomb. In K. Selden and M. Selden (eds), *The Atomic Bomb: Voices from Hiroshima and Nagasaki* (pp. 219–234), London: M.E. Sharpe, p. 127.

163 Others would be left to die in agony from radiation poising over the coming days, weeks, months, and years. Frank, *Downfall*, p. 265.

164 Ibid., p. 246.

Chapter 3

1 H.H. Arnold (1946). Air Force in the Atomic Age. In D. Masters and K. Way (eds), *One World or None* (pp. 70–90), New York: McGraw-Hill.

2 For reference to moral turmoil and the demand for international control from the period see H.S. Truman, M. King and C. Attlee (1945). Atomic Energy: Agreed Declaration by the President of the United States, the Prime Minister of the United Kingdom, and the Prime Minister of Canada, 18 November. *Department of State Bulletin*, Vol. 13 (334), pp. 1–5. For notions of strategic confusion see Freedman – in his influential text *The Evolution of Nuclear Strategy* (now in its third edition 1981, 1989, and 2003), Freedman takes issue with the adjective 'strategic' and its relationship to American nuclear 'strategy'. Specifically, he argued that the 'use of the adjective "strategic" has very little to do with the noun "strategy"', adding that it creates confusion when attempting to understand American nuclear strategy, as 'during the cold war, it was difficult to avoid this sort of use … it was the language in which nuclear issues were discussed'. As a result, Freedman declared that the 'muddled use of this fundamental term prepares us for the muddle of nuclear strategy itself'. This book would argue the converse. It is the notion of the American 'strategic', intrinsic to precision bombardment, which clarifies (and even drives) American nuclear strategy during this confusing and unique period. It is conceded that Freedman is, however, correct that use of the term 'strategic' to refer to the Strategic Arms Limitation Talks (SALT) does lead to later confusion in terminology. Yet this is not the same as confusion in strategy. See L. Freedman (2003). *The Evolution of Nuclear Strategy*, Basingstoke: Palgrave, p. xix.

3 Such notions are epitomised by the declarations of world leaders in 1945 regarding future warfare. As Attlee stated in November 1945, the use of the atomic bomb 'in war can only lead to mutual destruction and the collapse of civilisations'. C. Attlee (1945).

Notes

Memorandum by the Prime Minister: International Control of Atomic Energy, 5 November, London: His Britannic Majesty's Government. Retrieved from: http:// filestore.nationalarchives.gov.uk/pdfs/large/cab-129-4.pdf. Accessed: 2 July 2023. For calls to outlaw war see Chapter 1, Article 2 of the UN Charter. Brought into force in October 1945, it explicitly stated, '[m]embers shall refrain in their international relations from the threat or use of force against the territorial integrity or political independence of any state, or in any other manner inconsistent with the Purposes of the United Nations'. See United Nations (1945). *Charter of the United Nations*: Chapter 1, Article 2. Retrieved from: www.un.org/en/about-us/un-charter/chapter-1. Accessed: 2 July 2023. It was also Truman's view that there would be a 'permanent peace in the world'. See H.S. Truman (1945). Correspondence between Harry S. Truman and Clark Eichelberger, 7 December, Truman Papers, The Harry S. Truman Presidential Library and Museum, Independence. Retrieved from: www.trumanlibrary.gov/ library/research-files/correspondence-between-president-harry-s-truman-and-clark-ei chelberger. Accessed: 2 July 2023.

4 Early endeavours to understand the atomic bomb, which are somewhat differing in opinion, can be found in Brodie's edited collection from 1946. See also this collection for use of the term 'atomic age'. See B. Brodie (1946). War in the Atomic Age. In Bernard Brodie (ed.), *The Absolute Weapon* (pp. 21–69), New York: Harcourt, Brace and Company.

5 As Kennan stated, '[i]n foreign countries Communists will, as a rule, work toward destruction of all forms of personal independence, economic, political or moral. Their system can handle only individuals who have been brought into complete dependence on higher power. Thus, persons who are financially independent – such as individual businessmen, estate owners, successful farmers, artisans and all those who exercise local leadership or have local prestige, such as popular local clergymen or political figures, are anathema.' The threat posed by an expansionist USSR was the threat posed by communism. This ideology Kennan perceived to be at odds with the liberal Western values of capitalism, religious freedom, and cultural diversity. Yet perhaps most importantly, as Kennedy-Pipe adds, Kennan believed the USSR posed a 'threat to liberty and certain versions of justice and human rights'. Such threats were believed to be some of the most pressing and pertinent to future peace and stability. For Kennan see G.F. Kennan (1946). The Charge in the Soviet Union (Kennan) to the Secretary of State, *National Security Archive*. Retrieved from: www.gwu.edu/~nsarchiv/coldwar/ documents/episode-1/kennan.htm. Accessed: 16 April 2015. For Kennedy-Pipe see C. Kennedy-Pipe (2007). *The Origins of the Cold War*, Basingstoke: Palgrave, p. 2.

6 Although Kennan by no means sought to underplay the gravity of his concerns regarding the USSR, he was careful not to overstate the potency of such a threat to America in military terms. In fact, Kennan's wisdom lay in his ability to delineate between the potential threat to American influence and values posed by a Soviet-led communism and the direct threat of military aggression by the USSR to the United States. For example, although he was in little doubt that 'there can be no permanent *modus vivendi* that it is desirable and necessary that the internal harmony of our society be disrupted, our traditional way of life be destroyed', he also believed the USSR was 'still by far the weaker force' in comparison to the might of America and its allies. In addition, he believed the USSR was a nation which 'unlike that of Hitlerite Germany ... does not take unnecessary risks'. As such, for Kennan it was not a military solution which was most fitting. As he declared, the '[p]roblem of how to cope with this force [is]

Notes

undoubtedly the greatest task our diplomacy has ever faced and probably the greatest it will ever have to face. It should be the point of departure from which our political general staff work at present juncture should proceed. It should be approached with the same thoroughness and care as the solution of a major strategic problem in war, and if necessary, with no smaller outlay in planning effort. I cannot attempt to suggest all answers here. But I would like to record my conviction that the problem is within our power to solve – and that without recourse to any general military conflict.' Thus, for Kennan, the threat that an expansionist USSR posed was not one which needed to be countered through military force alone. Instead, in a world where the enemy was perceived to be militarily inferior, it was containment through diplomatic and political means which was paramount. For quotations see. Kennan, The Charge in the Soviet Union. See also 'X' [G.F. Kennan] (1947). The Sources of Soviet Conduct, *Foreign Affairs*. Vol. 25 (4), pp. 566–582.

7 Rosenberg stated that '[f]or two years after Nagasaki, the JCS did not collectively or formally review or approve any plan contemplating the use of atomic bombs'. Although Rosenberg is technically correct that no official war plans were accepted during this period, there were a lot of 'unaccepted' ones. It is important to study the 1946 PINCHER plans that were being constructed by the Joint Chiefs' planners during this period. It was these plans that laid the foundations for subsequent strategic planning. See D.A. Rosenberg (1983). The Origins of Overkill: Nuclear Weapons and American Strategy, 1945–1960, *International Security*. Vol. 7 (4), pp. 3–71.

8 Freedman, *The Evolution of Nuclear Strategy*, p. xix.

9 This use of the term panacea is in reference to Walter Lippmann's 1946 remarks in which he flippantly comments on the American societal perception of the atomic bomb. See W. Lippmann (1946). Why are we Disarming Ourselves?, *Redbrook Magazine*, September, p. 106.

10 Despite the 'failure' of not providing a permanent peace in the world, such a desire would go on to epitomise the founding document of the United Nations and shape international politics post-1945. As Morris stated, '[a] cardinal principle of the UN Charter – the key foundational document of the post-1945 international legal order against which the actions of states are primarily judged – is the prohibition of the use of force found in article 2(4)'. J. Morris (2013). Libya and Syria: The Spectre of the Swinging Pendulum, *International Affairs*. Vol. 89 (5), pp. 1265–1283. For above quotation see Truman, Correspondence between Harry S. Truman and Clark Eichelberger.

11 Truman, King and Attlee, Atomic Energy: Agreed Declaration, pp. 777–820.

12 A. Einstein (1946). The Way Out. In D. Masters and K. Way (eds), *One World or None* (pp. 209–214), New York: McGraw-Hill.

13 P. Morrison (1946). If the Bomb gets out of Hand. In D. Masters and K. Way (eds), *One World or None* (pp. 1–15), New York: McGraw-Hill.

14 Truman, Correspondence between Harry S. Truman and Clark Eichelberger.

15 Ibid.

16 Arnold had his doubts about the prospects of international control (having been a witness to similar attempts following the First World War) and knew the importance of 'peace time' war planning. It is for this reason that Arnold is shrewd in his use of language in the chapter's opening quotation. By phrasing the future deployment of force as a contingency 'pending the establishment' of international controls, he was able to do something many others could not ... begin the strategic thought on nuclear wars of tomorrow. H.H. Arnold (1951). *Global Mission*, London: Hutchinson & Co, pp. 265–267.

Notes

17 D. Masters and K. Way (eds) (1946). *One World or None*, New York: McGraw-Hill.

18 Ibid.

19 L. Szilards (1945). A Petition to the President of the United States, 3 July. Retrieved from: www.atomicarchive.com/Docs/ManhattanProject/SzilardPetition.shtml. Accessed: 12 January 2015.

20 Other contributors included Albert Einstein, Phillip Morris, E.U. Condon, Louis N. Ridenour, Frederick Seitz, Harlow Shapley, Harold C. Urey, Eugene P. Wigner, and Gale Young. Arnold was most definitely in esteemed company. Masters and Way, *One World or None*.

21 The *New York Times* review is found on the back cover of the 2007 reprint of the following book: Masters and Way, *One World or None*. In addition, the *Washington Post* pleaded with its readers, '[f]or the sake of the planet read *One World or None*', while the *New York Herald Tribune* stated that it was 'An illuminating, powerful, threatening, and hopeful statement which will clarify a lot of confused thinking about atomic energy'. Both of these reviews are retrieved from the above source.

22 Arnold, *Global Mission*, p. 268.

23 Ibid.

24 Unlike his namesake Benedict, General Henry H. Arnold was far from a turncoat. There is little doubt that he was pragmatic, hence his eventual deviation from a precision bombing doctrine which was perceived to be underachieving in 1944/45. Yet Arnold's moral and strategic ambition for precision had been present since the early days of air power and it was something that he wished to see achieved. Furthermore, it may be of interest to note that, as Arnold's biographer Daso stated, while he was a cadet at West Point H.H. Arnold had a number of nicknames. One of these was 'Benny' in reference to the infamous and 'obvious Benedict Arnold' associated with the military academy's history. Hence the reference to 'his namesake'. Other studies have claimed that both figures are related. Comprehensive support for this claim, however, has not been found and is beyond the scope of this study. D.A. Daso (2000). *Hap Arnold and the Evolution of American Airpower*, Washington, DC: Smithsonian Institution Press, p. 27.

25 As a 1958 RAND interview with Arnold's close colleague (and Secretary of War for Air during the Second World War) Robert Lovett revealed, during this period 'a predominant attitude to disengage from all wartime pursuits – a disengagement from reality' persisted within the Truman administration. N./N. (1958). Summary Notes on Telephone Discussion with Robert Lovett, Oct. 29, 1958 H.R.G 10/29/58, pp. 1–5. Lawrence Henderson Papers, History of RAND Corporations, 1954–1966, RAND Archives, Santa Monica.

26 Göring had further air power experience obtained from his days as a 'war hero' fighter pilot during the First World War. W. Hastings Burke (2010). Albert Göring, Hermann's Anti-Nazi Brother, *Guardian*, 20 February. Retrieved from: www.theguardian.com/lifeandstyle/2010/feb/20/albert-goering-hermann-goering-brothers. Accessed: 7 May 2015.

27 R. Overy (2012). *Goering: A Rediscovered Interrogation, I.B. Tauris blog*, 21 February. Retrieved from: http://theibtaurisblog.com/2012/02/21/goering-a-rediscovered-interrogation. Accessed: 30 April 2015.

28 This was vindication for Arnold and his drive for precision. It also pleased Arnold that Göring confirmed precision bombing had affected Luftwaffe training. As Göring stated, '[t]he attack on oil retarded the training, and our pilots could not get sufficient

training before they were put in the air, where they were no match for your flyers'. Excerpts from original interview found in Arnold, *Global Mission*, pp. 251–252.

29 As the historian Richard Overy corroborates, 'Göring was adamant that precision bombing was decisive.' Overy, *Goering: A Rediscovered Interrogation*.

30 Excerpts from original interview found in Arnold, *Global Mission*, pp. 251–252.

31 Göring (a man uncertain of his fate or future) was very complimentary about American air power ability to the American General Spaatz. As he declared, '[t]he American aeroplanes are superior technically, and in production. As for personnel, English, German and Americans are equal as fighters in the air.' As such, the veracity of his statements, made under duress, are open to challenge. Excerpts from original interview found in Arnold, *Global Mission*, pp. 251–252.

32 Rosenberg,. The Origins of Overkill.

33 Arnold, *Global Mission*, p. 251.

34 As Arnold stated, 'I have always regretted ... not to have had a chance to talk with Göring after the war was over.' Ibid., p. 250.

35 Ibid., p. 252.

36 It should be noted that the atomic bomb was seen as a popular weapon at a societal level in America due to its role in bringing about the end of a prolonged period of war. As Frank wrote, '[o]pinion polls showed overwhelming support (about 85 percent) for use of the bombs'. See R.B. Frank (2001). *Downfall: The End of the Imperial Japanese Empire*, London: Penguin, p. 331. Furthermore, the American press at the time were in 'unanimous agreement that in the event of war the American people would not only have no question as to the priority of the use of the atomic bomb, but would in fact expect it to be used'. Discussions quoted at the home of Philip Graham, publisher of the *Washington Post*, in R. Rhodes (1996). *Dark Sun: The Making of the Hydrogen Bomb*, New York: Touchstone, p. 327.

37 Arnold, Air Force in the Atomic Age. Also see S. Neale. Personal interview. 1 April 2010.

38 See T.M. Coffee (1982). *HAP: The Story of the US Air Force and the Man who Built it, General Henry H. 'Hap' Arnold*, New York: Viking Press, pp. 10–15.

39 Arnold, Air Force in the Atomic Age.

40 Ibid.

41 Ibid.

42 Ibid.

43 Ibid.

44 Specifically, Arnold mentioned the devastation inflicted by the Luftwaffe on British cities like Coventry. Similar examples can be seen in Hull or London. For more information on the level of destruction see R. Overy (2013). *The Bombing War*, London: Allen Lane.

45 Arnold, Air Force in the Atomic Age.

46 Truman, King and Attlee, Atomic Energy: Agreed Declaration, pp. 777–820.

47 Arnold, Air Force in the Atomic Age.

48 Ibid.

49 Ibid.

50 Ibid.

51 Ibid.

52 Ibid. For alternative definition see S.T. Barratt (2023). Online personal interview. 1 March.

53 Arnold, Air Force in the Atomic Age.

Notes

54 From the interview with Göring, Arnold had found out that this is what the Germans had already started to do in the previous war. As Göring made clear, 'German industry was going underground.' Excerpts from original interview found in Arnold, *Global Mission*, p. 251.

55 Arnold, Air Force in the Atomic Age.

56 Ibid.

57 Ibid.

58 Ibid.

59 Ibid.

60 Ibid.

61 'Active' is an understatement. Arnold's last actions in office in 1946 saw him push through $34 million for 'twenty-eight different AAF guided-missile projects' to ensure his quest for precision could soon become an achievable reality. He also established the RAND Corporation, as a US Air Force think tank, focused on early technical and strategic precision research. This story is explored in the following chapter. Daso, *Hap Arnold and the Evolution of American Airpower*, p. 213.

62 H. Vandenberg (1947). Memorandum to the Secretary of the Air Force, OPD 381, Record Group 341, 8 November. Papers of the Chief of Staff of the United States Air Force, Modern Military Branch, US National Archives, Washington, DC. Quotation originally found in Rosenberg, The Origins of Overkill.

63 C. Clausewitz (2008). *On War*. M. Howard and P. Paret (trans.). Oxford: Oxford University Press, p. 46.

64 Rosenberg, The Origins of Overkill.

65 Ibid.

66 Ibid.

67 It is important to note that, up until 1947, Truman had been unofficially briefed on the nuclear stockpile up to six times by Leahy and Eisenhower (to name but two). It is argued, however, that during these unofficial briefings Truman far from understood the full gravity of the changing atomic situation and technological evolution. Rosenberg is correct in as much that Truman was not 'officially' briefed until 1947. However, the situation was more complex, and it is perhaps more accurate to state that Truman did not fully understand the atomic situation until 1947. This only further adds to the uncertainty of the period. Rosenberg, The Origins of Overkill.

68 As Rosenberg explains, it was 'with the approval of the president [that the NSC] defined national security objectives'. Rosenberg, The Origins of Overkill.

69 S.T. Ross (1996). *American War Plans 1945–1950*, London: Frank Cass, p. 15.

70 Rosenberg, The Origins of Overkill, pp. 3–71.

71 As Tannenwald stated, 'using the bomb did trouble Truman'. See N. Tannenwald (2007). *The Nuclear Taboo: The United States and the Non-Use of Nuclear Weapons Since 1945*, Cambridge: Cambridge University Press, p. 88.

72 Ibid.

73 W.W. Butterworth (1948). Memorandum to James Q. Reber of the Executive Secretariat, Department of State. In United States Department of State (ed.), *Foreign Relations of the United States*, Vol. I (p. 630), Washington, DC: Government Printing Office, Department of State.

74 US Air Force (1954). *Biographies: General Hoyt S. Vandenberg*. Retrieved from: www.af.mil/AboutUs/Biographies/Display/tabid/225/Article/105311/general-hoyt-s-vandenberg.aspx. Accessed: 27 February 2023.

75 Vandenberg, Memorandum to the Secretary of the Air Force.

76 Ibid.

77 National Security Council (1948). United States Policy on Atomic Warfare: NSC-30. In United States Department of State (ed.), *Foreign Relations of the United States*, Vol. I (pp. 624–628). Washington, DC: Government Printing Office, Department of State.

78 Ibid.

79 Ibid.

80 Ibid.

81 Such lack of clarity was picked up on by high-level members of the American political elites. A case in point was Director of the Office of Far Eastern Affairs, Butterworth, who criticised NSC-30 and its lack of clarity and guidance by stating, 'the question to be decided is not whether we should or should not use atomic weapons ... The question is rather when and how such weapons should be used. Should we, for example, in the event of war, begin by bombing major centers of population in enemy territory or start with smaller centers important for transportation or specific industries?' Butterworth, Memorandum to James Q. Reber.

82 National Security Council (1948). US Objectives with Respect to the USSR to Counter Soviet Threats to US Security: NSC-20/4. In United States Department of State (ed.), *Foreign Relations of the United States*, Vol. I (pp. 663–669), Washington, DC: Government Printing Office, Department of State.

83 Ibid.

84 Ibid.

85 Rosenberg, The Origins of Overkill.

86 Lippmann's comment reflects his opinion on the atomic bomb. He was cynical and sceptical about the American focus and reliance on such weapons. Lippmann, Why are we Disarming Ourselves?, p. 106.

87 As the chapter proceeds to explain, these factors would soon be part of official American atomic strategy. This was no coincidence. Arnold, we must remember, was an influential member of the JCS while the first atomic strategy (PINCHER) was being formed. As Ross stated, '[i]n 1945 the service chiefs were men of vast experience. Generals Marshall and Arnold and Admirals King and Leahy and their successors Generals Eisenhower and Spaatz and Admiral Nimitz had guided America's armed forces to victory in the Second World War.' Ross, *American War Plans 1945–1950*, pp. 3–4.

88 F. Kaplan (1983). *The Wizards of Armageddon*, Stanford, CA: Stanford University Press, pp. 40–41.

89 Ibid.

90 Here Kaplan is channelling the popular strategic thought of Bernard Brodie. As is explained in Chapter 5, Brodie condoned such notions between 1946 and 1950. Kaplan, *The Wizards of Armageddon*, p. 38.

91 It is also worth noting that the air leaders of the period (such as Vandenberg, Spaatz, and Arnold) regarded atomic bombs as simply a more effective continuation of the bombs they had been using routinely in the previous war. As was made clear at a meeting between these men on 23 October 1945, '[t]he atomic bomb has not altered our basic concept of the strategic air offensive but has given us an additional weapon'. Thus, it is not surprising that, for these men, a strategy deemed effective for conventional weapons should seem fit for the deployment of atomic weapons. All three were signatories to this declaration. See B. Cillessen (1998). Embracing the Bomb: Ethics,

Notes

Morality, and Nuclear Deterrence in the US Air Force, 1945–1955, *Journal of Strategic Studies*. Vol. 21 (1), pp. 96–134.

92 Ross, *American War Plans 1945–1950*, p. 25.

93 Ibid., p. ix.

94 JSP 789, Concept of Operations for 'PINCHER' (2 March 1946).

95 Ibid.

96 Ibid.

97 Ibid.

98 Ibid.

99 Ross, *American War Plans 1945–1950*, p. 26.

100 JSP 789, Concept of Operations for 'PINCHER' (2 March 1946).

101 Ibid.

102 Ibid.

103 Ibid.

104 For instance, PINCHER stated the need to 'Provide for early destruction of Soviet naval forces and shipping. Ibid.

105 Ibid.

106 Ibid.

107 Ibid.

108 W. Mitchell (2009). *Winged Defence: The Development and Possibilities of Modern Air Power – Economic and Military*, Tuscaloosa: University of Alabama Press, p. 127.

109 E.S. Gorrell (1917). Strategical Bombardment. Reprinted in M. Maurer (ed.), *The US Air Service in World War I: Vol. II* (pp. 141–159). Washington, DC: Office of Air Force History, 1978, p. 151.

110 JSP 789, Concept of Operations for 'PINCHER' (2 March 1946).

111 Ibid.

112 Ibid.

113 Ibid.

114 Ibid.

115 Ibid.

116 Ibid.

117 As Ross stated, 'future war plans were … directly influenced by the PINCHER estimates and proposals'. Ross, *American War Plans 1945–1950*, p. 48.

118 Rosenberg, The Origins of Overkill.

119 JSPG 496/4, Joint Outline War Plan for Fiscal Year 1949 'BROILER' (18 December 1947).

120 Ibid.

121 Ibid.

122 Ibid.

123 Ibid.

124 Ibid.

125 Ibid.

126 Foreign Policy Studies Branch (1948). *The Berlin Crisis: Research Project No. 171*, Washington, DC: Department of State, p. 3.

127 H.S. Truman (1949). Statement by President Harry S. Truman Announcing the First Atomic Explosion in the USSR, 23 September, *Project of the Nuclear Age Peace Foundation*. Retrieved from: www.nuclearfiles.org/menu/key-issues/nuclear-weapons/history/cold-war/us-soviet-relations/statement-truman-ussr-first-atomic-explosion_1949-09-23.htm. Accessed: 27 February 2023.

128 Ibid.

129 Such tensions are epitomised by the illegal actions of Secretary of Defense Forrestal. On his own authority (and in frustration at Truman's earlier hesitation over planning for atomic war), Forrestal instructed the JCS to continue atomic war plan HALFMOON which followed BROILER. This was despite the fact that Truman had ordered them to work on conventional war plans instead. See Rhodes, *Dark Sun*, pp. 326–328.

130 Ibid., pp. 327–328.

131 This is not to say that criticism did not exist. As Chapter 4 demonstrates, LeMay and SAC were challenging the reliance on precision bombing and attempting to gain support for their own largely indiscriminate alternative bombing plan.

132 M. Mandelbaum (1979). *The Nuclear Question: The United States and Nuclear Weapons 1946–1976*, Cambridge: Cambridge University Press, p. 44.

133 Kaplan, *The Wizards of Armageddon*, p. 40.

134 Discussions were held regarding the virtue of bombing whole cities, especially as many of the targets were in urban locations. Nevertheless, as Kennan is quoted to have stated when briefed '[i]f you drop atomic bombs on Moscow, Leningrad, and the rest ... you will simply convince the Russians that you are barbarians trying to destroy their very society and they will rise up and wage an indeterminate guerrilla war against the West'. Subsequently, the striking of whole cities instead of discriminate targets was rejected. Kennan quoted in R.F. Futrell (1989). *Ideas, Concepts, Doctrine: Basic Thinking in the United States Air Force 1907–1960*, Vol. 1, Alabama: Air University Press, p. 238.

135 Neither did his subordinate, General Lauris Norstad (another former ACTS man) who was a 'brilliant staff planner' and Vandenberg's Vice Chief of Staff. Both contributed greatly to the continued push for discriminate precision targeting. Kaplan, *The Wizards of Armageddon*, p. 38.

136 Taken from the Air Intelligence Division's targeting plan, which was later approved by the JCS and incorporated into OFFTACKLE (reference in the footnote below). Originally obtained from Kaplan, *The Wizards of Armageddon*, pp. 41–42.

137 JCS 1844/46, Joint Outline Emergency War Plan 'OFFTACKLE' (SHAKEDOWN-CROSSPIECE) (8 November 1949). Later, this would be modified and become JCS 1844/55, Directives for the Implementation of 'OFFTACKLE' (18 February 1950).

138 Ibid.

139 E. Kaplan (2015). *To Kill Nations: American Strategy in the Air-Atomic Age and the Rise of Mutually Assured Destruction*, Ithaca, NY: Cornell University Press.

140 Such notions were also discussed under the leadership of Spaatz between 1947 and 1948. Futrell, *Ideas, Concepts, Doctrine*, p. 238.

141 JCS 1844/46, Joint Outline Emergency War Plan 'OFFTACKLE' (SHAKEDOWN-CROSSPIECE) (8 November 1949). Later, this would be modified and become JCS 1844/55, Directives for the Implementation of 'OFFTACKLE' (18 February 1950).

Chapter 4

1 J.R. McCarthy (February 9, 1950). *'Enemies from Within': Senator Joseph R. McCarthy's Accusations of Disloyalty* [transcript: Enemies from Within Speech], 9 February, Wheeling, West Virginia. Retrieved from: http://historymatters.gmu.edu/d/6456. Accessed: 2 March 2016.

2 Ibid.

Notes

3   The reference to communism as a parasite alludes to Kennan's statements in his 'Long Telegram'. G.F. Kennan (1946). The Charge in the Soviet Union (Kennan) to the Secretary of State, *National Security Archive*. Retrieved from: www.gwu.edu/~nsarchiv/coldwar/documents/episode-1/kennan.htm. Accessed: 16 April 2015.

4   The language used in NSC-68 summed up such anxiety and fear. As its emotive language made clear, the USSR was perceived to be '[t]he gravest threat to the security of the United States'. National Security Council (1950). *NSC 68: United States Objectives and Programs for National Security: A Report to the President Pursuant to the President's Directive of January 31, 1950*, Washington, D.C.: National Security Council, p. 60.

5   One contributing factor, as Gaddis wrote, was the 'new insecurities created by the Soviet atomic breakthrough'. J.L. Gaddis (2005). *The Cold War*, London: Allen Lane, p. 36.

6   As McCarthy stated in his 'Enemies within Speech', '[t]he reason why we find ourselves in a position of impotency is not because our only powerful potential enemy has sent men to invade our shores ... but rather because of the traitorous actions of those who have been treated so well by this Nation. It has not been the less fortunate, or members of minority groups who have been traitorous to this Nation, but rather those who have had all the benefits that the wealthiest Nation on earth has had to offer ... the finest homes, the finest college education and the finest jobs in government we can give.' McCarthy, *'Enemies from Within'*.

7   As a study of the NSC papers from 1950 highlighted, the intent to announce a 'Proclamation of National Emergency' was being considered from 11 December. Of such severity was the situation that the proclamation was made by Truman on 16 December. H.S. Truman (December 16, 1950). Proclamation 2914 – Proclaiming the Existence of a National Emergency, 16 December, *The American Presidency Project*. Retrieved from: www.presidency.ucsb.edu/ws/index.php?pid=13684. Accessed: 30 February 2016. For relevant NSC documents see National Security Council (December 11, 1950). Minutes of National Security Council Meeting, 11 December, President's Secretary's Files, Korean War Collection, Truman Papers, The Harry S. Truman Library and Museum, Independence. Retrieved from: www.trumanlibrary.gov/library/research-files/minutes-national-security-council-meeting. Accessed: 2 July 2023.

8   As Robert Jervis rightly points out, although these comments were made in 1947 'they also apply in later years'. See R. Jervis (1980). The Impact of the Korean War on the Cold War, *Journal of Conflict Resolution*. Vol. 24 (4), pp. 563–592.

9   N.H. Peterson, J.P. Glennon, D.W. Mabon, R.R. Goodwin and W.Z. Slany (1998). *Foreign Relations of the United States, 1950, National Security Affairs; Foreign Economic Policy, Vol. I*, Washington, DC: Government Printing Office, pp. 145–146. See also Jervis, The Impact of the Korean War.

10   As the US Embassy in Moscow stated, 'Moscow is steering a course as close as possible to full-scale war short of actually precipitating it', Peterson et al., *Foreign Relations of the United States*, pp. 145–146.

11   National Security Council, *NSC 68*, p. 4.

12   Not to forget the 'loss of China' to communism in the Chinese Civil War during this period. See J.L. Gaddis (1982). *Strategies of Containment: A Critical Appraisal of American National Security Policy During the Cold War*, Oxford: Oxford University Press, p. 90.

13   Jervis, The Impact of the Korean War. The directive by the President was as follows: 'That the President direct the Secretary of State and the Secretary of Defense to undertake a re-examination of our objectives in peace and war and of the effect of these objectives on our strategic plans, in the light of the probable fission bomb capability

and possible thermonuclear bomb capability of the Soviet Union'. National Security Council, *NSC 68*, p. 3.

14 Ibid.

15 As Kaplan stated, 'Nitze's first task: Scare the daylights out of Truman, so he'd raise the military budget. NSC-68 was the vehicle for doing so'. F. Kaplan (2004). Paul Nitze: The Man Who Brought us the Cold War, *Slate*. Retrieved from: www.slate.com/articles/news_and_politics/obit/2004/10/paul_nitze.html. Accessed: 27 May 2015.

16 National Security Council, *NSC 68*, p. 3.

17 Kaplan, Paul Nitze.

18 The exact reasoning behind Kennan's departure is open for debate. Gaddis argued, 'NSC-68 was not intended as a repudiation of Kennan. He was consulted at several stages … But the very fact of reducing the strategy to writing exposed the differences that had begun to develop between Kennan and the administration.' Others stated, however, that one reason for Kennan's departure was due to the fact he and Acheson disagreed on the manner in which America should counter the USSR. As Kaplan stated, '[a]t the beginning of 1950, Acheson fired Kennan and put Nitze in his place. Nitze, a former Wall Street banker, had been one of Kennan's deputies, but openly sympathized with Acheson.' For Gaddis see Gaddis, *Strategies of Containment*, p. 90. For Kaplan see Kaplan, Paul Nitze.

19 N. Thompson (2009). *The Hawk and the Dove: Paul Nitze, George Kennan and the History of the Cold War*, New York: Henry Hold and Company, pp. 1–4.

20 Ibid., p. 2. For details on the committee see Gaddis, *Strategies of Containment*, pp. 106–107.

21 Department of State (1976). *Foreign Relations of the United States, 1950, National Security Affairs; Foreign Economic Policy, Vol. I*, Washington, DC: Government Printing Office, Department of State. See also Jervis, The Impact of the Korean War.

22 Paul. H. Nitze. Interview by National Security Archive. 4 April 1999. Retrieved from: http://nsarchive.gwu.edu/coldwar/interviews/. Accessed: 1 June 2015.

23 Kaplan, Paul Nitze.

24 It should be mentioned that Nitze did not create NSC-68 alone. He led a committee that authored the document. Much in line with Nitze, Gaddis wrote that these 'authors' believed 'American interests could not be defined apart from the threat the Soviet Union posed to them'. Gaddis, *Strategies of Containment*, p. 95.

25 Edward W. Barrett (Assistant Secretary of State for Public Affairs) even went as far as referring to NSC-68 as being part of a 'psychological scare campaign'. Quoted in ibid., p. 105.

26 D. Acheson (1969). *Present at the Creation: My Years in the State Department*, London: W.W. Norton & Company, p. 375.

27 Ibid., p. 374.

28 It is perhaps also interesting to note that the document asserted the importance of swaying public opinion towards such a change in policy direction. As Jervis wrote, '[t]he need for a new policy would have to seem imperative, not merely desirable, and domestic opinion would have to abandon the view that multiple commitments and high defence budgets were intolerable'. Jervis, 'The Impact of the Korean War'. See also page 39 of NSC-68 that stated 'it is important that the United States employ military force only if the necessity for its use is clear and compelling and commends itself to the overwhelming majority of our people'. National Security Council, *NSC 68*, p. 39.

29 Ibid., p. 4.

30 It should be mentioned that Gaddis might disagree with this author's use of 'Nitze's' instead of 'the authors'. This is because (as mentioned above) NSC-68 was created by committee and thus cannot represent one opinion alone. It is the premise of this study, however, that (more in line with Kaplan's thought) Nitze's views, as head of the committee, steered the narrative. For more on Gaddis see Gaddis, *Strategies of Containment*, pp. 90–95. For Kaplan see Kaplan, Paul Nitze.

31 National Security Council, *NSC 68*, p. 7.

32 Ibid.

33 Ibid., p. 12.

34 Ibid.

35 Ibid., p. 7.

36 The narrative of 'good versus evil', in essence, fighting for what is sacred, is common to almost all justifications for war. American rhetoric regarding military build-up is no exception. The impact of this narrative should not be understated. As Lynch argued, '[s]acred forms generate their own visions of evil (the "profane"), and establish moral boundaries beyond which lie people who are regarded as "inhuman" or "animals"'. See G. Lynch (2012). *On the Sacred*, Durham: Acumen, p. 11.

37 National Security Council, *NSC 68*, p. 12.

38 Ibid., p. 5.

39 As Mearsheimer stated, 'Kennan recoiled at this patronizing way of dealing with other countries and called for "greater humility in our national outlooks".' For Mearsheimer quotation see G.F. Kennan (2012). *American Diplomacy*, sixtieth-anniversary expanded edition, London: University of Chicago Press. For the Kennan quotation see page 192 of the same book. Also, for more on the importance of the American 'sacred' see Lynch, *On the Sacred*.

40 National Security Council, *NSC 68*, p. 62. See also page 64 where it builds on this notion by stating '[i]n summary, we must, by means of rapid and sustained build-up of the political, economic, and military strength of the free world, and by means of an affirmative program intended to wrest the initiative from the Soviet Union'.

41 It must also be mentioned that significant attention was paid to the need for the build-up of conventional as well as atomic force. As Jervis stated, 'most significant was the call for an increased conventional capability'. Jervis, The Impact of the Korean War.

42 National Security Council, *NSC 68*, p. 39.

43 Ibid.

44 Ibid., p. 37.

45 Ibid.

46 Ibid., p. 38.

47 Ibid.

48 Kaplan, Paul Nitze.

49 It is this change at a strategic level, within JCS war planning, which is the focus of Chapter 5.

50 Jervis, The Impact of the Korean War.

51 As Daniel Yergin stated, '[w]ith the Korean conflict, a new phase had opened in the cold war'. D. Yergin (1990). *Shattered Peace: The Origins of the Cold War*, revised edition, London: Penguin, pp. 460–466.

52 Gaddis is but one perspective on Korea. For peacemaking in Korea see R. Foot (1990). *A Substitute for Victory: The Politics of Peacemaking at the Korean Armistice Talks*, Ithaca, NY: Cornell University Press. For in-text quotation see Gaddis, *Strategies of Containment*, p. 109.

Notes

53 The original version of NSC-68 was released on 7 April 1950. P. Nitze and S.N. Drew (1996). *NSC-68: Forging the Strategy of Containment*, Washington, DC: National Defense University Press, pp. 17–19.

54 There were a number of amended versions of NSC-68. The original document was referred by Truman to the NSC for further clarification on 'what programs would be involved and their costs'. NSC-68/1 was then created in September 1950 to describe the programmes and their financial implications. On receiving presidential approval of these details, NSC-68/2 was formed (in the same month) and passed over to 'the ad hoc group' for further revision. In December, a new version containing ad hoc group revisions was created and named NSC-68/3. This was then resubmitted to the President and his National Security Council for approval. On approval, in December 1950, NSC-68/4 was formed to reflect this 'presidential approval of NSC-68/3'. Later in December, the President declared a state of emergency due to the war in Korea and urged the American people to 'make the sacrifices necessary to implement NSC-68's strategy of global containment'. For all quotations see Nitze and Drew, *NSC-68*, pp. 17–19.

55 Ibid.

56 Jervis, The Impact of the Korean War.

57 Office of Reports and Estimates (1947). Central Intelligence Group: The Situation in Korea, 3 January. President's Secretary's Files, Korean War Collection, Truman Papers, The Harry S. Truman Library and Museum, Independence. Retrieved from: https://digitalarchive.wilsoncenter.org/document/central-intelligence-group-ore-51-situation-korea. Accessed: 2 July 2023.

58 Ibid.

59 Previously known as the 'Central Reports Staff', the 'Office of Reports and Estimates' was home to the analysis division in the Central Intelligence Agency. Thus, when studying American military and political perceptions of Korea, the ORE is a useful and relevant source. See W. Kuhns (2007). *The Beginning of Intelligence Analysis in CIA: The Office of Reports and Estimates: CIA's First Center for Analysis*. Retrieved from: www.cia.gov/resources/csi/studies-in-intelligence/volume-66-no-3-september-2022/the-beginning-of-intelligence-analysis-in-cia-the-office-of-reports-and-estimates-cias-first-center-for-analysis/. Accessed: 2 July 2023.

60 Office of Reports and Estimates, Central Intelligence Group: The Situation in Korea.

61 Ibid.

62 Ibid.

63 Ibid.

64 Ibid.

65 Department of State (1950). Memorandum of Conversation: Korean Situation, 25 June. Retrieved from: https://history.state.gov/historicaldocuments/frus1950v07/d86. Accessed: 2 July 2023. Also see M. Hunt (1992). Beijing and the Korean Crisis, June 1950–June 1951, *Political Science Quarterly*. Vol. 107 (3), pp. 453–478.

66 N. Khrushchev (1970). *Khrushchev Remembers*, Boston, MA: Little Brown & Company, pp. 367–369.

67 It is interesting to note that 'the Truman administration assumed almost immediately that it had been inspired directly by Moscow and Beijing as part of a dangerous and aggressive new worldwide push for extending Communist influence'. J. McMahon (1988). The Cold War in Asia: Towards a New Synthesis?, *Diplomatic History*. Vol. 12 (3), pp. 307–327.

Notes

68 This was despite the warnings by the ORE. See Office of Reports and Estimates, Central Intelligence Group: The Situation in Korea.

69 D. MacArthur (1950). Correspondence between Harry S. Truman and Douglas MacArthur, 19 July, President's Secretary's Files, Korean War Collection, Truman Papers, The Harry S. Truman Library and Museum, Independence. Retrieved from: www.trumanlibrary.gov/library/research-files/correspondence-between-harry-s-truman-and-douglas-macarthur?documentid=NA&pagenumber=5. Accessed: 2 July 2023.

70 Other options, including atomic options and the destruction of nearby Soviet air forces bases, were considered. As General Vandenberg stated, such destruction 'could be done if we used A-Bombs'. Department of State, Memorandum of Conversation: Korean Situation. Also see MacArthur, Correspondence between Harry S. Truman and Douglas MacArthur. For more on the Inchon Landings see A.R. Lewis (2012). *The American Culture of War: The History of US Military Force from World War II to Operation Enduring Freedom*, London: Routledge, pp. 98–99.

71 Secretary of Defense Marshall gave MacArthur permission to proceed stating, '[w]e want you to feel unhampered tactically and strategically to proceed north of the 38th parallel'. Quoted in S. Weintraub (2000). *MacArthur's War: Korea and the Undoing of an American Hero*, New York: Simon & Schuster, pp. 157–158.

72 E.L. Daily (1999). *MacArthur's X Corps in Korea: Inchon to the Yalu, 1950*, Paducah, KY: Turner Publishing Company, p. 43.

73 MacArthur's successes were openly praised by Truman, as the President stated in a letter in October 1950: 'Dear General MacArthur: The progress the forces under your command have made since we met at Wake continues to be most remarkable and once again I offer you my hearty congratulations. The military operations in Korea under your command will have a most profound influence for peace in the world. Very sincerely yours, Harry S. Truman.' D. MacArthur (1950). Message from Douglas MacArthur to Harry Truman, 30 October. President's Secretary's Files, Korean War Collection, Truman Papers, The Harry S. Truman Presidential Library and Museum, Independence. Retrieved from: http://ww2db.com/doc.php?q=378. Accessed: 30 March 2016.

74 MacArthur, Message from Douglas MacArthur to Harry Truman.

75 The Chinese Civil War had only ended in May 1950. See O.A. Westad (2003). *Decisive Encounters: The Chinese Civil War, 1946–1950*, Stanford, CA: Stanford University Press.

76 Lewis, *The American Culture of War*, p. 106.

77 Ibid.

78 The initial delay in realising Chinese intervention is not surprising. As Whiting stated, 'the Chinese Communist intervention was initially cautious and limited'. A.S. Whiting (1968). *China Crosses the Yalu: The Decision to Enter the Korean War*, Stanford, CA: Stanford University Press, p. 117.

79 D. Wainstock (1999). *Truman, MacArthur and the Korean War*, Westport, CT: Greenwood Press, p. 139.

80 Lewis, *The American Culture of War*, p. 107.

81 MacArthur quoted in W. Courtney (1956). *MacArthur: His Rendezvous with History*, New York: Alfred A. Knopf, p. 421.

82 C.J. Lee (1996). *China and Korea: Dynamic Relations*, Stanford, CA: Hoover Press, p. 25.

83 Lewis, *The American Culture of War*, pp. 106–107.

84 Lee, *China and Korea*, p. 25.

85 Lewis, *The American Culture of War*, p. 107. Also see Lee, *China and Korea*, pp. 25–26.

Notes

86 S. Sandler (2013). *The Korean War: An Encyclopaedia*, Abingdon: Routledge, p. 82.

87 J. Chen (1992). China's Changing Aims during the Korean War, 1950–1951, *Journal of American–East Asian Relations*. Vol. 1 (1), pp. 8–41.

88 Ibid.

89 In fact, for clarity of the greater context, it is perhaps important to note that 'Seoul fell to Chinese and North Korean troops on 4 January 1951, and the Chinese-North Korean troops continued operations crossing the Han River. By 8 January, the combat line had moved southward to the 37th Parallel.' Ibid. See also R. Spurr (2010). *Enter the Dragon: China's Undeclared War Against the US in Korea, 1950–51*, New York: Newmarket Press, p. 190.

90 As Gaddis stated, a number of Truman's 'advisors had seen difficulties in getting Congress to fund it [NSC-68]'. It was for this reason he had delayed the approval of the document in April. Nevertheless, 'the attack across the 38th parallel greatly simplified that task'. Gaddis, *Strategies of Containment*, p. 109.

91 Ibid.

92 This may also have been due to the fact that NSC-68 all but mirrored the events that had transpired.
    As Gaddis went on to clarify, the adoption of NSC-68 'happened in large part because of the remarkable manner in which the Korean War appeared to validate several of NSC-68's most important conclusions'. Ibid., p. 109.

93 J. Pollack (1989). The Korean War and Sino-American Relations. In Harry Harding and Yuan Ming (eds), *Sino-American Relations, 1945–1955: A Joint Reassessment of a Critical Decade* (pp. 213–237). Wilmington, DE: Scholarly Resources, p. 224.

94 As Kaplan concluded, '[t]he Korean War forced a reassessment of US policy. NSC-68 may not have been the best fit for the circumstances, but it was there … The defense budget climbed – not just to beat back North Korea, but to tackle communism everywhere – and didn't come down again for decades.' Kaplan, Paul Nitze.

95 It would take until 10 July 1951, however, for the Korean armistice negotiations to begin. In this time the situation would only get worse, allowing the support for military options to grow. See R.A. Pape (1996). *Bombing to Win: Air Power and Coercion in War*, New York: Cornell University Press, pp. 137–138.

96 Truman, Proclamation 2914.

97 Such notions are backed by Freedman who stated that 'the United States had no choice but to rely on its nuclear arsenal, and extend its breathing space by maintaining, for as long as possible, a clear superiority in nuclear capabilities over the Soviet Union'. See L. Freedman (2003). *The Evolution of Nuclear Strategy*, Basingstoke: Palgrave, p. 67. For Truman's proclamation see Department of State, *Foreign Relations of the United States, 1950*, pp. 481–482.

98 D.A. Rosenberg (1983). The Origins of Overkill: Nuclear Weapons and American Strategy, 1945–1960, *International Security*. Vol. 7 (4), pp. 3–71.

99 Another issue that arguably motivated Truman's move towards the atomic bomb was a report conducted by the CIA. Specifically, the CIA published their 'Estimate of the Effects of the Soviet Possession of the Atomic Bomb upon the Security of the United States and upon the Probability of Direct Soviet Military Action' report (top secret) in April 1950. The historian Richard Rhodes analyses this report and its impact in his text *Dark Sun* (1996). He stated that this 'study estimate[d] that two hundred atomic bombs exploded over the major cities of the United States might well knock the US out of [a] war'. From his reading of this report he highlights that it was believed that the Soviets might have had that many bombs 'sometime between mid-1954 and the end of 1955'.

Notes

Such a capability, Rhodes highlighted, would mean 'the continental US will be for the first time liable to devastating attack'. Rhodes proceeded to declare that it was perceptions such as this that heightened the anxiety regarding the threat the USSR posed to the US. He concluded by stating that, as a result of this report, 1954 was deemed the year of 'maximum danger' in the Truman administration. Anxiety had increased and the atomic option became a necessity. R. Rhodes (1996). *Dark Sun: The Making of the Hydrogen Bomb*, New York: Touchstone, pp. 440–442.

Chapter 5

1 C.S. Grey (2012). *Airpower for Strategic Effect*, Alabama: Air University Press, p. 184.
2 For an example of inter-service rivalry between the Air Force and Navy during this period see the so-called 'Admirals Revolt'. This is commonly seen as the epitome of inter-service rivalry over the allocation of atomic strategic bombardment resources. The revolt occurred when the new Secretary of Defense, Johnson, (traditionally seen as an advocate of the Air Force) cut funding to the Navy and increased Air Force spending. In response, an anonymous document was 'delivered to several members of Congress. It alleged that serious improprieties had occurred in the Air Force's procurement of the B-36 bomber' and implied that Johnson had been party to this. The author was subsequently 'revealed to be Cedric R. Worth, the special assistant to Under Secretary of the Navy Dan A. Kimball'. Consequently, the House Armed Services Committee held two sets of hearings about the controversy. The Navy used the attention to make clear its concerns about the reliance on (and competency of) the Air Force to deliver atomic weapons within American national security strategy. The American press labelled this the 'Admirals Revolt'. Subsequently, the Chief of Naval Operations was fired. For all quotations above and for a far more detailed study of this event see J.G. Barlow (2013). *The Revolt of the Admirals: The Fight for Naval Aviation, 1945–1950*, Washington, DC: Naval Historical Center, pp. 10–20.
3 As Rhodes stated, 'LeMay was a realist and understood that bombing at night by radar in a strange country over which you have never previously flown meant unavoidable inaccuracy'. R. Rhodes (1996). *Dark Sun: The Making of the Hydrogen Bomb*, New York: Touchstone, p. 440.
4 More details of these SAC concerns are given through the study of the following document as the chapter proceeds: Strategic Air Command (1950). *Presentation by the Strategic Air Command: Commanders Conference United States Air Force*, Ramey Air Force Base, April. SAC No. BA-B2.
5 This was especially the case in regard to OFFTACKLE. As Kaplan stated, LeMay 'had no objection to the Air Staff's predilection for destroying liquid-fuel industries, for that seemed to have been effective in Germany and, besides, there were many other choice targets by those factories. But atomic-energy facilities and electro-power plants? Who knew how many the Soviets had or where they all were? Even if somebody did know, they would be difficult for pilots to find. Most of the plants that anybody did know something about were sited outside cities, some of them in the middle of nowhere. What was the point of dropping something as big as the atom bomb just to hit one target?' Thus, for LeMay, it was the big targets, such as cities, that were deemed of most value for atomic bombardment. F. Kaplan (1983). *The Wizards of Armageddon*, Stanford, CA: Stanford University Press, p. 44.

Notes

6 LeMay had been raising similar issues for many years. As RAND documents, declassified in 2017, show, LeMay was pragmatic about the fact there was 'no special reconnaissance aircraft' and insisted RAND research the development of an all-in-one bomber that could do the job and fill the capacity gap. F.R. Collbohm (1966). *Memorandum for the Trustees*, 5 August. Washington, DC: RAND, p. 11. Lawrence Henderson Papers, History of RAND Corporations, 1954–1966, RAND Archives, Santa Monica.

7 C.E. LeMay (1951). Diary 3, 23 January, Curtis E. LeMay Papers, Library of Congress, Washington, DC. Box B-64, Folder: 1951.

8 As stated within the initial 1946 document outlining the remit and purpose of SAC, '[t]he mission of this Wing and other Wings to follow is for this unit to be capable of immediate and sustained VLR [very long range] offensive operations in any part of the world, either independently or in cooperation with land and naval forces, utilizing the latest and most advanced weapons'. C.E. LeMay (1946). US Army Deputy Chief of Air Staff for Research and Development General Curtis E. LeMay to Commanding General, Strategic Air Command Colonel Kenneth H. Gibson, 13 June, Mission of the 58th Bombardment Wing. Air Force Declassification Archive, Bolling Field, DC. Retrieved from: www.secretsdeclassified.af.mil/shared/media/document/AFD-100504-057.PDF. Accessed: 17 July 2015 (no longer available).

9 D.A. Rosenberg (1983). The Origins of Overkill: Nuclear Weapons and American Strategy, 1945–1960, *International Security*. Vol. 7 (4), pp. 3–71.

10 Kaplan, *The Wizards of Armageddon*, p. 42.

11 This was, for many reasons, background career progression, but perhaps most importantly that LeMay was from a different generation to Arnold et al. Born in 1906 (compared to Arnold, born in 1886), LeMay had a different perspective from those who had served in the First World War. W. Kozak (2011). *LeMay: The Life and Wars of General Curtis LeMay*, Washington, DC: Regnery Publishing, pp. 16–29.

12 US Airforce (2022). General Curtis Emerson Lemay, *USAF*. Retrieved from: www.af.mil/About-Us/Biographies/Display/Article/106462/general-curtis-emerson-lemay/. Accessed: 20 July 2022. Also see A.A. Narvaez (1990). Gen. Curtis LeMay, an Architect Of Strategic Air Power, Dies at 83, *New York Times*, 2 October. Retrieved from: www.nytimes.com/1990/10/02/obituaries/gen-curtis-lemay-an-architect-of-strategic-air-power-dies-at-83.html. Accessed: 19 July 2015.

13 Kozak, *LeMay*, pp. 196–199.

14 Kaplan, *The Wizards of Armageddon*, p. 43.

15 Ibid.

16 LeMay, *Diary 3, Curtis E. LeMay Papers*.

17 It should not be overlooked that such talk of 'bonuses' was a line of thought akin to the political directive outlined by Nitze and approved by Truman in NSC-68 and thus not unpalatable to the administration.

18 Rhodes, *Dark Sun*, p. 440.

19 Ibid.

20 Major General Kenneth Nichols was an engineer in the US Army who worked as a Deputy District Engineer on the Manhattan Project. In the early 1950s he became the Deputy Director of the Guided Missiles Division of the Department of Defense. As such, Nichols had sufficient knowledge of the debate around targeting. For more on Kenneth Nichols see K. Nichols. Interview by Stephane Groueff. January 4, 1965. Retrieved from: https://ahf.nuclearmuseum.org/voices/oral-histories/general-kenneth-nicholss-interview-part-1/. Accessed: 2 July 2023. See also K.D. Nichols (1987).

The Road to Trinity: A Personal Account of How America's Nuclear Policies Were Made, New York: William Morrow & Company.

21 Rhodes, *Dark Sun*, p. 440.

22 Kaplan, *The Wizards of Armageddon*, p. 42.

23 Ibid.

24 Ibid., pp. 42–43.

25 Ibid.

26 LeMay, *Diary 3, Curtis E. LeMay Papers*.

27 Furthermore, LeMay stated that through the destruction of this selection of major cities, America could not only ensure victory, but would also be able to 'conserve [its] stockpile of atomic weapons' for future and further destruction. See LeMay, *Diary 3, Curtis E. LeMay Papers*.

28 Strategic Air Command (1949). *SAC Emergency War Plan 1–49*, EWP 1–49. For more details see T. Englehardt (2007). *The End of Victory Culture: Cold War America and the Disillusioning of a Generation*, Amhurst: University of Massachusetts Press, p. 155.

29 Kaplan, *The Wizards of Armageddon*, p. 44.

30 For more on Ramey Air Force Base see A.T. Stein (2005). *Into the Wild Blue Yonder: My Life in the Air Force*, College Station: Texas A&M University Press.

31 Strategic Air Command, *Presentation by the Strategic Air Command*, pp. 5–8.

32 Ibid.

33 As the presentation stated, the purpose was to outline 'those deficiencies which face us today'. Ibid., p. 18.

34 Ibid., pp. 5–6.

35 Ibid.

36 Ibid., pp. 6–8.

37 Ibid.

38 As the presentation went on to reiterate, '[s]everal of the target areas assigned by "OFFTACKLE" lie outside the boundaries of Russia proper'. Ibid., p. 6.

39 Ibid., pp. 12–13.

40 The RB-29 is in reference to the older US Air Force B-29 bombers from the Second World War. The RB designation is for reconnaissance.

41 Ibid., p. 13.

42 Ibid., pp. 12–13.

43 Early pressure had arisen in May 1949 from the Harmon Report, which warned against reliance on the proposed atomic bombing offensive (although it did not reject the principal importance of atomic weapons per se). Specifically, the report argued that such an offensive would not, by itself, 'bring about the capitulation, destroy the roots of Communism, or critically weaken the power of the Soviet leadership to dominate the people'. JCS 1953/1, Bulky Package (12 May 1949). Further support came in January 1950 from the Weapons System Evaluation Group (WESG) report. This report 'only reinforce[ed] the already pessimistic conclusions of the Harmon report' by stating that 'because of the current levels of accuracy of air force bombardiers, only between one-half and two-thirds of industrial installations in the target areas would be beyond repair'. Such conclusions were also given for increased investment in the hydrogen bomb, as a means to ensure destruction. For quotations see D.A. Rosenberg (1979). American Atomic Strategy and the Hydrogen Bomb Decision, *Organization of American Historians*. Vol. 66 (1), pp. 62–87.

44 In regard to the ambition for precision, Brodie stated: '[t]he atomic bomb in its various forms may well weaken our incentive to choose targets shrewdly and carefully … But

such an event would argue a military failure as well as a moral one.' B. Brodie (1950). Strategic Bombing: What It Can Do, *Reporter*, 15 August. Retrieved from: www.unz.org/Pub/Reporter-1950aug15-00028. Accessed: 8 August 2016.

45 Kaplan, *The Wizards of Armageddon*, pp. 44–45.
46 Ibid., p. 47.
47 Ibid.
48 Ibid., pp. 44–45.
49 As Kaplan stated, '[t]o SAC, that was simply not the way to fight a war'. Ibid., pp. 42–43.
50 Proceedings of LeMay meeting with Air Staff Targeting Panel. See Rhodes, *Dark Sun*, p. 440.
51 Ibid.
52 Proceedings of LeMay meeting with Air Staff Targeting Panel. See ibid.
53 Rosenberg expanded on the meeting by stating that LeMay also argued that '[v]isual prestrike reconnaissance would be required for a disproportionately large number of targets; isolated target complexes like electric power stations would be difficult for air crews to locate visually or with radar in unfamiliar and hostile terrain'. Why take such a risk when the very survival of the state would be at risk? See D.A. Rosenberg (1987). US Nuclear War Planning, 1954–1960. In Desmond Ball and Jeffery Richardson (eds), *Strategic Nuclear Targeting* (pp. 35–57). Ithaca, NY: Cornell University Press.
54 Ibid.
55 Although it should be noted that the broader targeting categories (BRAVO, DELTA, ROMEO) were kept. LeMay could now decide, however, how to interpret such categories.
56 J.L. Gaddis (1982). *Strategies of Containment: A Critical Appraisal of American National Security Policy During the Cold War*, Oxford: Oxford University Press, pp. 148–152.
57 P. Sellers and S. Hayden, perf. *Dr Strangelove or: How I Learned to Stop Worrying and Love the Bomb*. Hawk Films, 1964. Released in 1964, Stanley Kubrick's renegade and war-mongering American generals, Ripper and Turgidson, are said to have been inspired in part by the actions and persona of General Curtis E. LeMay. Although it is perhaps unfair to say that LeMay was a renegade, there can be little doubt that he favoured a certain amount of autonomy when it came to nuclear planning. For more on these comparisons see Kozak, *LeMay*, p. 311. Thanks to the board of the Kubrick Papers in the University of the Arts London who provided me with access to Kubrick's notes on the film-making process. These papers reaffirmed the influence of RAND (and people like Thomas Schelling) on the production of the film. Stanley Kubrick Archive, Archives and Special Collections Centre, University of the Arts London, Elephant and Castle, London.
58 Further to this, during his time as Army Chief of Staff throughout 1946, Eisenhower 'had jurisdiction over the Manhattan Engineer District and was the sole channel to high civilian policymakers for nuclear stockpile information'. Rosenberg, The Origins of Overkill (1983). See also R.S. Norris and H.M. Kristensen (2009). Nuclear Notebook: US Nuclear Warheads, 1945–2009, *Bulletin of the Atomic Scientists*. Vol. 65 (4), pp. 72–81.
59 Meeting between Eisenhower and his Cabinet (March 1953). Quoted in E.J. Hughes (1964). *The Ordeal of Power*, New York: Dell Books, p. 88.
60 It should also be mentioned that the Eisenhower administration saw nuclear weapons as a way to balance a defence budget that had been exponentially inflated under Truman. In essence, as Secretary of State, Dulles stated in January 1954 to the Council

Notes

on Foreign Relations in New York, that nuclear weapons and allied cooperation offered 'a maximum deterrent at a bearable cost'. J.F. Dulles (1954). *Speech to the Council of Foreign Relations: The Evolution of Foreign Policy*, Press Release No. 81, 12 January. Washington, DC: Department of State.

61 For a more recent take on massive retaliation and the evolution of American nuclear strategy and technology during this period see E. Schlosser (2014). *Command and Control: Nuclear Weapons, the Damascus Accident, and the Illusion of Safety*, London: Penguin, p. 130.

62 Hagerty, J. (13 December 1954), quoted in Gaddis, *Strategies of Containment*, p. 150.

63 Dulles, J.F. *Speech to the Council of Foreign Relations.*

64 Eisenhower did not officially approve the option of a preventative strike against the USSR. Pre-emption of attack remained, however, a core motivation behind strategic planning. As General Thomas White (Chief of Staff of the Air Force 1957–61) stated in his public testimony to Congress in 1959, after receiving 'tactical or strategic warning' the US would 'destroy the enemy's capability to destroy us'. For White's quotation and more information see S.D. Sagan (1989). *Moving Targets: Nuclear Strategy and National Security*, Princeton, NJ: Princeton University Press, pp. 21–24.

65 NSC-162/2 stated the need for: '1) A strong military posture, with emphasis on the capability of inflicting massive retaliatory damage by offensive striking power; 2) U.S. and allied forces readiness to move rapidly initially to counter aggression by Soviet bloc forces and to hold vital areas and lines of communication; and 3) A mobilisation base, and its protection against crippling damage, adequate to insure victory in the event of general war.' See National Security Council (1953). *NSC-162/2: Statement of Policy by the National Security Council: Basic National Security Policy, October 30th 1950*, Washington, DC: National Security Council, pp. 5–6.

66 The decision to proceed with the development of thermonuclear weapons was made by President Truman during the increasingly anxious context of 1950. Specifically, he stated on 31 January 1950 that he had 'directed the Atomic Energy Commission to continue its work on all forms of atomic weapons, including the so-called hydrogen or super-bomb'. See H.S. Truman (1950). Statement by the President on the Hydrogen Bomb, 21 January. Truman Papers, The Harry S. Truman Presidential Library and Museum, Independence. Retrieved from: www.presidency.ucsb.edu/documents/statement-the-president-the-hydrogen-bomb. Accessed: 2 July 2023.

67 Specific priority was given to the development of 'U.S. strategic air power' capabilities within the Air Force as a means to ensure that the massive retaliation offensive could be successfully and rapidly delivered. Furthermore, the defence programme focused on increased investment in 'intelligence systems' so the Air Force could detect when 'Soviet bloc forces' were preparing an offensive and so that the Air Force could identify where the appropriate targets for massive retaliation were located. Finally, the programme concentrated on the fostering of 'scientific research and development' to ensure that the United States had the 'superiority in quantity and quality of weapons systems' (such as thermonuclear weapons) and thus could achieve 'victory in the event of general war' through the deployment of these weapons. Overall, the defence programme largely monopolised investment within sectors that would most benefit the Air Force as a means of ensuring that a massive retaliation offensive could be successfully undertaken. See National Security Council, *NSC 162/2*, pp. 5–7.

68 There was an interesting shift in direction by SAC during this period. The prioritising of 'Air Power targets' became common rhetoric. In reality, however, as documents from 1956 highlight (declassified in 2015 and studied later in the chapter), such

classification gave SAC the justification to assign the targeting of H-Bombs onto whole cities (due to the preponderance of Air Power and other sensitive targets in these locations). Targeting such as this, when deployed in practice, would have wrought mass destruction in the largest population centres of China and the Soviet bloc (even if China was not 'in the war'). See Strategic Air Command (1956). *The SAC Atomic Weapons Requirements Study for 1959*, B-54300. See also D.A. Rosenberg (1981–82). *A Smoking Radiating Ruin at the End of* Two Hours: Documents on American Plans for Nuclear War with the Soviet Union, 1954–1955, *International Security*. Vol. 6 (3), pp. 3–38.

69 For original report see Strategic Air Command (1959). *Historical Study 73A, SAC Targetting Concepts*, April. Offutt: Historical Division, Headquarters, pp. 2–7. For quotation see Rosenberg, The Origins of Overkill (1983).

70 Ibid.

71 I. Chernus (2008). *Apocalypse Management: Eisenhower and the Discourse of National Insecurity*, Stanford, CA: Stanford University Press, p. 82.

72 Eisenhower's remarks were documented in correspondence between US Army General Lyman L. Lemnizer and Chief of Staff of the US Army General Ridgeway. See L.L. Lemnizer (1954). Letter to Matthew Ridgeway, 21 June. Ridgeway Papers, United States Army Military History Institute, Carlisle. Box 30, Folder: January to June 1954.

73 This idea of using a little more imagination to come up with a better plan than to merely resort to blowing up a nation was not uncommon in Eisenhower's rhetoric. As he is quoted as later stating to an audience of Marines: 'I repeat there is no victory in any war except through our imaginations, through our dedication, and through our work to avoid it.' See R.H. Ferrell (1983). *The Diary of James C. Hagerty: Eisenhower in Mid-Course, 1954–1955*, Bloomington: Indiana University Press, p. 69.

74 Rosenberg, The Origins of Overkill (1983).

75 Admiral Roy Johnson. Interview by John T. Mason, Jr. 6 December 1980. Retrieved from: http://nsarchive.gwu.edu/nukevault/ebb236/#1. Accessed: 22 January 2016.

76 Ibid.

77 JCS 2057/71, CSS 373.11 (12–14–48) Joint Chiefs of Staff Document (18 October 1954).

78 Sagan, *Moving Targets*, p. 19.

79 Ibid.

80 Rosenberg, The Origins of Overkill (1983).

81 William Burr. Personal interview. 12 December 2015.

82 See Rosenberg, The Origins of Overkill (1983).

83 See ibid. See also Sagan, *Moving Targets*.

84 William Burr. Personal interview. 12 December 2015. Also Nate Jones. Personal interview. 11 December 2015.

85 Strategic Air Command (1961). *History of the Joint Strategic Target Planning Staff and Preparation of SIOP-62 (B82767)*. Offutt: History and Research Division, Headquarters, p. 1.

86 Ibid., pp. 1–5.

87 Ibid., p. 1.

88 Ibid., p. 2.

89 As the official history stated, this would have been sent in Europe to 'Commander in Chief Naval Forces Eastern Atlantic and Mediterranean (CINCNELM), Commander in Chief Forces Europe (CINCEur) and Commander in Chief Strategic Air Command (CINCSAC), and in the Far East, Commander in Chief Pacific (CINCPac), Commander in Chief Alaska (CINCAl), and CINCSAC. Ibid., p. 2.

90 Ibid., p. 3.
91 Ibid.
92 E.C. Unger. Interview by E.R. Caywood. 12–14 July 1961. See also Strategic Air Command, *History of the Joint Strategic Target Planning Staff*, p. 4.
93 Strategic Air Command, *History of the Joint Strategic Target Planning Staff*, p. 4.
94 E.C. Unger. Interview by E.R. Caywood. 12–14 July 1961. See also Strategic Air Command, *History of the Joint Strategic Target Planning Staff*, p. 4.
95 Strategic Air Command, *History of the Joint Strategic Target Planning Staff*, pp. 4–5.
96 D. Eisenhower (1958). President's Message to Congress: Defense Reorganization Act of 1958, 3 April, *The American Presidency Project*. Retrieved from: www.presidency.ucsb.edu/documents/special-message-the-congress-reorganization-the-defense-establishment. Accessed: 2 July 2023.
97 Strategic Air Command, *History of the Joint Strategic Target Planning Staff*, pp. 4–6.
98 Ibid.
99 Ibid., p. 4.
100 Organised by CINCSAC, to consolidate all atomic bombardment plans and assets. See General White's comments. JCS 1620/250, Command and Control of Strategic Forces (28 April 1959).
101 For Navy plans regarding Polaris weapons systems see JCS 1620/223, Concept of Employment and Command Structure for the Polaris Weapons System (22 January 1959).
102 For more information and quotation see Strategic Air Command, *History of the Joint Strategic Target Planning Staff*, p. 4. See also JCS 1620/254, Concept of Employment and Command Structure for the Polaris Weapons System (20 April 1959).
103 Admiral Arleigh Burke (1949). Testimony, October. *Hearings before the Committee of Armed Services, House of Representatives, 85th Congress, 2nd Session. Reorganisation of DOD, No. 83*, pp. 6344–6391.
104 Strategic Air Command, *History of the Joint Strategic Target Planning Staff*, pp. 6–7.
105 The positions of the Army, Navy, Marine Corps and Air Force went to Secretary of Defense Gates as JCSM 171-59 (8 May 1959).
106 Strategic Air Command, *History of the Joint Strategic Target Planning Staff*, pp. 9–10.
107 JCS 314–682–60, Target Coordination and Associated Problems (15 July 1960).
108 Strategic Air Command, *History of the Joint Strategic Target Planning Staff*, pp. 10–11.
109 Ibid.
110 D.A. Rosenberg (1984). The Origins of Overkill: Nuclear Weapons and American Strategy, 1945–1960. In S. Miller (ed.), *Strategy and Nuclear Deterrence: An International Security Reader* (pp. 133–183). Princeton, NJ: Princeton University Press.
111 Ibid.
112 J.H. Rubel (2008). *Doomsday Delayed: USAF Strategic Weapons Doctrine and SIOP-62, 1959–1962*, Lanham, MD: Hamilton Books, p. vii.
113 Strategic Air Command, *History of the Joint Strategic Target Planning Staff*, pp. 1–5. See also Department of State (1996). NSC Memorandum. Discussion at the 387th Meeting of the National Security Council. In *Foreign Relations of the United States, 1958–60*, Vol. III (pp.148–152), Washington, DC: Government Printing Office, Department of State.
114 Rosenberg, The Origins of Overkill (1983).
115 JCS 1907/266, Memorandum for the Secretary of Defense: Berlin Contingency Planning (26 June 1961).
116 Rosenberg, The Origins of Overkill (1984).

Notes

117 JCS 1907/266, Memorandum for the Secretary of Defense: Berlin Contingency Planning (26 June 1961).

118 Rosenberg, The Origins of Overkill (1983).

119 JCS 1907/266, Memorandum for the Secretary of Defense: Berlin Contingency Planning (26 June 1961).

120 Ibid. For more details on this topic (and for the team that should be credited with securing access to documents such as this) see W. Burr (2011). US War Plans Would Kill an Estimated 108 million Soviets, 104 million Chinese, and 2.6 million Poles: More Evidence on SIOP-62 and the Origins of Overkill, *National Security Archive*, 8 November. Retrieved from: https://nsarchive.wordpress.com/2011/11/08/u-s-war-plans-would-kill-an-estimated-108-million-soviets-104-million-chinese-and-2-3-million-poles-more-evidence-on-siop-62-and-the-origins-of-overkill/#_edn3. Accessed: 24 January 2016.

121 Strategic Air Command, *History of the Joint Strategic Target Planning Staff*, pp. 9–15.

122 JCS 1907/266, Memorandum for the Secretary of Defense: Berlin Contingency Planning (26 June 1961).

123 W. Burr (2015). US Cold War Nuclear Target Lists Declassified for First Time, *National Security Archive*, 22 December. Retrieved from: http://nsarchive.gwu.edu/nukevault/ebb538-Cold-War-Nuclear-Target-List-Declassified-First-Ever/. Accessed: 20 March 2016.

124 Ibid.

125 Strategic Air Command, *Atomic Weapons Requirements Study for 1959*.

126 Burr, US Cold War Nuclear Target Lists Declassified for First Time.

127 There were aspects of both countervalue (the direct targeting of the enemy's population) and counterforce targeting (the targeting of the opponent's military-industrial site) in SIOP-62. These terms are not, however, widely used in this chapter. Use of these two targeting frameworks is most associated with the dominant debates of the 1960s. See W.A. Stewart (1967). *Counterforce, Damage-Limiting, and Deterrence*. Santa Monica, CA: RAND. Retrieved from: www.rand.org/content/dam/rand/pubs/papers/2008/P3385.pdf. Accessed: 26 June 2016.

128 JCS 1907/266, Memorandum for the Secretary of Defense: Berlin Contingency Planning (26 June 1961).

129 Ibid.

130 Ibid.

131 It was during this period that US–Soviet relations were once again taking a turn for the worse. From the capture of U-2 spy plane pilot Gary Powers in 1958, to Premier Khrushchev's demand for the United States, Great Britain, and France to remove their forces from West Berlin within six months, it was indeed a tense period. Thus, nuclear planning became of increased importance in the face of such tension and demands. The situation was not helped by Khrushchev's comments to US Ambassador Llewellyn E. Thompson Jr. on 1 January 1960 when he is said to have threatened that '[w]e have thirty nuclear weapons earmarked for France, more than enough to destroy that country. We are reserving fifty each for West Germany and Britain.' For this quotation and more information on this period see F. Kempe (2012). *Berlin 1961: Kennedy, Khrushchev, and the Most Dangerous Place on Earth*, New York: Berkley Books, pp. 1–5. For quotation see Burr, US War Plans.

132 For 1956 see Strategic Air Command, *The SAC Atomic Weapons Requirements Study*. For figures see JCS 1907/266, Memorandum for the Secretary of Defense: Berlin Contingency Planning (26 June 1961).

133 JCS 1907/266, Memorandum for the Secretary of Defense: Berlin Contingency Planning (26 June 1961).

134 Ibid.

135 Ibid.

136 For quotation see Burr, US War Plans.

137 Ibid.

138 JCS 1907/266, Memorandum for the Secretary of Defense: Berlin Contingency Planning (26 June 1961).

139 These figures are presented by William Burr of the National Security Archive based on details in JCS 1907/266, Memorandum for the Secretary of Defense: Berlin Contingency Planning (26 June 1961). For online access to this document and Burr's report see Burr, US War Plans.

140 JCS 1907/266, Memorandum for the Secretary of Defense: Berlin Contingency Planning (26 June 1961).

141 These figures are presented by William Burr of the National Security Archive based on details in JCS 1907/266, Memorandum for the Secretary of Defense: Berlin Contingency Planning (26 June 1961). For online access to this document and Burr's report see Burr, US War Plans.

142 JCS 1907/266, Memorandum for the Secretary of Defense: Berlin Contingency Planning (26 June 1961).

143 Strategic Air Command, *Atomic Weapons Requirements Study for 1959*. See also Burr, US Cold War Nuclear Target Lists Declassified for First Time.

144 For information on the origins of overkill see W. Burr (2004). The Creation of SIOP-62: More Evidence on the Origins of Overkill, *National Security Archive*, 13 July. Retrieved from: http://nsarchive.gwu.edu/NSAEBB/NSAEBB130/index.htm#26. Accessed: 20 March 2015.

145 SIOP-62 was completed in December 1960 and officially implemented by Eisenhower in July 1961. See Strategic Air Command, *History of the Joint Strategic Target Planning Staff*, pp. 1–5.

Chapter 6

1 Shoup documented his concerns in JCS 2056/220. See JCS 2056/220 (11 February 1961). Memorandum by the Commandant of the Marine Corps. Serial 0003B1961. For quotation see F. Kaplan (1983). *The Wizards of Armageddon*, Stanford, CA: Stanford University Press, p. 270.

2 Even Eisenhower became critical of the excesses of SIOP-62 during this period. Building upon his earlier warnings, in his farewell address on 17 January 1961 he stated that within 'the councils of government, we must guard against the acquisition of unwarranted influence, whether sought or unsought, by the military-industrial complex. The potential for the disastrous rise of misplaced power exists and will persist.' This emotive speech has often been interpreted as a warning about SIOP-62's excessive destructive power and SAC bootstrapping. For quotation see D.D. Eisenhower (1961). President Dwight D. Eisenhower's Farewell Address, 17 January, Eisenhower Presidential Library and Archives. Retrieved from: www.archives.gov/milestone-documents/president-dwight-d-eisenhowers-farewell-address#transcript. Accessed: 2 July 2023.

3 S.D. Sagan (1989). *Moving Targets: Nuclear Strategy and National Security*, Princeton, NJ: Princeton University Press.
4 Strategic Air Command (January 1964). *History of the Joint Strategic Target Planning Staff: Preparation of SIOP: 63*, Offutt: History & Research Division, Headquarters, pp. 1–5.
5 Ibid., pp. 1–3.
6 'It's Kennedy for Me!' (Kennedy Campaign Song, 1960). Retrieved from: www.youtube.com/watch?time_continue=32&v=7DoUiNxh6_o. Accessed: 26 February 2016.
7 'Keeping the peace without surrender', like he had done 'alongside Eisenhower', was the dominant message of Nixon's election campaign. See Nixon's campaign video: R. Nixon (1960). *Richard Nixon/Henry Cabot Lodge Campaign Advertisement.* Retrieved from: www.youtube.com/watch?v=j3cpQnVvXSs. Accessed: 1 August 2016.
8 This was a narrow, yet influential, victory. It highlighted the divisions and tensions within American society. For more on this see Freedman's analysis of the North–South divide in America during this period and the differing perceptions of economic and foreign policy manifest in the 'political marketplace'. L. Freedman (2000). *Kennedy's Wars: Berlin, Cuba, Laos and Vietnam*, Oxford: Oxford University Press, pp. 5–8.
9 This is a select list of arguably the most influential events. For more see S. Hall (2016). *1956: The World in Revolt*, London: Faber & Faber. Also see D.A. Nichols (2012). *Eisenhower 1956: The President's Year of Crisis – Suez and the Brink of War*, London: Simon & Schuster.
10 Headlines like 'Why Did the US Lose the Race?' define the perceptions of Sputnik's launch in the US during this period. C.C. Furnas (1957). Why Did the US Lose the Race? Critics Speak Up, *Time*, 21 October, pp. 22–23.
11 For a detailed (and personal) recollection of the period see F.G. Powers (1970). *Operation Overflight: The U-2 Spy Pilot Tells His Story for The First Time*, New York: Holt, Rinehart and Winston.
12 For statements by Khrushchev and Eisenhower on this issue see N. Khrushchev (1960). Nikita Khrushchev: Summit Conference Statement, *New Times*, 16 May, pp. 34–36. D.D. Eisenhower (1960). Dwight Eisenhower: Summit Conference Statement, *Department of State Bulletin*, 6 June, pp. 904–905.
13 S.D. Sagan (1987). SIOP-62: The Nuclear War Plan Briefing to President Kennedy, *International Security*. Vol. 12 (1), pp. 22–51.
14 John F. Kennedy Presidential Library and Museum (2015). *Campaign of 1960*. Retrieved from: www.jfklibrary.org/JFK/JFK-in-History/Campaign-of-1960.aspx. Accessed: 29 February 2016.
15 This has been a broad history of the period as a means to provide the societal mood music to the change in strategy that occurred during this period. For more detailed studies of this period see G.A. Donaldson (2000). *The First Modern Campaign: Kennedy, Nixon, and the Election of 1960*, Plymouth: Rowman & Littlefield. For in-text quotation see A. Abella (2008). *Soldiers of Reason: The RAND Corporation and the Rise of the American Empire*, London: Harcourt, p. 133.
16 Sagan, SIOP-62.
17 See Kennedy's election videos, for example: 'It's Kennedy for Me!' (1960). Retrieved from: www.youtube.com/watch?time_continue=32&v=7DoUiNxh6_o. Accessed: 26 February 2016. Also see headlines from the period. J. Reston (1960). Kennedy's Victory Won by Close Margin; He Promises Fight for World Freedom; Eisenhower Offers 'Orderly Transition', *New York Times*, 18 November. Retrieved from: https://

Notes

archive.nytimes.com/www.nytimes.com/learning/general/onthisday/big/1108.html?
module=inline. Accessed: 8 August 2016.

18 Sagan, SIOP-62.
19 JCS (13 September 1961). JCS 2056/281 (SIOP-62 Briefing). In ibid., pp. 22–51.
20 Ibid.
21 Ibid.
22 Ibid.
23 Ibid.
24 Strategic Air Command, *History of the Joint Strategic Target Planning Staff*, pp. 1–5.
25 Elected on the platform of change and in search of 'more freedom of action', Kennedy quickly set about conducting a 'reappraisal of defence policies'. Ibid., p. 1.
26 As Alain Enthoven stated, 'Kennedy objected to this policy because it faced the president with a choice between "suicide and surrender".' As such, the President wanted more choice, more flexibility. Alain Enthoven. Personal interview. 9 August 2016.
27 W.W. Rostow (1972). *The Diffusion of Power*, New York: Macmillan, pp. 172–173.
28 Strategic Air Command, *History of the Joint Strategic Target Planning Staff*, p. 1.
29 JSTPS. Document 24B: Memorandum for the Record, Secretary McNamara's Visit to the JSTPS, 4 February 1961 (6 February 1961).
30 W. Burr (2004). The Creation of SIOP-62: More Evidence on the Origins of Overkill, *National Security Archive*, 13 July. Retrieved from: http://nsarchive.gwu.edu/NSAEBB/NSAEBB130/index.htm#26. Accessed: 20 March 2015.
31 J.G. Blight and J.M. Lang (2005). *The Fog of War: Lessons from the Life of Robert S. McNamara*, Oxford: Rowman & Littlefield, pp. 5–10.
32 See R. McNamara, Interview by PBS. Washington, DC (1986). War and Peace in the Nuclear Age; At The Brink; Interview with Robert McNamara, 1986 [2], *Openvault*, 28 March. Retrieved from: http://openvault.wgbh.org/catalog/V_823171 90244B46168DFDFB0314E8E7B8#at_4364.416_s. Accessed: 2 August 2016. Also see T. Weiner (2009). Robert S. McNamara, Architect of a Futile War, Dies at 93, *New York Times*, 6 July. Retrieved from: www.nytimes.com/2009/07/07/us/07mcnamara.html?pagewanted=all&_r=0. Accessed: 26 June 2016.
33 In his article 'The McNamara Phenomenon' Bernard Brodie described the reputation for hard work and excellence that McNamara had made for himself. As Brodie stated, 'there were stories of his tremendous zeal for getting on top of his new job. Senior members of his staff hurrying to the Pentagon on Sunday mornings would feel the hood of the Secretary's car, to determine by its temperature how long he had been at work. Usually they found the metal distressingly chilled.' B. Brodie (1965). The McNamara Phenomenon, *World Politics*. Vol. 17 (4), pp. 672–686.
34 Weiner, Robert S. McNamara.
35 Kaplan, *The Wizards of Armageddon*, p. 262.
36 T. Coffey (2015). *American Arsenal: A Century of Waging War*. Oxford: Oxford University Press, p. 287. Also see W.A. Stewart (1967). *Counterforce, Damage-Limiting, and Deterrence*. Santa Monica, CA: RAND. Retrieved from: www.rand.org/content/dam/rand/pubs/papers/2008/P3385.pdf. Accessed: 26 June 2016.
37 Kaplan, *The Wizards of Armageddon*, p. 251.
38 Arnold believed in the value of harnessing scientific research and industry during peacetime as a means to ready the nation for wartime. He was heeding lessons from the inter-war period after the First World War. As he stated in his chapter in *One World or None*, 'research must continue during peacetime and cannot be slighted until

Notes

the war clouds are seen to be gathering'. H.H. Arnold (1946). Air Force in the Atomic Age. In D. Masters and K. Way (eds), *One World or None* (pp. 70–90), New York: McGraw-Hill.

39 Donald Douglas (the aircraft manufacturer and founder of the Douglas Aircraft Company) would also help found Project RAND with Arnold. The two had a history of collaboration and had been working on missile technologies since the 1910s. As one civilian engineer (F.W. Conant) working for Arnold at the Douglas Aircraft factory during the Second World War recalled, '[y]ou never thought the things he asked you to do were possible ... but then you went out and did them'. For quotation see D. Daso (1997). Origins of Airpower: Hap Arnold's Command Years and Aviation Technology, 1936–1945, *Airpower Journal*. Vol. 11 (1), pp. 94–113. For more on Arnold and Douglas see B. Yenne (2013). *Hap Arnold: The General Who Invented the US Air Force*, Washington, DC: Regnery History, p. 33.

40 Others involved in setting up RAND were 'Major General Curtis LeMay; General Lauris Norstad, Assistant Chief of Air Staff, Plans; Edward Bowles of the Massachusetts Institute of Technology, consultant to the Secretary of War; Arthur Raymond, chief engineer at Douglas; and Franklin Collbohm, Raymond's assistant'. See RAND (2022). A Brief History of RAND, *RAND*. Retrieved from: www.rand.org/about/history.html. Accessed: 26 July 2022.

41 W.H. Ware (2008). *RAND and the Information Evolution: A History in Essays and Vignettes*, Santa Monica, CA: RAND, p. 6.

42 The Ford Foundation would invest an initial $1,000,000, but most of the investment would come from Arnold's military budget. As Frank Collbohm explained, Arnold instructed that $30 million be put in his name from the Air Force budget ready for use across three projects. $10 million of this would be used for Project RAND. F.R. Collbohm (1954). Statement by Mr Frank R. Collbohm, Director, The RAND Corporation, on the origins and history RAND, with special reference to the roles played by Mr. H. Rowan Gaither, the Ford Foundation and by Mr Collbohm. Lawrence Henderson Papers, History of RAND Corporations, 1954–1966, RAND Archives, Santa Monica, pp. 6–7.

43 It is interesting to note that as a means to learn from the experiences (and mistakes) of Second World War American bombardment, RAND hired 'several targeters from World War II strategic-bombing campaigns as consultants or full-time employees'. These included economist Charles Hitch and mathematician John Williams. Kaplan, *The Wizards of Armageddon*, p. 206. Not only this, but as Robert Lovett revealed, the advancement of the jet engine and the German V rockets also inspired Arnold. N./N. (1958). Summary Notes on Telephone Discussion with Robert Lovett, Oct. 29, 1958 H.R.G 10/29/58, pp. 1–5. Lawrence Henderson Papers, History of RAND Corporations, 1954–1966, RAND Archives, Santa Monica.

44 Arnold had been working on precision bombardment through missile technologies since 1917. As he reported on early tests of the Kettering Bug (what P.W. Singer refers to as 'an early cruise missile'), 'this flying bomb was sufficiently accurate to reach a point within a hundred yards of its target after a forty-mile run'. If Arnold is correct in his recollection, such precision bombardment over this distance was indeed remarkable for the period (and many decades before its time). Nevertheless, tests show this was either embellished or rare. See H.H. Arnold (1951). *Global Mission*, London: Hutchinson & Co., p. 64. For Singer quotation see P.W. Singer (2010). *Wired for War: The Robotics Revolution and Conflict in the 21st Century*, New York: Penguin, p. 47.

Notes

45 Frank Collbohm explained that, in his first meeting with Arnold about establishing RAND, the general 'emphasized the need for a research project which would go beyond the bounds of conventional bomb delivery and which would include intercontinental pilotless missiles and related techniques, as well and new and more effective countermeasures'. Collbohm, Statement by Mr. Frank R. Collbohm, p. 5.

46 See Chapter 3 of this book.

47 See Chapter 3 of this book.

48 N./N. Summary Notes on Telephone Discussion with Robert Lovett. (Interview likely carried out by F.R. Collbohm.)

49 A.F. Krepinevich and B.D. Watts (2015). *The Last Warrior: Andrew Marshall and the Shaping of Modern American Defence Strategy*, New York: Basic Books, p. 20.

50 For the evolution of early RAND work on missile technologies see J. Neufeld (1990). *The Development of Ballistic Missiles in the United States Air Force 1945–1960*, Washington, DC: Office of Air Force History, pp. 67–68.

51 Bruno Augenstein was a physicist at RAND for forty six years. He was a 'central figure in the development of U.S. space and missile programs'. RAND (1996). *50th Anniversary Project AIR FORCE 1945–1996*. Santa Monica, CA: RAND. Retrieved from: www.rand. org/content/dam/rand/www/external/publications/PAFbook.pdf. Accessed: 3 July 2016. For Augenstein's work on missile technologies see B.W. Augenstein (1954). *A Revised Development Program for Ballistic Missiles of Intercontinental Range*. RM-1191. Santa Barbara, CA: RAND.

52 RAND, *50th Anniversary Project AIR FORCE 1945–1996*.

53 Kaplan, *The Wizards of Armageddon*, p. 60.

54 Vannevar Bush stated: '[i]n its purpose RAND represents a type of activity that I have long believed to be sorely needed throughout the Military Establishment. If we are to bring planning to a desirable state of efficiency and reliability at all levels, we must somehow achieve a thorough analytical and quantitative basis for it.' V. Bush (1948). Lett to Brig. General D.L. Putt Director of Research and Development, US Air Force, p. 1. Lawrence Henderson Papers, History of RAND Corporations, 1954–1966, RAND Archives, Santa Monica.

55 Kaplan, *The Wizards of Armageddon*, p. 59.

56 G. Martin-Lyons (1969). *The Uneasy Partnership: Social Science and the Federal Government in the Twentieth Century*, New York: Russell Sage Foundation, p. 143.

57 Kaplan, *The Wizards of Armageddon*, p. 62.

58 D. Jardini (2013). *Thinking Through the Cold War: RAND, National Security and Domestic Policy*, e-book (n.p.): Smashwords, pp. 51–53.

59 RAND (1948). *New York Conference of Social Scientists*, RAND Report R-106. Santa Monica, CA: RAND, pp. 1–9.

60 Ibid., pp. 1–9.

61 Weaver had published on the theory of air power in January 1946. He was approached as a potential director of RAND, yet declined and took up the directorship at the Rockefeller Foundation. Jardini, *Thinking Through the Cold War*, p. 27. (Thanks to Mr Jardini for supplying a copy of his thesis and ebook.)

62 Weaver was well versed in air power, war, and strategy. His early report on the matter is housed within the NASM. W. Weaver (1947). Comments on a General Theory of Air Warfare. E.L. Bowles Papers, National Air and Space Museum, Washington, DC. Box U, Folder: Air Warfare: Warren Weaver.

63 RAND, *New York Conference of Social Scientists*, pp. 1–9.

Notes

64 Ibid., pp. 1–9.

65 Jardini, *Thinking Through the Cold War*, pp. 52–53.

66 J. Cook (1990). Hans Speier, Author, Exile School Founder and Sociologist, 85, *New York Times*, 23 February. Retrieved from: www.nytimes.com/1990/02/23/obituaries/hans-speier-author-exile-school-founder-and-sociologist-85.html. Accessed: 1 August 2016.

67 Hitch and his colleagues worked on cost–benefit analysis, optimisation methods, and systems analysis. Out of this work emerged their seminal work, *The Economics of Defense in the Nuclear Age*, which became the 'operation manual for the "McNamara revolution" in the Kennedy administration's Pentagon'. For quotation and expanded details see Jardini, *Thinking Through the Cold War*, p. 58.

68 This was helped by multidisciplinary aspects at RAND such as the high-level Strategic Objectives Committee (SOC). This consisted, over time, of Andrew Marshall, Bernard Brodie, Charles Hitch (the SOC's first chairman), Arnold Kramish, James Digby (and electrical engineer), Alex Mood (a statistician), John Williams, Herman Kahn, and economist Malcolm Hoag. This is exemplified by Brodie's acknowledgements in *Strategy in the Missile Age* where he pays thanks to Wohlstetter, Spier, Schelling, Rowen, Kaufmann, Kahn, Digby, and many more RAND scholars across a number of departments. See B. Brodie (1959). *Strategy in the Missile Age*, R-335, Santa Monica, CA: RAND. Also see Krepinevich and Watts, *The Last Warrior*, p. 34.

69 M. Howard (1992). Brodie, Wohlstetter and American Nuclear Strategy, *Survival*. Vol. 34 (2), pp. 107–116.

70 It is Stewart in his 1967 RAND report who most succinctly surmises counterforce and countervalue. As he stated, '[t]he strategist can elect to strike at his opponent's military forces. This is counterforce and in the nuclear age people tend to think of it as a single blow against enemy "strategic" nuclear forces. Alternatively, the strategist can undertake to strike at the source of his opponent's national strength, i.e., his economic resources or population. In the Nuclear age this is labelled as countervalue strategy.' Of course, it is worth noting that a strategy, as Kaufmann would ultimately show, does not have to choose between the two. Both can serve a purpose for the means and achievement of an effective deterrence. See Stewart, *Counterforce, Damage-Limiting, and Deterrence*.

71 Howard, Brodie, Wohlstetter and American Nuclear Strategy.

72 Described by Brodie as 'the eminent Albert Wohlstetter', Wohlstetter was one of the most influential thinkers on American nuclear strategy at RAND (and beyond). Arguably, his most influential text was A. Wohlstetter (1958). *The Delicate Balance of Terror*, Santa Monica, CA: RAND. Retrieved from: www.rand.org/about/history/wohlstetter/P1472/P1472.html. Accessed: 8 July 2016. For Brodie see Brodie, The McNamara Phenomenon. For in-text quotation see A. Wohlstetter, Interview by PBS. Boston, MA (1986). War and Peace in the Nuclear Age; Education of Robert McNamara, The; Interview with Albert Wohlstetter, 1986, *Openvault*, 26 February. Retrieved from: http://openvault.wgbh.org/catalog/V_2C5EF61C59EE44CB89CD8 6E62F2AD4C4. Accessed: 2 August 2016.

73 Henry S. Rowen and Alain C. Enthoven (both young economists) worked alongside Wohlsetter and would 'become important members of McNamara's staff'. Brodie, The McNamara Phenomenon.

74 A literary expert with a passion for Shakespeare's Hamlet, Roberta turned her interest in tragedy towards learning lessons from Pearl Harbor (at the recommendation of Andrew Marshall). This research would see her come head to head with the

Notes

Eisenhower-Nixon administration. Indeed, Roberta had warned that the US was still vulnerable to surprise attack – a message that was not welcomed by the powers that be. As David Sherman wrote in his 2022 article on the topic: 'Wohlstetter's seminal analysis was relegated to the classified archives of the Department of Defense for several years after she finished the manuscript in the mid-1950s.' It would not be until the RAND team were brought in from the cold during the Kennedy administration that the book would be published just prior to the Cuban Missile Crisis. The work is now considered 'a classic of intelligence literature' and Second World War history. D. Sherman (2022). An Intelligence Classic that Almost Never Was – Roberta Wohlstetter's *Pearl Harbor: Warning and Decision, Intelligence and National Security*, Vol. 37 (3), pp. 331–345.

75 Hoffman was another young economist who published the influential *Protecting US Power to Strike Back in the 1950s and 1960s* alongside Wohlstetter and Rowen. A.J. Wohlstetter, F.S. Hoffman and H.S. Rowen (1956). *Protecting US Power to Strike Back in the 1950s and 1960s*, R-290, Santa Monica, CA: RAND.

76 As Chapter 3 has highlighted, some of these ideas were expressed by General Arnold in his post-war strategic writings, especially the importance of force protection, which was put forward in detail by Arnold. It should also be noted that Wohlstetter's recommendations for the protection of bomber forces were not accepted by LeMay. As Brodie recalled when discussing Wohlstetter's recommendations in his 1978 article, '[t]he Air Force still has no shelters for these bombers and does not contemplate any'. B. Brodie (1978). The Development of Nuclear Strategy, *International Security*. Vol. 2 (4), pp. 65–83. For Wohlstetter see Wohlstetter, *The Delicate Balance of Terror*.

77 Brodie, The Development of Nuclear Strategy.

78 See Chapter 4 of this book. Howard also stated that Brodie 'complained bitterly about what he saw as the ossified nature of the military mind, the absence of flexibility and critical analysis in their thinking'. Howard, Brodie, Wohlstetter and American Nuclear Strategy. Also see B.H. Steiner (1991). *Bernard Brodie and the Foundations of American Nuclear Strategy*, Lawrence: University of Kansas Press.

79 Brodie's early reports at RAND were greatly assisted by Andrew Marshall and Victor Hunt. See Kaplan, *The Wizards of Armageddon*, pp. 204–205.

80 The social sciences at RAND included Nathan C. Leites, Paul Kecskemeti, and Brodie's protégé William Kaufmann. Brodie also inspired many key strategists across RAND's departments. As Thomas C. Schelling stated, '[h]e, more than anyone else, helped us learn to think about surviving in a nuclear weapon world'. For quotation see T.C. Schelling (1979). *A Tribute to Bernard Brodie and (Incidentally) to RAND*. Santa Monica, CA: RAND. Retrieved from: www.rand.org/content/dam/rand/pubs/papers/2006/P6355.pdf. Accessed: 8 August 2016. For the work of Leites see N. Leites (1951). *The Operational Code of the Politburo*, New York: McGraw Hill. For Kecskemeti see P. Kecskemeti (1958). *Strategic Surrender: The Politics of Victory and Defeat*, Santa Monica, CA: RAND. Retrieved from: www.rand.org/pubs/reports/R308.html. Accessed: 8 July 2016.

81 Howard, Brodie, Wohlstetter and American Nuclear Strategy.

82 B. Brodie (1950). Strategic Bombing: What It Can Do, *Reporter*, 15 August. Retrieved from: www.unz.org/Pub/Reporter-1950aug15-00028. Accessed: 8 August 2016.

83 From being a proponent of city bombing, to condemning strategic justification for nuclear bombardment, Brodie's ideas about nuclear strategy evolved over time. Ultimately, he increasingly believed that only diplomacy could be justified in regard to nuclear weapons. For the change in Brodie's perceptions of nuclear strategy see Brodie,

Strategic Bombing: What It Can Do. Also see Brodie, The Development of Nuclear Strategy. For a collection of Brodie's work of nuclear strategy from the 1950s see B. Brodie (1958). *The Anatomy of Deterrence*, RM-2218, Santa Monica, CA: RAND.

84 Brodie, Strategic Bombing: What It Can Do.

85 As stated above, Brodie deviated from his earlier proposals 'relying primarily on tacit agreements and diplomacy to avoid this on both sides'. Howard, Brodie, Wohlstetter and American Nuclear Strategy.

86 Brodie, *Strategy in the Missile Age*, p. 293.

87 Ibid., p. 289.

88 To further highlight his critique of the SAC plan Brodie compared his 'no cities' approach to 'withdrawal before ejaculation', while the SAC plan was more likened to 'going all the way'. Such 'imaginative' representations would come to catch the mood within the social sciences section of RAND and would feed into critique provided to SAC officers during briefings on nuclear war plans. As Brodie's RAND colleague Herman Kahn famously stated to SAC officers: '[g]entlemen, you don't have a war plan, you have a war orgasm'. This was later shortened to 'wargasm'. Kahn would expand upon this argument and highlight it in a more nuanced manner. As he flippantly stated in his 1960 RAND report (P-1888-RC): '[i]f it be granted that each side can utterly destroy the other, then expensive preparations to reduce casualties, lessen damage, and facilitate postwar recuperation are useless. Can we not spare ourselves the financial burden of such preparations?' For Brodie quotes regarding sex and nuclear war see Kaplan, *The Wizards of Armageddon*, p. 223. For Kahn see H. Kahn (1960). *The Nature and Feasibility of War and Deterrence*, P-1888-RC, Santa Monica, CA: RAND, p. 2.

89 As is explained towards the end of this chapter, due to the legacies of precision, the case may indeed be made for Albert Wohlstetter to hold this title.

90 Brodie, The McNamara Phenomenon. Kaufmann received his PhD from Yale in International Relations in 1948. W. Kaufmann. Interview by PBS. Boston, MA (1986). War and Peace in the Nuclear Age; Education of Robert McNamara, The; Interview with William Kaufmann, 1986, *Openvault*, 5 March. Retrieved from: http://open vault.wgbh.org/catalog/V_D1FA1FDE1AF4474A8C40165A496EEAEB. Accessed: 2 August 2016.

91 Kaplan, *The Wizards of Armageddon*, p. 194.

92 Kaufmann, Interview by PBS.

93 Kaplan, *The Wizards of Armageddon*, p. 190.

94 W. Kaufmann (1964). *The McNamara Strategy*, London: Harper & Row, p. 11.

95 The work was originally published in a small report-sized format in 1954. It was published again in 1956 and 1958 in different formats. W. Kaufmann (1956). The Requirements of Deterrence. In William W. Kaufmann (ed.), *Military Policy and National Security* (pp. 12–38). Princeton, NJ: Princeton University Press.

96 Kaufmann's counterforce strategy was influenced by Wohlstetter's force protection for second strike capabilities and Brodie's city avoidance (to name but two influences). Kaufmann understood the deterrence factor of second strike capabilities and agreed with Brodie about city avoidance. As he stated: 'cities virtually guaranteed that your own cities would be attacked. Therefore, you really wanted to avoid those cities in order not just to be a nice guy ... But because you wanted to try and limit damage to your own cities.' Kaufmann, Interview by PBS.

97 F. Kaplan (2009). *1959: The Year Everything Changed*, Hoboken, NJ: John Wiley & Sons, p. 68.

Notes

98 Kaufmann, Interview by PBS.
99 W. Kaufmann, Interview by the National Security Archive (1996). Interview with Professor William Kaufmann – 8 August. Retrieved from: https://nsarchive.gwu.edu/coldwar/interviews/episode-12/kaufmann3.html. Accessed: 2 August 2016.
100 Kaplan, *1959*, p. 68.
101 Ibid.
102 As Wohlstetter stated '[a] force cannot deter an attack, which it cannot survive'. Wohlstetter, Interview by PBS. For Kaplan quotation see Kaplan, *1959*, p. 68.
103 W. Kaufmann (1958). *The Evolution of Deterrence 1945–1958*, Santa Monica, CA: RAND, p. 2.
104 Kaplan, *1959*, p. 68.
105 Kaufmann, Interview by PBS.
106 Ibid.
107 Strategic Air Command, *History of the Joint Strategic Target Planning Staff.*
108 Brodie, The McNamara Phenomenon.
109 J. Lepgold (1990). *The Declining Hegemon: The United States and European Defence, 1960–1990*, London: Greenwood Press, p. 121. As Baylis stated, it was 'flexibility in strategic planning which the Secretary of Defense was striving to achieve in his reform of SIOP'. J. Baylis (1995). *Ambiguity and Deterrence: British Nuclear Strategy 1945–1964*, Oxford: Clarendon Press, p. 313.
110 Lepgold, *The Declining Hegemon*, p. 121.
111 Kaufmann, Interview by PBS.
112 It is important not to ignore the inter-service rivalry aspects in the Air Force appeal towards counterforce at this time. As has often been the case, many in the Air Force were aware of the increasing pressure being place on them by the Army, Navy, and political elites who wanted them to justify the scale of their war plans. Polaris and the increased capability of missile technologies created options for smaller, yet effective, non-Air Force forces. Kaufmann, Interview by PBS.
113 Ibid.
114 Ibid.
115 Coffey, *American Arsenal*, p. 287.
116 Kaplan, *The Wizards of Armageddon*, p. 246
117 In the letter, Jackson requests that Collbohm (and his RAND researchers) look over a report from the Subcommittee on National Policy Machinery. H. Jackson (1959). Letter from Henry Jackson to Frank J. Collbohm, December 10, 1959. H. Rowan Gaither Papers, Box 001. RAND Archives, Santa Monica.
118 In one letter dated 10 June 1959, Jackson thanks Brodie for his comments on his [Jackson's] speech to 'the National War College on April 16'. H. Jackson (1959). Letter from Henry M. Jackson USS to Mr Bernard Brodie, June 10, 1959. H. Rowan Gaither Papers, Box 001. RAND Archives, Santa Monica.
119 Ibid. Also see F. Collbohm (1960). Letter from Frank J. Collbohm to the Honorable Henry M. Jackson, January 7, 1960. H. Rowan Gaither Papers, Box 001. RAND Archives, Santa Monica; H.M. Jackson (1959). Letter from Henry M. Jackson to Dr William W. Kaufmann. July 30, 1959. H. Rowan Gaither Papers, Box 001. RAND Archives, Santa Monica.
120 According to Panagiotis Hatzis, Theodore Sorensen classified Henderson as a 'coordinator and expediter'. In addition (and by her own admission) Deirdre also acted as the 'legs and arms' of the advisory group. See. P. Hatzis (1996). The Academic Origins

Notes

of John F. Kennedy's New Frontier, MA Thesis, Department of History, Concordia University, Montreal.

121 D. Henderson. Personal interview. 6 July 2021.

122 This history is fully documented in my forthcoming chapter 'Kennedy's Road to the White House: Paved with Good Advice' which has been accepted for publication in an edited book on the Kennedy years, due for release in 2024.

123 D. Henderson. Personal interview. 6 July 2021. Also see Deirdre Henderson Personal Papers, Kennedy Library and Archives, Boston, MA, Box 002 – Archibald Cox (DHPP-002–012).

124 For the original letters of recommendation see Deirdre Henderson Personal Papers, Kennedy Library and Archives, Boston, MA, Box 001 – Appointment Memos (DHPP-001–004).

125 D. Henderson. Personal interview. 6 February 2019.

126 For their influential role in US defence policy, both Albert and Roberta Wohlstetter would be awarded the Presidential Medal of Freedom by President Ronald Reagan. However, it should be noted there were many women working at RAND during these years, most of whom are missing from the historiography. These include, but are by no means limited to, Fawn Brodie, Doris Iklé, and Bernice B. Brown. I hope to one day be able to write their history.

127 Others from RAND would walk the halls of power. The so-called Whiz Kids that surrounded McNamara during this period have been well documented, and many were originally RAND researchers. There were also those from RAND who continued to make their influence known in corresponding administrations. These included Harold Brown, Henry Rowen, William Kaufmann, Ivan Selin, and Daniel Ellsberg (to name a few), with scholars such as Albert Wohlstetter and Bernard Brodie advising on the sidelines. *Time* (1962). The Pentagon's Whiz Kids, *Time*, 3 August. Retrieved from: https://content.time.com/time/magazine/article/0,9171,896423,00.html. Accessed: 27 March 2023.

128 As Enthoven stated, Kaufmann, 'a good friend and colleague of mine, had been studying this whole question, and had developed a briefing on the concept of war planning and what the use of weapons ought to be. In 1961 and 1962 Kaufmann made various briefings around the Pentagon. It was probably 1961 that he briefed McNamara.' A. Enthoven, Interview by PBS. Boston, MA (1986). War and Peace in the Nuclear Age; Education of Robert McNamara, The; Interview with Alain Enthoven, 1986. *Openvault*, 22 February. Retrieved from: http://openvault.wgbh.org/catalog/V_75CBC1D800E24C0EA2F792AEE69CF778#at_1460.144_s. Accessed: 2 August 2016.

129 Kaufmann, Interview by PBS.

130 Ibid.

131 Ibid.

132 Ibid.

133 As Kaufmann stated, McNamara 'wanted to know whether he was entering an area where there was going to be an endless open-ended kind of expenditure or whether one … would ever get into an area of diminishing returns'. Ibid.

134 In Kaufmann's text *The McNamara Strategy* (1964) he elaborated a little on McNamara's line of thought, stating that 'McNamara, naturally, was predisposed toward the alternative of the flexible response with the options that it contained.' To provide context, this was in comparison to the options of massive retaliation or minimum deterrence as outlined by WSEG 50. WSEG 50 was a ten-volume report briefed to McNamara

before the Kaufmann briefing. It recommended limitation on weapons (appealing to McNamara) but did not recommend counterforce. Instead, the report highlighted the benefit of 'minimum deterrence'. Kaufmann, *The McNamara Strategy*, pp. 52–53. For more information on WSEG 50 see Kaplan, *The Wizards of Armageddon*, p. 258. For in-text quotations see Kaufmann, Interview by PBS.

135 R. McNamara (1961). Appendix I to Memorandum for the President: Recommended Long Range Nuclear Delivery Forces 1963–1967, 23 September. The Robert S. McNamara Papers Part I: 89. Department of Defense Memoranda for the President, 1961–1969. Retrieved from: https://nsarchive.files.wordpress.com/2014/11/foia-release-mcnamara-memo.pdf. Accessed: 3 March 2016. This notion is further supported by McNamara's biographer Deborah Shapley: '[i]n characteristic fashion, he adopted Kaufmann's plan wholesale. Counterforce-no cities-thus was transformed into US nuclear doctrine at the flick of his pen.' Quotation taken from J.J. Mearsheimer (1993). McNamara's War, *Bulletin of the Atomic Scientist*. Vol. 49 (3), pp. 49–53. For original text see D. Shapley (1993). *Promise and Power: The Life and Times of Robert McNamara*, London: Little Brown and Company.

136 McNamara, Appendix I to Memorandum for the President.

137 Ibid.

138 The context in which counterforce was devised is best explained by one of McNamara's closest advisors, Enthoven, who stated: 'Herman Kahn, a famous RAND strategist and author, upon reviewing our strategic nuclear war plan said, to General Thomas Power, the Commander in Chief of the Strategic Air Command, "You don't have a war plan, you have a wargasm", otherwise characterized as "a spasm response".' McNamara sought a plan that would permit us to respond to any attack with 'control and deliberation'. Alain Enthoven. Personal interview. 9 August 2016.

139 Robert S. McNamara (23 February 1961). Testimony before the committee on Armed Services, House of Representatives. Originally quoted in Kaufmann, *The McNamara Strategy*, p. 53.

140 Ibid.

141 R. Rhodes (1995). The General and World War III. *New Yorker*, 11 June. Retrieved from: www.newyorker.com/magazine/1995/06/19/the-general-and-world-war-iii. Accessed: 2 April 2023. Also see D.A. Brugioni (1992). *Eyeball to Eyeball: The Inside Story of the Cuban Missile Crisis*, London: Random House.

142 Ibid. For original quote see J.G. Blight and D.A. Welch (1989). *On the Brink: Americans and Soviets Reexamine the Cuban Missile Crisis*, New York: Hill & Wang.

143 Rhodes, The General and World War III.

144 W. Kozak (2011). *Curtis LeMay: Strategist and Tactician*, Washington, DC: Regnery, p. 328.

145 The Joint Strategic Target Planning Staff (JSTPS) was 'an inter-service group of intelligence and operations specialists' (with SAC and Air Force personnel making up the majority of membership) who were charged with analysing and appraising strategic nuclear targeting. Strategic Air Command, *History of the Joint Strategic Target Planning Staff*. For in-text quotation see page 3 of the SIOP-63 document.

146 Ibid., p. 14.

147 Ibid., p. 14.

148 Cities could still be targeted, but only at the final stage of escalation, not as the first port of call as was detailed in SIOP-62. Ibid., pp. 10–20.

149 Ibid., pp. 20–25.

Notes

150 The speech was written by another former RAND analyst Daniel Ellsberg (famous for releasing the Pentagon Papers in 1971). Kaufmann had taken issue with the public declaration believing such a move would cause domestic political issues for the British and French. As Kaufmann succinctly explained, 'there are a lot of things that you can say privately to your friends which they will accept, but if you say them in public and then have a world wide audience ... you create a number of political problems for the officials in those countries'. Kaufmann, Interview by PBS.

151 R.S. McNamara (1962). 'No Cities' Speech by Sec. of Defense McNamara, 9 July. Retrieved from: www.atomicarchive.com/Docs/Deterrence/Nocities.shtml. Accessed: 19 August 2016. The reception to counterforce was by no means totally positive. On the one hand the Europeans believed that McNamara had reduced the potency of deterrence and SAC saw a reduction in force/power. On the other, critics abhorred any plan that still allowed for millions of civilians to be killed. For an interesting breakdown of the British reaction to this period see Docktrill's review in the Journal of Cold War Studies. S. Docktrill (2005). Kennedy, Macmillan and the Cold War: The Irony of Interdependence, *Journal of Cold War Studies*. Vol. 7 (4), pp. 160–162.

152 Public support for war-mitigating and damage-limiting nuclear policies were, unsurprisingly, popular at this time. (Kennedy was, in part, elected to implement such change.) Although initially welcomed by many members of the public in 1962, counterforce (as the chapter proceeds to explain) became synonymous with making nuclear war more likely. As reports from the Historical Office within the Office of the Secretary of Defense stated, 'McNamara soon deemphasized the no cities approach, for several reasons: public fear that planning to use nuclear weapons in limited ways would make nuclear war seem more feasible.' For quotation and more information see Office of the Secretary of Defense (2015). *Robert S. McNamara: John F. Kennedy / Lyndon Johnson Administration: January 21, 1961–February 29, 1968.* Retrieved from: http://history.defense.gov/Multimedia/Biographies/Article-View/Article/571271/robert-s-mcnamara. Accessed: 7 September 2016.

153 Beatrice Heuser argued in her text *The Bomb: Nuclear Weapons in their Historical, Strategic and Ethical Context* that counterforce has much earlier origins in American strategic thought. As Heuser outlined, '[m]any related concepts of nuclear targeting also predated the development of nuclear weapons. Counterforce and Countervalue strategies had been developed, as had deterrence.' Heuser relates these back to the Second World War. B. Heuser (2014). *The Bomb: Nuclear Weapons in their Historical, Strategic and Ethical Context*, London: Routledge, p. 97.

154 Alain Enthoven. Personal interview. 9 August 2016.

155 R. Zarate (2009). Albert and Roberta on Nuclear-Age Strategy. In Robert Zarat and Henry Sokolski (eds), *Nuclear Heuristics: Selected Writings of Albert and Roberta Wohlstetter* (pp. 1–90). Carlisle: Strategic Studies Institute, p. 49.

156 The 'eminent Wohlstetter' was, according to Brodie, 'the leader' of the RAND group of strategists who, in part, pioneered counterforce. As Brodie continued, though Wohlstetter had been invited he 'chose not to become a member of the new Administration but consulted with its leaders and also remained in very close contact with others in his old group, especially Henry S. Rowen and Alain C. Enthoven, who did become important members of McNamara's staff. Brodie, The Development of Nuclear Strategy.

157 It should be stated that Wohlstetter disliked using the term 'counterforce' and much preferred to discuss the utility of 'accuracy' and later 'precision'. Wohlstetter, Interview by PBS.

Notes

158 Ibid.

159 For more on the Wohlstetter School see Howard, Brodie, Wohlstetter and American Nuclear Strategy.

160 For more on 'declaratory nuclear policy' see R.S. Norris and H.M. Kristensen (2014). *Reviewing Nuclear Guidance: Putting Obama's Words Into Action.* Retrieved from: www.armscontrol.org/act/2011_11/Reviewing_Nuclear_Guidance_Putting_Obama_Words_Into_Action. Accessed: 2 July 2023.

161 The origins of MAD can be seen from 1964–65. For analysis of the speech see C.H. Fairbank Jr. (2004). MAD and US Strategy. In Henry D. Sokolski (ed.), *Getting MAD: Nuclear Mutual Assured Destruction, Its Origins and Practice* (pp. 137–149), Ann Arbor: University of Michigan Library Press.
For the full speech see R. McNamara (1967). Remarks by Secretary of Defense Robert S. McNamara, September 18, 1967, *Bulletin of the Atomic Scientists*. Vol. 23 (10), pp. 26–31.

162 McNamara, Remarks by Secretary of Defense Robert S. McNamara.

163 Ibid.

164 Ibid.

165 Wohlstetter, Interview by PBS.

166 Ibid.

167 Not only were the European powers not a fan of the limited counterforce ethos, the Air Force (especially SAC) found a novel way of interpreting it that went against McNamara's intentions. As Harold Brown (McNamara's Director of Defense Research and Engineering from 1961 to 1965 and former Secretary of Defense under President Carter) stated, 'the city avoidance approach, military targets only approach, certainly opened the door to unlimited requests for force'. H. Brown. Interview by PBS. Boston, MA (1986). War and Peace in the Nuclear Age; Education of Robert McNamara, The; Interview with Harold Brown, 1986. *OpenVault*, 13 March. Retrieved from: http://openvault.wgbh.org/catalog/V_CF179614E1CD43A292F04877A2DC1189#at_2389.207_s. Accessed: 2 August 2016.

168 It is interesting to note, as Rosenberg does, that despite the desire to limit damage and weapons procurement levels, such ambitions were only partially successful. Although McNamara's MAD became the 'nation's basic military posture in 1964–65' it came, as Rosenberg explains, 'after the SIOP and missile programs based on the twin pillars of damage limiting and assured destruction had operationally established levels of force far above what critics of SAC offensive, including Eisenhower towards the close of his administration, considered necessary'. Thus, the desires (and the policy) may have differed drastically to the operational reality. For Rosenberg see D.A. Rosenberg (1983). Towards Armageddon: The Foundations of United States Nuclear Strategy, 1945–1961. Unpublished PhD Dissertation, University of Chicago, p. 311.

169 As Charles H. Fairbanks Jr. stated, '[t]he price tag for the weapons on this [counterforce] wish list was frightfully large'. Fairbank, MAD and US Strategy.

170 Alain Enthoven. Personal interview. 9 August 2016.

171 Ibid.

172 Ibid.

173 McNamara, Interview by PBS.

174 Office of the Secretary of Defense, *Robert S. McNamara: John F. Kennedy / Lyndon Johnson Administration.*

175 Ibid.

176 McNamara, Interview by PBS.

177 Ibid.
178 Official estimates gave strength to the argument that a shift away from reliance on nuclear weapons towards conventional forces would, due to the sheer strength of the Warsaw Pact, leave the US and its allies unable to match the might of the USSR. McNamara and his staff believed differently, however. Not only did they believe the Soviet forces were smaller than predicted, but they believed with an increase in conventional force investment they could counter the Warsaw Pact. As Enthoven confirmed, '[o]fficial estimates of the size and strength of the Warsaw Pact forces relative to NATO exaggerated Pact capabilities to an extreme extent. People thought that, when in doubt, the safe thing was to overestimate the enemy. As McNamara pointed out, 'it can be just as dangerous to overstate as to understate the enemy' because that can lead to strategies of desperation (like nuclear war when we could have won a non-nuclear war)'. Alain Enthoven. Personal interview. 9 August 2016.
179 Department of Defense (1962). *Memorandum for the President: Recommended FY 1964–FY 1968 Strategic Retaliatory Forces*, 21 November. Retrieved from: https://archive.org/ details/DraftMemorandumforthePresidentRecommendedFY1964toFY1968Strategic RetaliatoryForces. Accessed: 8 August 2016.
180 McNamara, Interview by PBS.
181 Ibid.
182 For more on the consequences of this conventional shift, especially in regard to Vietnam, see Freedman, *Kennedy's Wars*. Also see R.A. Pape (1996). *Bombing to Win: Air Power and Coercion in War*, New York: Cornell University Press; M. Hastings (2019). *Vietnam: An Epic History of a Divisive War 1945–1975*, New York: Harper Collins. For more on the parallel history of RAND and the Vietnam war see K. Husain (2003). Neocons: The Men Behind the Curtain, *Bulletin of the Atomic Scientists*. Vol 59 (6), pp. 62–71.
183 The Kennedy administration's decision to embark upon the Vietnam War somewhat epitomises this focus. For more on the application of 'limited warfare' to the case of Vietnam during this period see A.R. Lewis (2012). *The American Culture of War: The History of US Military Force from World War II to Operation Enduring Freedom*, London: Routledge, pp. 201–208. Also see McNamara, Interview by PBS.
184 Alain Enthoven. Personal interview. 9 August 2016. For more on Enthoven's policies during this period see A.C. Enthoven and K. Wayne-Smith (1971). *How Much is Enough?: Shaping the Defence Program (1961–1969)*, Santa Monica, CA: RAND.
185 This idea, according to Enthoven, gained bipartisan support from prominent Republican's, such as 1964 presidential nominee Barry Goldwater, who commended both McNamara and Enthoven for their reorientation of policy. As Enthoven recalled '[t]o my surprise, he said he liked the lecture [on the change in policy], that he never did agree with Eisenhower's policy of cutting back our conventional forces, and that he agreed with our build-up of conventional forces and the philosophy I had articulated. Given the political situation, that came as a big surprise. Goldwater expressed the same thought as McNamara when McNamara was testifying before his committee. When McNamara got back to the Pentagon, he laughed and joked and stated "Alain, it causes me to call into question the wisdom of your advice." We had a good laugh and also a feeling of relief that we were not likely to be attacked on this aspect of our defense policy.' Alain Enthoven. Personal interview. 9 August 2016.
186 Wohlstetter, Interview by PBS.

Notes

187 Ibid.

188 Ibid.

189 Wohlstetter also believed that, in a similar vein to the criticism of massive retaliation, MAD may make smaller aggression by the USSR more likely due to the fact it was an unrealistic 'bluff' that the US would inflict 'unacceptable' destruction (which would ensure mutual destruction) for smaller incursions. As Wohlstetter hypothetically questioned, 'how do you make threats to respond that are believable ... if you were saying that you were going to respond by unleashing uncontrollable destruction that would engulf you as well?'. Ibid.

190 Ibid.

191 Ibid.

192 Ibid.

193 Ibid.

194 For more recent debates see A. Long and B. Rittenhouse Green (2015). Stalking the Secure Second Strike: Intelligence, Counterforce, and Nuclear Strategy, *Journal of Strategic Studies*. Vol. 38 (1–2), pp. 38–73. Also see H.M. Kristensen and M. Korda (2023). Nuclear Notebook: United States Nuclear Weapons, 2023, *Bulletin of the Atomic Scientists*, 16 January. Retrieved from: https://thebulletin.org/premium/2023-01/nuclear-notebook-united-states-nuclear-weapons-2023/. Accessed: 4 April 2023.

195 See J.P. Sterba (1986). Between MAD and Counterforce: In Search of a Morally and Strategically Sound Nuclear Defense Policy, *Social Theory and Practice*. Vol. 12 (2), pp. 173–199. Also see K.A. Lieber and D.G. Press (2014). The End of MAD? The Nuclear Dimension of US Primacy, *International Security*. Vol. 30 (4), pp. 7–44; F.J. Gavin (2022). Time to Rethink America's Nuclear Strategy, *Foreign Affairs*, 5 September. Retrieved from: www.foreignaffairs.com/united-states/time-rethink-america-nuclear-strategy. Accessed: 22 January 2023.

196 Wohlstetter, Interview by PBS.

197 N. Swidey (2003). *The Analyst: Strategy Guru Albert Wohlstetter*. Retrieved from: https://archive.boston.com/news/globe/ideas/articles/2003/05/18/the_analyst. Accessed: 19 August 2016.

198 A.J. Bacevich (2005). *The New American Militarism: How Americans are Seduced by War*, Oxford: Oxford University Press, p. 161. For in-text Wohlstetter quotation referred to by Bacevich see A. Wohlstetter (1974). Threats and Promises of Peace: Europe and America in the New Era, *Orbis*. Vol. 17 (4), pp. 1107–1144.

199 S.M. Hersh (2003). Lunch with the Chairman: Why was Richard Perle meeting with Adnan Khashoggi?, *New Yorker*, 17 March. Retrieved from: www.newyorker.com/magazine/2003/03/17/lunch-with-the-chairman. Accessed: 23 August 2016.

200 M. Shareef (2014). *The United States, Iraq and the Kurds: Shock, Awe and Aftermath*, Abingdon: Routledge, p. 30.

201 Z. Khalilzad (2016). *The Envoy: From Kabul to the White House, My Journey Through a Turbulent World*, New York: St Martin's Press.

202 As he stated in critique of the accuracy (or lack thereof) in American Thor and Jupiter missile technology during the late 1950s: '[n]evertheless, if the Thor and Jupiter have these defects, might not some future weapon be free of them? Some of these defects, of course, will be overcome in time. Solid fuels or storable liquids will eventually replace liquid oxygen, reliabilities will increase, various forms of mobility or portability will become feasible, accuracies may even be so improved that such weapons can be used in limited wars.' Wohlstetter, *The Delicate Balance of Terror*.

Notes

203 A. Wohlstetter (1968). *Strength, Interest and New Technologies*, Santa Monica, CA: RAND. Retrieved from: www.rand.org/about/history/wohlstetter/DL16624/DL16624.html. Accessed: 18 August 2016.

204 Ibid.

205 Ibid.

206 Ibid.

207 DARPA and DNA (1975). *Summary Report of the Long Range Research and Development Planning Programme*, DNA-75-03055, 7 February, Falls Church, VA: Lulejian & Associates. Also see A. Wohlstetter (1975). Defense implications of technologies of precision and discrimination. Declassified. Albert J. Wohlstetter Papers (97076.12), Hoover Institution Library and Archives, Stanford University, Stanford, CA.

208 F.C. Ikle and A. Wohlstetter (1988). *Discriminate Deterrence: Report of the Commission on Integrated Long-Term Strategy*, January, AD-A277 478, Washington, DC: Government Printing Office.

209 DARPA and DNA, *Summary Report of the Long Range Research and Development Planning Programme*, p. iii.

210 Ibid.

211 Ibid.

212 Ibid.

213 Ibid., p. 45.

214 Ikle and Wohlstetter, *Discriminate Deterrence*, p. 8.

215 Ibid., p. 2.

216 Ibid., p. 15.

217 Ibid., p. 21.

218 Ibid., p. 1.

Epilogue

1 D. Deptula. Interview with James Rogers for the Warfare podcast (2021). Gulf War: Inside the Planning Room, *Warfare* podcast. Retrieved from: https://open.spotify.com/episode/1eiprsQZwrVjFTuwXtUWZZ?si=sLTzfIyhRV-OqQ93iNXAkA&nd=1 Accessed: 7 April 2023.

2 D. Tierney (2011). 'The Mother of All Battles': 20 Years Later, *Atlantic*, 28 February. Retrieved from: www.theatlantic.com/national/archive/2011/02/the-mother-of-all-battles-20-years-later/71804/. Accessed: 8 April 2023.

3 For more on the parallel history of how RAND researchers directly contributed to the RMA see K. Husain (2003). Neocons: The Men Behind the Curtain, *Bulletin of the Atomic Scientists*. Vol 59 (6), pp. 62–71.

4 More broadly, advancements in stealth technologies and command and control reliability and resilience also contributed to mission success.

5 R. Sisk (2021). 'Most Successful War of the 20th Century': What the US Did Right in Desert Storm, *Military.com*, 18 January. Retrieved from: www.military.com/daily-news/2021/01/18/most-successful-war-of-20th-century-what-us-did-right-desert-storm.html. Accessed: 8 April 2023.

6 M.W. Browne (1991). Invention that Shaped the Gulf War: The Laser-Guided Bomb, *New York Times*, 26 February. Retrieved from: www.nytimes.com/1991/02/26/science/invention-that-shaped-the-gulf-war-the-laser-guided-bomb.html. Accessed: 8 April 2023.

Notes

7 Total estimated by the Iraqi government and reported by PBS. PBS (n.d.). Iraqi Death Toll, *PBS*. Retrieved from: www.pbs.org/wgbh/pages/frontline/gulf/appen dix/death.html. Accessed: 8 April 2023.

8 J.T. Correll (2003). Casualties, *Air and Space Forces Magazine*, 1 June. Retrieved from: www.airandspaceforces.com/article/0603casualties/. Accessed: 8 April 2023. Also see reports on the legacy impact of cluster bomb use during the conflict. J. Ismay (2019). America's Dark History of Killing its Own Troops with Cluster Munitions, *New York Times*, 4 December. Retrieved from: www.nytimes.com/2019/12/04/magazine/clus ter-munitions-history.html Accessed: 8 April 2023.

9 J.G. Heidenrich (1993). The Gulf War: How Many Iraqis Died?, *Foreign Policy*. Vol. 90, pp. 108–126.

10 L.A. West (2020). *An Analysis of the Al Firdos Bunker Strike*, Fort Leavenworth, KS: US Army Command and General Staff College.

11 P.J. Sloyan (2003). What I Saw was a Bunch of Filled-In Trenches with People's Arms and Legs Sticking Out of Them. For All I Know, We Could Have Killed Thousands, *Guardian*, 14 February. Retrieved from: www.theguardian.com/world/2003/feb/14/iraq.features111. Accessed: 8 April 2023.

12 T.A. Keaney and E.A. Cohen (1993). *Gulf War Air Power Survey Summary Report*, Washington, DC: US Government Printing Office, p. 66–69.

13 D. Rice (1990). *The Air Force and US National Security: Global Reach–Global Power*, White Paper. Washington, DC: Department of the Air Force.

14 Deptula, Interview with James Rogers for the Warfare podcast.

15 Ibid.

16 Ibid.

17 Ibid.

18 Ibid.

19 Ibid.

20 Ibid.

21 W.J. Crowe (2003). Foreword. In S.D. Wrage, *Immaculate Warfare* (pp. i–viii), Westport, CT: Praeger Publishers, p. viii. Thanks to Jeanette Patton for her valuable research assistance in this section.

22 D. Axe (2021). *Drone War Vietnam*, Annapolis, MD: Naval Institute Press.

23 C. Fuller (2017). *See It/Shoot It: The Secret History of the CIA's Lethal Drone Programme*, New Haven and London: Yale University Press.

24 James Neal and Linden Blue, who purchased the defence company General Atomics, are also important to mention as the industrialists behind the Predator. For more on this period see R. Whittle (2015). *Predator: The Secret Origins of the Drone Revolution*, New York: Henry Holt & Co.; C. Lee (2019). The Role of Culture in Military Innovation Studies: Lessons Learned from the US Air Force's Adoption of the Predator Drone, 1993–1997, *Journal of Strategic Studies*, Vol. 46 (1), pp. 115–149.

25 Other branches of the US military – such as the US Navy and US Army – will have overlapping, yet markedly different, intellectual histories behind the development and adopt of precision technologies and strategies. Ideal topics for a future academic study.

26 A. Wohlstetter (1993). Bosnia as Future. In Z.M. Khalilzed (ed.), *Lessons from Bosnia* (pp. 30–33), Santa Monica, CA: RAND.

27 R.P. Hallion (1995). *Precision Guided Munitions and the New Era of Warfare*, APSC Paper No. 53, Fairbairn, Australia: Air Power Studies Centre. Retrieved from: www.fas.org/man/dod-101/sys/smart/docs/paper53.htm. Accessed: 26 July 2022.

Notes

28 As Chris Wood's research has documents, the CIA was also given permission to launch a handfull of its new experimental unarmed GNAT drones over the conflict. The GNAT is best seen as an early version of the Predator. C. Woods (2015). The Story of America's Very First Drone Strike, *Atlantic*, 30 May. Retrieved from: www.theatlantic. com/international/archive/2015/05/america-first-drone-strike-afghanistan/394463/. Accessed: 23 April 2023.

29 NATO (2022). Kosovo Air Campaign (March–June 1999): Operation Allied Force, *NATO*. Retrieved from: www.nato.int/cps/en/natohq/topics_49602.htm. Accessed: 19 April 2023.

30 J.A. Tirpak (1999). Washington Watch: Victory in Kosovo, *Air & Space Forces Magazine*, 1 July. Retrieved from: www.airandspaceforces.com/article/0799watch/. Accessed: 19 April 2023.

31 Crowe, Foreword, p. viii; Axe, *Drone War Vietnam*.

32 Human Rights Watch concluded that 'as few as 489 and as many as 528 Yugoslav civilians were killed in the ninety separate incidents in Operation Allied Force'. HRW (2000). The Crisis in Kosovo, *Human Rights Watch*. Retrieved from: www.hrw.org/reports/2000/nato/Natbm200-01.htm. Accessed: 19 April 2023.

33 Attacks by Osama bin Laden and his al-Qaeda terrorist organisation were far from new by 2001. In 1998, bin Laden targeted US diplomatic sites in Kenya and Tanzania with Vehicle-Borne Improvised Explosive Devices (VBIEDs). Unsurprisingly, in response, President Clinton chose precision strikes as a way to mitigate the emerging threat. Within hours of the attacks, seventy-five Tomahawk cruise missiles had been launched from 'a submarine and several surface warships in the USS Abraham Lincoln battle group' located in the Red Sea and Arabian Sea. B. Gellman (1998). US Strikes Terrorist-Linked Sites in Afghanistan, Factory in Sudan, *Washington Post*, 21 August. Retrieved from: www.washingtonpost.com/wp-srv/inatl/longterm/eafricabombing/stories/strikes082198.htm. Accessed: 19 April 2023.

34 R. Wohlstetter (1962). *Pearl Harbour: Warning and Decision*, Stanford, CA: Stanford University Press, p. 1.

35 National Archives (n.d.). 'A Date Which Will Live in Infamy': The First Typed Draft of Franklin D. Roosevelt's War Address, *National Archives*. Retrieved from: www.archives.gov/education/lessons/day-of-infamy. Accessed: 21 April 2023.

36 As stated by Elaine Woo, Roberta's work helped 'to draw parallels to the 2001 terrorist strikes, which raised similar questions about military preparedness, intelligence, and politics'. E. Woo (2007). Roberta Wohlstetter; Her Book on Faulty US Analysis Before WWII Resonates Today, *Los Angeles Times*, 16 January. Retrieved from: https://archive.boston.com/news/globe/obituaries/articles/2007/01/16/roberta_wohlstetter_her_book_on_faulty_us_analysis_before_wwii_resonates_today/. Accessed: 20 April 2023.

37 National Security Archive (1997). Episode 19: Interview with Richard Perle, *Freeze*, NSA. Retrieved from: https://nsarchive2.gwu.edu/coldwar/interviews/episode-19/perle1.html. Accessed: 20 April 2023. Also see B. Wattenberg (2003). Richard Perle: The Making of a Neoconservative [transcript of interview], *Think Tank*, PBS. Retrieved from: www.pbs.org/thinktank/transcript1017.html. Accessed: 20 April 2023.

38 US Department of Defense (2010). Defense Policy Board, *USDOD*. Retrieved from: https://policy.defense.gov/OUSDP-Offices/Defense-Policy-Board/. Accessed: 21 April 2023.

Notes

39 S.M. Hersh (2003). Lunch with the Chairman: Why was Richard Perle meeting with Adnan Khashoggi?, *New Yorker*, 17 March. Retrieved from: www.newyorker.com/magazine/2003/03/17/lunch-with-the-chairman. Accessed: 23 August 2016.

40 Z. Khalilzad (2016). *The Envoy: From Kabul to the White House, My Journey Through a Turbulent World*, New York: St Martin's Press.

41 Z. Nazar (2022). Former US Envoy Defends Controversial Peace Deal with Taliban, *Radio Free Europe*, 14 August. Retrieved from: www.rferl.org/a/afghanistan-khalilzad-defends-taliban-deal/31988305.html. Accessed: 21 April 2023.

42 Wattenberg, Richard Perle.

43 World Bank (n.d.). Explore History: Paul D. Wolfowitz, *World Bank*. Retrieved from: www.worldbank.org/en/archive/history/past-presidents/paul-dundes-wolfowitz. Accessed: 21 April 2023.

44 Ibid.

45 P. Wolfowitz (2016). Online personal interview by James Rogers. 21 September.

46 P. Wolfowitz (2003). Interview by Sam Tannenhaus, *Vanity Fair*, 9 May. Retrieved from: www.sscnet.ucla.edu/polisci/faculty/trachtenberg/useur/wolfowitztanenhaus.html. Accessed: 21 April 2023.

47 Ibid.

48 Hoover Institution (2023). Ambassador Paul Wolfowitz, *Hoover Institution, Stanford*. Retrieved from: www.hoover.org/profiles/paul-wolfowitz. Accessed: 20 April 2023.

49 Voice of America (VOA) (2003). Pentagon to Rely on Speed, Precision Weaponry in Future Conflicts, says Official, *VOA*, 18 June. Retrieved from: www.voanews.com/a/a-13-a-2003-06-18-8-pentagon-67312972/381490.html. Accessed: 20 April 2023.

50 Ibid.

51 R. Grant (2003). Hand in Glove: In Gulf War II, the Air Force and Army Discovered a New 'Sweet Spot' in Combat Cooperation, *Air and Space Forces Magazine*, 20 July. Retrieved from: www.airandspaceforces.com/PDF/MagazineArchive/Documents/2003/July%202003/0703glove.pdf. Accessed: 21 April 2023.

52 eMediaMillWorks (2001). US Secretary of Defense Donald Rumsfeld's News Conference on US Retaliatory Attacks on the Taliban [transcript], *Washington Post*, 8 October. Retrieved from: www.washingtonpost.com/wp-srv/nation/specials/attacked/transcripts/rumsfeldtext_100801.html. Accessed: 21 April 2023.

53 R. Grant (2003). The Redefinition of Strategic Airpower, *Air and Space Forces Magazine*, 1 October. Retrieved from: www.airandspaceforces.com/article/1003strategic/. Accessed: 21 April 2023.

54 Ibid.

55 C-SPAN (2022). First Predator Drone Mention [speech by President George Bush at the Citadel, 12 December 2001], *C-SPAN*. Retrieved from: www.c-span.org/video/?c5042957/user-clip-predator-drone-mention. Accessed: 23 April 2023.

56 Woods, The Story of America's Very First Drone Strike.

57 US Air Force (n.d.). Lt. Gen. David A. Deptula, *US Air Force*. Retrieved from: www.af.mil/About-Us/Biographies/Display/Article/104634/lieutenant-general-david-a-deptula/. Accessed: 21 April 2023.

58 Woods, The Story of America's Very First Drone Strike.

59 Ibid.

60 Ibid.

61 L. Ferran and B. Candea (2015). Taliban Leader Mullah Omar Died 2 Years Ago, Afghan Officials Say, *ABC News*, 29 July. Retrieved from: https://abcnews.go.com/

Notes

International/taliban-leader-mullah-omar-dead-afghan-officials/story?id=32751650. Accessed: 23 April 2023.

62 P. Rogers (2013). Security by 'Remote Control': Can it Work?, *RUSI Journal*, Vol. 158 (3), pp. 14–20. Retrieved from: www.tandfonline.com/doi/abs/10.1080/03071847.2013 .807581. Accessed: 23 April 2023.

63 As Chris Woods stated, Bush was a 'fan of the Predator'. In a December 2001 address to cadets at The Citadel, Bush announced that drones were now 'able to circle over enemy forces, gather intelligence, transmit information instantly back to commanders, then fire on targets with extreme accuracy'. Woods, The Story of America's Very First Drone Strike.

64 The total number is estimated at between fifty-four and fifty-seven drone strikes killing '296 terrorists and 195 civilians'. M. Zenko (2016). Obama's Embrace of Drone Strikes Will Be a Lasting Legacy. *New York Times*, 12 January. Retrieved from: www. nytimes.com/roomfordebate/2016/01/12/reflecting-on-obamas-presidency/obamas-embrace-of-drone-strikes-will-be-a-lasting-legacy. Accessed: 23 April 2023.

65 B. Obama (2013). *Obama's Speech on US Drone Policy* [transcript], *New York Times*, 23 May. Retrieved from: www.nytimes.com/2013/05/24/us/politics/transcript-of-obamas-speech-on-drone-policy.html?pagewanted=all. Accessed: 1 July 2022.

66 BBC (2019). Trump Revokes Obama Rule on Reporting Drone Strike Deaths, *BBC*, 7 March. Retrieved from: www.bbc.com/news/world-us-canada-47480207. Accessed: 24 April 2023.

67 Zenko, Obama's Embrace of Drone Strikes Will Be a Lasting Legacy.

68 J. Kantor (2008). Teaching Law, Testing Ideas, Obama Stood Slightly Apart, *New York Times*, 30 July. Retrieved from: www.nytimes.com/2008/07/30/us/politics/30law. html. Accessed: 23 April 2023.

69 Obama, *Speech on US Drone Policy*.

70 J. Rogers (2023). Rethinking Remote Warfare, *International Politics*. Online First. https:// doi.org/10.1057/s41311-023-00449-5.

71 A. Khan (2021). Hidden Pentagon Records Reveal Patterns of Failure in Deadly Airstrikes, *New York Times*, 18 December. Retrieved from: www.nytimes.com/inter active/2021/12/18/us/airstrikes-pentagon-records-civilian-deaths.html. Accessed: 24 April 2023.

72 Of course, the drone also allowed Obama to fulfil his promise to the American people by reducing the need to deploy and risk large deployments of US troops in regions of uncleared conflict, such as Somalia and Yemen. For fatality stat see BBC, Trump Revokes Obama Rule on Reporting Drone Strike Deaths.

73 S. Kreps, P. Lushenko and S. Raman (2022). Biden can Reduce Civilian Casualties during US Drone Strikes. Here's How, *Brookings*, 19 January. Retrieved from: www. brookings.edu/articles/biden-can-reduce-civilian-casualties-during-us-drone-strikes-heres-how/. Accessed: 24 April 2023.

74 Ibid.

75 K.D. Atherton (2020). Trump Inherited the Drone War but Ditched Accountability, *Foreign Policy*, 22 May. Retrieved from: https://foreignpolicy.com/2020/05/22/obama-drones-trump-killings-count/. Accessed: 24 April 2023.

76 A. Callamard and UN Human Rights Council (2020). *Use of Armed Drones for Targeted Killings: Report of the Special Rapporteur on Extrajudicial, Summary or Arbitrary Executions*, A/ HRC/44/38, Geneva: UNGA. Retrieved from: www.ohchr.org/en/documents/ thematic-reports/ahrc4438-use-armed-drones-targeted-killings-report-special-rappor teur. Accessed: 2 July 2023.

Notes

77 J. Rogers (2022). The Third Drone Age: Visions Out to 2040, *CIGI*, 28 November. Retrieved from: www.cigionline.org/articles/the-third-drone-age-visions-out-to-2040/. Accessed: 24 April 2023.

78 Z. Cohen, H. Alkhshali, K. Khadder, and A. Dewan (2020). US Drone Strike Ordered by Trump Kills Top Iranian Commander in Baghdad, *CNN*, 4 January. Retrieved from: www.cnn.com/2020/01/02/middleeast/baghdad-airport-rockets/index.html. Accessed: 23 April 2023.

79 Callamard and UN Human Rights Council, *Use of Armed Drones for Targeted Killings*.

80 J. Rogers (2017). Drone Warfare: The Death of Precision, *Bulletin of the Atomic Scientists*, 12 May. Retrieved from: https://thebulletin.org/2017/05/drone-warfare-the-death-of-precision/. Accessed: 24 March 2023.

81 K.B. Lillis (2022). Biden Finalizes New Rules for US Drone Strikes, *CNN*, 7 October. Retrieved from: www.cnn.com/2022/10/07/politics/drone-strikes-counterterrorism-white-house-biden-new-rules/index.html. Accessed: 24 April 2023.

82 Ibid.

83 Z. Miller (2022). New Biden Counterterror Strategy puts Limits on Drone Use, *AP News*, 7 October. Retrieved from: https://apnews.com/article/biden-ayman-al-zawahri-don ald-trump-terrorism-counterterrorism-7c5c6dfd112a3b0440714a4514ff800. Accessed: 24 April 2023.

84 Lillis, Biden Finalizes New Rules for US Drone Strikes.

85 E. Schmitt (2021). Deadly Kabul Strike, Pentagon Chief Decides, *New York Times*, 13 December. Retrieved from: www.nytimes.com/2021/12/13/us/politics/afghanistan-drone-strike.html. Accessed: 24 April 2023.

86 Ibid.

87 Ibid.

88 N. Merchant and L.C. Baldor (2022). Explainer: A Look at the Missile that Killed al-Qaida Leader, *AP News*, 3 August. Retrieved from: https://apnews.com/article/hellfire-r9x-al-zawahri-dod25b7ed4059750b4add024322fe17c. Accessed: 24 April 2023.

89 J. Biden (2022). Remarks by President Biden on a Successful Counterterrorism Operation in Afghanistan, *The White House*, 1 August. Retrieved from: www.whitehouse. gov/briefing-room/speeches-remarks/2022/08/01/remarks-by-president-biden-on-a-successful-counterterrorism-operation-in-afghanistan/. Accessed: 24 April 2023.

90 Ibid.

91 For the export of Switchblade drones to Ukraine see D. Hambling (2022). Shadowy Switchblade Kamikaze Drones on their Way to Ukraine: Here's What We Know About Them, *Forbes*, 17 March. Retrieved from: www.forbes.com/sites/davidham bling/2022/03/17/shadowy-switchblade-munition-on-its-way-to-ukraine/?sh=46a584 275e13. Accessed: 24 April 2023. For agreed export of MQ9-B Sea Guardians to Taiwan see A. Wilson (2022). Taiwan Agrees to Buy Four American-Made Naval Surveillance Drones for $555 Million, *Stars and Stripes*, 1 September. Retrieved from: www.stripes.com/theaters/asia_pacific/2022-09-01/taiwan-seaguardian-surveillance-drones-china-7176170.html. Accessed: 24 April 2023.

92 For more on Russian drone technology see S. Bendett (2022). The Ukraine War and Its Impact on Russian Development of Autonomous Weapons, *The Atlantic Council*, 30 August. Retrieved from: www.atlanticcouncil.org/content-series/airpower-after-ukraine/the-ukraine-war-and-its-impact-on-russian-development-of-autonomous-wea pons/. Accessed: 24 April 2023. For China see C. Alden, L. Fiala, E. Krol, and R. Whittle (2020). *Wings Along the BRI: Exporting Chinese UCAVs and Security?*, London: LSE

IDEAS. Retrieved from: www.lse.ac.uk/ideas/Assets/Documents/updates/LSE-IDEAS-Wings-Along-the-BRI.pdf. Accessed: 24 April 2023. For more on the future of drone warfare see Rogers, The Third Drone Age.

93 J. Rogers (2023). The Second Drone Age: Defining War in the 2020s, *Defense and Security Analysis*. Vol. 39 (2), pp. 256–259.

94 F.C. Ikle and A. Wohlstetter (1988). *Discriminate Deterrence: Report of the Commission on Integrated Long-Term Strategy*, January, AD-A277 478, Washington, DC: Government Printing Office.

95 Ibid.

96 Ibid.

97 Ibid.

98 D. Gettinger (2020). *The Drone Databook*, Annandale-On-Hudson: Center for the Study of the Drone.

99 Thanks to Gettinger for providing the 113 figure to the author prior to the publication of the updated *Drone Databook*. For more details see J. Rogers (2022). Arria-Formula Meeting on Transnational Terrorist Threats [Address to UN Security Council Arria-Formula: video]. *UNSC*, 31 August. Retrieved from: https://media.un.org/en/asset/k1q/k1qcqls4b9. Accessed: 17 February 2023. Also see Callamard and UN Human Rights Council, *Use of Armed Drones for Targeted Killings*.

100 Thanks to Chávez and Swed for providing the 65 figure as part of their ongoing research. K. Chávez and O. Swed (2021). The Proliferation of Drones to Violent Nonstate Actors, *Defence Studies*. Vol. 21 (1), pp. 1–24.

101 J. Rogers and D. Kunertova (2022). *The Vulnerabilities of the Drone Age: Established Threats and Emerging Issues out to 2035*, NATO SPS/CSS/CWS. Zurich: ETH Zurich. Retrieved from: www.research-collection.ethz.ch/handle/20.500.11850/556165. Accessed: 24 April 2024.

102 J. Rogers (2021). Future Threats: Military UAS, Terrorist Drones, and the Dangers of the Second Drone Age. In A. Haider (ed.), *A Comprehensive Approach to Countering Unmanned Aircraft Systems* (pp. 481–509). Kalkar: NATO Joint Air Power Competence Centre.

103 J. Rogers (2021). Last Month, Three Drones Attacked an Israeli Tanker. Here's Why That's Something New, *Washington Post*, 19 August. Retrieved from: www.washingtonpost.com/politics/2021/08/19/last-month-three-drones-attacked-an-israeli-tanker-heres-why-thats-something-new/. Accessed: 24 April 2023.

104 Ibid.

105 P. Iddon (2022). Wing Loong 3: The Emergent Threat of Long-Range 'Intercontinental' Attack Drones, *Forbes*, 21 November. Retrieved from: www.forbes.com/sites/pauliddon/2022/11/21/wing-loong-3-the-emergent-dangers-of-long-range-intercontinental-attack-drones/?sh=36b3ccca3d2f. Accessed: 24 April 2023; R. Schapiro and T. Capra (2018). Terrorists Likely to Attack US with Drones, says FBI Director, *NBC News*, 10 October. Retrieved from: www.nbcnews.com/politics/national-security/terrorists-likely-attack-u-s-drones-says-fbi-director-n918586. Accessed: 24 April 2023.

106 YouTube (2022). General Milley Delivers 2022 West Point Commencement Speech [video], *Union Herald*. Retrieved from: www.youtube.com/watch?v=FGAXyrP-Lm4. Accessed: 23 April 2023.

107 Ibid.

Figures

Acknowledgements

This book, like all books, was not written alone. It is thanks to the support of friends and family, the advice of colleagues, the patience of the publisher, and the intellectual inspiration offered by expert researchers and practitioners, that the book was completed. While it is impossible to name each individual who has helped along the way, I wish to acknowledge a few select people and institutions who greatly influenced the finished product.

First, I would like to thank Manchester University Press for their time and support. Most notably, Tony Mason, Rob Byron, Alun Richards, Rebecca Parkinson, David Appleyard and Anthony Mercer, who worked hard to produce an accessible and well produced academic text. Second, I would like to thank the research and archival institutions that supported the research. The project began at the University of Hull and was aided by the vibrant War Studies community and resources that were established by Colin Grey, developed by Justin Morris, and greatly expanded by Caroline Kennedy-Pipe. Following my time there, my employment and research stays at the University of York, University of Oxford, SDU, Yale, Stanford, the US Air Force Air Command and Staff College, and Cornell provided the time and support needed to get the book over the finish line. In regards to archival institutions, I would like to thank the Library of Congress, the National Archives, the National Air and Space Museum's Archives Division, the Brynmor Jones Library, the Huntington Library Collection, The John F. Kennedy Library and Archives, the Hoover Archives at Stanford University, the Imperial War Museum Oral History Archives, the British Library, the Air Force Historical Research Agency, The Harry S. Truman Presidential Library and Museum, the Manuscripts and Archives Division within the Sterling Memorial Library at Yale University, the Eisenhower Presidential Library and Archives, the Hiroshima Peace Memorial Museum, National Security Archive (GWU) and

Acknowledgements

the Liddell Hart Centre for Military Archives at King's College London. I would also like to thank the RAND Archives in Santa Monica and the Stanley Kubrick Archive at the Archives and Special Collections Centre within the London College of Communication for granting privileged access to the material they hold.

I would also like to thank those who took the time to be interviewed during the research stage. This included, but was not limited to, Alain Enthoven, Dierdre Henderson, Tami Biddle, Stephen Bourque, William Burr, Nate Jones, Paul Wolfowitz, Chuck Richardson, David Deptula, Peter Jakub and Keiko Orgura. Thanks are also given to Richard P. Hallion, Alan Vick, Richard Betts, James Connelly, and Paul G. Thornhill, who took the time to offer early guidance that was vital to the final direction of the work. Sarah Kreps, Theo Farrell, and Christopher Fuller are thanked for reviewing the manuscript and offering words of support, as are the anonymous reviewers, chosen by Manchester University Press, who rigorously peer-reviewed the work. The Air Command and Staff College, located at Maxwell Air Force Base in Montgomery, Alabama, is worthy of a special note of appreciation. It was here, where the ambition to achieve precision bombing was developed during the 1920s, that this book underwent rigorous academic peer-review during a dedicated workshop that was designed as a hard test of the book's core thesis. Thanks are due to J. Wesley Hutto for his personal support, for making my wife and I so welcome in Montgomery, and for organising the workshop. To those who gave their time to participate in the workshop – Richard Mueller, Kathryn M. G. Boehlefeld, Sterling Michael Pavelec, and, of course, J. Wesley Hutto – I will be forever grateful. Thanks are also offered to Michael Cox, Nuno Monteiro, and Nicholas Rengger who all supported the work through excellent advice, feedback, and simply the time to discuss the topic.

Finally, I would like to thank my mentor and dear friend, Caroline Kennedy-Pipe, for her years of support, advice, and friendship. Without you I would not be where I am today.

Index

Index

Index

Index